The War on California

The War on California

DEFEATING OIL, OLIGARCHS AND THE NEW TYRANNY

Bruce H. Jennings

ISBN: 0692860088
ISBN 13: 9780692860083
Library of Congress Control Number: 2017903957
Collective Political Strategies, Santa Rosa, CA

Table of Contents

Introduction · ix

Chapter 1 Climate of Conflict · 1

Chapter 2 Inside the Law Machine · 14

Chapter 3 Taking the Initiative · 27

Chapter 4 So Far from California · 43

Chapter 5 The Path Not Taken · 54

Chapter 6 A Tale of Two Lobbies · 70

Chapter 7 Market Solutions for Market Failures · · · · · · · · · · · · · 87

Chapter 8 The Climate of Subversion · 107

Chapter 9 Hazardous Traits · 121

Chapter 10 Cassandra Does Sacramento · · · · · · · · · · · · · · · · · · 137

Chapter 11 The Climate of Austerity · 151

Chapter 12 Private Profits and a Punished Public · · · · · · · · · · · · · 160

Chapter 13 Adding Fuels to the Fire · 176

Chapter 14 Race, Poverty and Trading · 185

Chapter 15 Climate of Compromise · 196

Chapter 16 The Pontiff, Politicians, and Paris · · · · · · · · · · · · · · · · 208

Chapter 17 Buying Our Way Out · 217

Chapter 18 Dismantling Democracy · 226

Chapter 19 The War on California · 237

Chapter 20 The Climate of Change · 250

Serving the Public Interest: Profiles of Advocates · · · · 265

Acknowledgements · 273

About the Author · 277

End Notes · 279

In the sixties, there was a sense of reform in the air.... We would transcend mere profit. Subsequent years brought about a growing skepticism that's still with us. So there was a transition from a belief in government and public interest to this powerful doctrine that the market, buying and selling, is the principle that will make everything work at the end of the day. That's the dominant ideology that we live with in America today. That's our new religion. That's our mythology.[1]

The Honorable Jerry Brown 2003

Introduction

The shock expressed by so many with the election of Donald Trump as the 45th President of the United States was followed by a slow motion realization that a volatile billionaire/reality television-host was no longer a punchline on late night television, but a leader of our nation. The early days of his presidency were so filled with a series of missteps verging on a Constitutional crisis (e.g., the nexus of conflicts of interests, receiving payments from foreign interests, refusals to fully disclose extensive financial holdings), one prominent legal scholar summarized his presidency with a sound bite approximating the newly elected leader's infamous tweets: "Trump is simply violating the law, everyday!"[2]

Despite the theatrical flourishes surrounding his early days, many of President Donald Trump's actions echoed themes of earlier Republican administrations: downsizing government and reversing wide swaths of regulatory law; promoting the privatization of public services and education; increasing support for prisons, police, and the American military; expanding the ties between select religions and the state; and, endorsing tax schemes benefitting corporations and the wealthy. His earlier proclamations of "draining the swamp" of corruption in D.C. coupled with vows to represent "ordinary Americans" quickly morphed into an agenda benefitting America's elite. If certain facets of his hypocrisy seemed greater than past presidents, it was perhaps only a matter of degree; the collection of cabinet appointees would be recorded as among the most-wealthy in American history – holding personal assets reaching into the many billions of dollars.[3] Before completing his first 100 days in office, both the media and many of his political opponents seemed resigned to the reality of dealing with another bumbling political leader, except for one distinctive feature of the new century: a fossil-fueled catastrophe threatening the survival of the planet.

One of the indelible marks of the Trump administration was a clear and enthusiastic support for fossil fuels. If many in the nation's capitol were calculating how to find common ground with the mercurial man in the Oval Office, tens of millions of residents on the Pacific coast sensed the makings of a growing and irreconcilable conflict. By 2017 the clash over the direction of the national economy and politics had no better poster child for opposition than roughly forty million Californians. Only days after his inauguration and just prior to the televised airing of the Super Bowl, the President declared to a national audience: "California is out of control."[4] Apparently provoked by the state Senate vote to expand protections for undocumented residents, Trump's response contained a thinly veiled threat to withhold federal funding.[5]

Residents openly worried as a new President and his Congress prepared to reverse broad swaths of California law ranging from support for undocumented immigrants to women's reproductive health services, to restrictive gun controls, to consumer warnings on hazardous products, to regulations on payday lending shops, to the expansion of bilingual education, to funds for mass transit, to prohibitions against the use and transport of coal, to the promotion of clean fuels, to protections for endangered species, to limitations on private prisons, to the legalization of marijuana, to enforcement actions against banking fraud, to expanded equal pay provisions... seemingly without end.

National policies on fossil fuels demonstrated a plan sharply divergent from California's clean energy devised over a period of decades. President Trump and his cabinet readily embraced an agenda scripted "straight from the talking points of top energy industry officials and their lavishly financed allies in Congress"... "to lift environmental restrictions on oil and natural gas extraction, build the Keystone XL and Dakota Access pipelines, open more federal lands to drilling, withdraw from the Paris climate agreement, kill Obama's Clean Power Plan, revive the coal mining industry..."[6] Scott Pruitt, Trump's nominee to head the U.S. Environmental Protection Agency, succinctly characterized his role as a soldier in the emerging war on alternative energy, in 2015, by declaring: "the Clean Power Plan an unlawful attempt to expand federal bureaucrats' authority over states' energy economies in order to shut coal-fired power plants and eventually other sources of fossil-fuel generated electricity."[7]

Californian's successes in cleaning the air, water and the environment, along with creating safer workplaces, healthy communities, and the green sprouts of an economy dismantling fossil fuels in favor of renewable energy all meant that Trump's war centered on California: And with good reason. California held a leading majority of those voters who caused the latest president to lose the popular vote (achieving office only by archaic and tortured Electoral College calculations). For the new and notoriously thin-skinned President, California encapsulated his political failure; as "Trump drew a smaller percentage of the California vote - 31.6% - than any GOP presidential candidate in 160 years."[8] The divide between Trump and California, however, ran much deeper.

The historic underpinnings of this undeclared war included the successes of organized labor and the blossoming of a vast network of public interest activists who shaped thousands of individual laws and, by so participating, fostered more expansive notions of democratic practice. The decades of activism by nurses, school teachers, farm/service workers, and millions of allied voters advanced a central principle: *the public rights of citizens over the private rights of corporations.* After decades of victories, citizens understood how the state's prominence as one of the largest and most dynamic economies in the world had resulted from the interplay of a public continuously engaged in directing the content and nature of private sector activities. By the beginning of the 21st century, the fruits of a decades-long struggle to control the increasingly negative consequences of fossil fuels resulted in an obvious political imperative: creating a thriving economy based on clean energy entails defeating the political power of *petroleros:* big oil, and their corporate allies.

Californians found themselves on a collision course with a regime that, in place of this state's design for a post-fossil fuel economy, quickly advanced multifaceted plans for purging clean energy programs while increasing federal support for dirty fuels. Anticipating useful targets, the state's environmental leadership loomed large for the new president. It came as little surprise that the new President's first budget proposed a draconian 30 per cent reduction for the U.S. Environmental Protection Agency with deeper cuts or even the elimination of climate-related programs; many federal programs originated with laws crafted by California's public interest advocates. In response, many Californians reacted with a renewed and vigorous opposition.

At this juncture in the story, one might expect a more intensive focus on Donald Trump, the Republican Congress and partisan battles with other political celebrities. Such reporting, however, would miss the most important parts of a much more dramatic tale. The backdrop to the current crises spawned by fossil fuels has a much longer trajectory than the most recent election cycle. Indeed, a longer perspective on what has gone so terribly wrong in a world facing cataclysms threatening the future of this planet is only distantly related to something brought about by celebrity politicians. Donald Trump, his billionaire cabinet, and the Republican Congress may accurately represent the faces of ignorance and oppression, a point I am not interested in disputing. How do these characteristics explain why the end of human history appears on the horizon? Or consider our situation according to the classic American political formulation: What difference would it make if the Trumpians were swept away and replaced by their Democratic counterparts?

The stories that follow reveal a different set of responses than commonly found in mainstream political journalism. Without giving away their stories, one of the answers can be found in the quote that begins this work: the myth of markets. It is precisely the *political* role of markets, especially when combined with those who dominate the economic and political spheres of life that defines so much of our contemporary crises. Reading from the headlines, it seems preposterous that, while much attention has focused on whether powerful political figures accept the basic scientific premises of a climate crisis, the vast differences regarding *what to do about the worsening threat* of burning fossil fuels have borne very little scrutiny. One of the purposes of this work is to bring greater attention to the Golden State's recent political history, to understand other dimensions of the conflict and consequences. To fully appreciate the politics of fossil-fueled crisis, there may be no better place to begin than California's most recent and immodest contribution to the world community.

California's Celebrated Climate Solution

"I don't give a damn if you believe in climate change." The message posted on his Facebook page was vintage Arnold Schwarzenegger and many could imagine hearing the unmistakable voice of California's former governor at the 2015 Paris meetings discussing a global climate treaty.[9] His words captured a common political shift across the globe: something needed to be done about the worsening environment.

The actor/former governor began by arguing in simple terms of public health damage. "First – do you believe it is acceptable that 7 million people die every year from pollution?... Every day, 19,000 people die from pollution from fossil fuels. Do you accept those deaths? Do you accept that children all over the world have to grow up breathing with inhalers?" He had only begun his message.

"Now, my second question: do you believe coal and oil will be the fuels of the future?"

Unlike legions of scientists, technocrats, and policy wonks who would promptly lose the attention of any audience, Arnold displayed his finely honed skills as a political speaker. "I, personally, want a plan. I don't want to be like the last horse and buggy salesman who was holding out as cars took over the roads....That's exactly what is going to happen to fossil fuels."

If his followers were not yet convinced, Arnold pursued an argument that had served as the bedrock for achieving his stunning victory in the election to recall a sitting governor from office: the promise of unrestrained markets and private sector innovations as the answer to any problem, including the threat of global warming. "A clean energy future is a wise investment, and anyone who tells you otherwise is either wrong, or lying....Renewable energy is great for the economy, and you don't have to take my word for it...Our economy has not suffered. In fact, our economy in California is growing faster than the U.S. economy. We lead the nation in manufacturing, agriculture, tourism, entertainment, high tech, biotech, and, of course, green tech."

For those who might conclude that this was simply another exercise in self-congratulation, Schwarzenegger acknowledged that the plan to address global warming belonged to a state with a remarkable set of laws to guide others around the planet. "California has some of the most revolutionary environmental laws in the United States, we get 40% of our power from renewables, and are 40% more energy efficient than the rest of the country. We were an early-adopter of a clean energy future." His conclusion was even more concise, calling on everyone to join in advancing "a smarter, cleaner, healthier, more profitable energy future."[10] The simplicity of this solution, however, masked a more divisive political story. At the heart of this soliloquy was a question. Could one necessarily rely on energy corporations and markets to deliver a clean energy future and still manage to avoid a worsening global environment?

As Governor Schwarzenegger was making the case for faith in market solutions combined with California's environmental laws, his successor, Governor Jerry Brown was voicing a similar missive at another meeting across Paris. Brown's message to a multitude of cities and states gathered in Paris was equally to the point: California possessed many solutions to a worsening climate crisis. The evening celebrating the California's policy innovations at the posh hotel, however, was punctuated with the unscripted remarks by community-based organizers from the Golden State, including a youth organizer, Rossmery Zayas, from Los Angeles: "We're from California, and let us tell you the truth about what's happening in our communities."[11] In representing a decades-old California public interest group, Communities for a Better Environment, Rossmery Zayas was part of a coalition of globally-linked community activists at the Paris climate meetings. Among the central issues at the heart of the critique of those talks was the approach that both Governors Brown and Schwarzenegger advanced as an export model law for solving climate change: a program called cap-and-trade.[12]

For all the cheerleading by its two most recent Governors, California's export model for guiding other climate policies around the planet disguised serious political fault lines that had been unfolding in the capitol over many years. The most notable of these conflicts appeared between the Golden State's public interest advocates' vision of the future versus that represented by lobbyists for many of the world's larger corporate interests. The winners and losers in these clashes were recorded annually in the hundreds of bills either vetoed or signed into law. Less noticed were the nuanced as well as not so subtle changes made to hundreds of bills during their journey. Indeed, it had only been a few short months since a group of global energy corporations had depleted a proposed California law that many public interest groups were hoping to showcase for everyone gathered in Paris.

Back in September, 2015 in Sacramento, seated across from one particular reporter in his expansive capitol office, was one of California's most important political figures, State Senator Kevin de León. The leader for one of the state's legislative bodies possessed enormous political power, over hundreds of legislative measures affecting everyday life for one of the world's larger economies. Amidst the trappings of power, President Pro Tempore Kevin de León was fuming over what insiders regard as a rare political setback, when forced by a group of global corporations to dramatically alter his climate legislation.

Among the many hundreds of laws manufactured each year in California, in early 2015, Senator de León introduced measures with the promise of achieving global recognition. The proposed law's potential to dramatically change how fossil fuels are regulated in one of the world's largest economies drew the attention of leading figures. De León recounted the supporters of his measure as including U.S. Senators Barbara Boxer and Dianne Feinstein, Representative Nancy Pelosi, Governor Jerry Brown, and President Barack Obama.

Yet, for all of this political might, Senator de León was forced to abandon a key provision in this legislation instructing some of the world's largest oil producers to dramatically reduce their use of petroleum over the next fifteen years. After leaving the capitol office, a veteran political reporter captured the Senator's assessment of how such a grand coalition of public interest, legislative, executive, and citizen support for his measure could be defeated – "They didn't matter, not compared to the power of oil."[13]

Fossil-Fueled Crises

And so we witness a dawning recognition that the crises of our time are unlike anything in the past. A review of the unfolding climate cataclysms of the 21st century documents that the destruction of our oceans, forests, water and food sources, species and habitats, and broad ecologies proceed at an astonishing rate, with each passing year. Distressing annual projections have given way to a greater certainty that humanity may well be confronting more extreme conditions, threatening the very foundations of human civilization unless more dramatic and urgent actions are immediately taken to exit the era of fossil fuels.[14]

For all the dire warnings, the response thus far has been a muddled one. Calls for urgent action by governments meet with equally vigorous demands that nothing should interfere with free markets and a faith in market-based solutions.[15] This abiding trust is sustained by a corresponding narrative that many past crises have emerged as a kind of unforeseen accident, "how could we have known?"

But, the climate crisis of our day, as it turns out, has been long recognized not only by a large body of scientists, but even by certain of the principal energy corporations responsible for unleashing damaging consequences on a global scale. Recent evidence reveals that by the late 1970s one of America's leading petroleum corporations, Exxon, was informed by its own research team that potentially catastrophic consequences would likely result from the continued use of fossil fuels. Even so, near the end of the 1980s Exxon joined with other energy corporations to block public efforts to restrict fossil fuel emissions in the face of overwhelming scientific evidence of increasingly damaging consequences.[16]

Pivotal to understanding the nature of the problem as well as viable solutions is corporate global energy's unleashed, unrelenting campaign to perpetuate its uses. The worsening climate crises of our time are neither a natural event nor a mere accident. Rather, the product of deception initiated and perpetuated largely by a group of global corporations, our so-called 'climate crisis' might be more accurately understood by substituting another appellation: fossil-fueled storms.[17]

Understanding climate change as *fossil-fueled crises* introduces a radically different approach than that articulated in many forums, including the 2015 Paris climate treaty discussions.

Whereas phrasing problems in terms of "climate change" posits a societal responsibility; "fossil-fueled crises" directs our attention at the relationships and rules governed by those exercising control over fuels. When we know that "eight of the world's largest oil companies account for as much of the climate-damaging pollution spewed into the atmosphere as the entire U. S.,"[18] we begin to see how assigning the public a nebulous responsibility for the climate change problem has disguised the actions of private interests. It also explains how the early avoidance of clean energy alternatives has transformed the challenging problems of fossil-fueled economies into catastrophic events.

The record of conflicts surrounding laws impinging on fossil fuels reveals a political struggle between public and private interests. In place of more nebulous terms such as climate change or global warming, fossil-fueled crises underscore that the worsening condition of the global atmosphere, oceans, habitat, public health and environmental health is embedded in political struggle. The climate events surrounding the combustion of fossil fuels are but one dimension of deeper social conflicts. A less recognized crisis involves private interest campaigns achieving more than isolated legislative victories, but dominating democratic arenas where public advocates might challenge and defeat global energy corporations.

Political leaders lamenting their relative absence of political leverage as compared to the power of oil – is only the most superficial dimension of a larger conflict. Contemporary fossil-fueled crises have less of the character of unintended consequences and more of the features of what a few experts term as the world's greatest market disaster. These are crises more closely resembling a kind of doomsday machine requiring a fundamental transformation in politics in order to expeditiously deploy alternatives while dismantling fossil-fueled economies.

A New Solution or New Tyranny?

In the coming century, there will be many stories recounting how this tale evolves. Various accounts will focus on pivotal political battles; conflicts in which subsequent generations will talk about a path not taken. The consequences of today will be scrutinized and studied regarding what went right as well as what went so terribly wrong. Lost among the statements issued by leaders, however, are the results of daily toiling by public interest advocates, over many years.

California's environmental laws are frequently described as leading the nation and the world with innovative solutions. In the 1960s, the state initiated what would gradually become a suite of laws addressing global warming. With concerns arising from smog and air pollution, California expanded the scope of its work to address efficiency standards for appliances and new buildings, toxic air contaminants, leaded gasoline formulations, vessel and port emissions, renewable portfolio standards, vehicle emission testing and controls, and a bevy of related laws. Characterizations as a global environmental leader disguise the fierce and continuing political struggles in the State's approach to climate change. In various instances the interplay at the heart of what to do about climate change underscores fundamentally divergent paths between "free" market approaches versus democratic controls over the nature and direction of the economy.

In a nutshell, California's Global Warming Solutions Act, AB 32, was broadly conceived to allow businesses a flexibility to engage in trades in specialized markets as a means of gradually reducing emissions of gases harmful to the global atmosphere. In place of relying on legally defined standards imposing strict date certain limits, the Solutions Act opened the door on use of market mechanisms to address the state's climate problems. This Act illustrates the stark contradiction of California's model for the 21st century; operating from a framework imposing an overall cap on emissions, private sector enterprises were given broad latitude in determining how to address emissions released from factories, refineries, and other major sources.

Signed by Governor Arnold Schwarzenegger, the law was seen as a compromise solution, earning the support of both environmental and business interests. Largely ignored by Governor Schwarzenegger was the fact that California already possessed a robust legal architecture for combatting many facets of fossil fueled crises. Yet, political leaders often placed its Global Warming Solutions Act at the forefront of international agreements encompassing states and provinces from North America, South America, Europe, and Africa.[19] The law immediately served as the model for fashioning Congressional legislation to address climate change, but the measure lacked sufficient votes to gain passage.

Beneath the seemingly progressive bent of California's so-called solution are fundamental questions regarding, "who is responsible for threats to the Earth's climate," " who should pay the price for current and future damages," and perhaps most crucially, "who controls California's economy?" Where AB 32 suggests that we are all responsible (i.e., by way of market mechanisms), a closer historical review reveals a fossil fuel industry at work for decades to disguise the impacts of its products, aggressively subverting political efforts to control and restrain their industry.

The general acceptance that humanity could rely on market forces as an act of faith may well have remained invisible from public view except for a statement issued by one of the world's principal religious leaders, Pope Francis. In June 2015, the leader of more than one billion followers effectively condemned the basic architecture underpinning California's Global Warming Solutions Act. Addressing the imperative for the people of the world to decisively address the looming apocalypse of global climate disruption, Pope Francis identified the basic approach contained in California's Global Warming Solutions Act as subterfuge, a device that would misdirect the public away from the fundamental and radical changes necessary to alter the sources of the fossil-fueled crises.[20]

The chasm between California's former governor and the Pope mirrors a deepening political fault line across America. Where many private interests readily engineer market-based approaches for organizing society, a growing coalition of public interest advocates challenge this view. Absent a process that embraces the rights of citizens, conflicts arising from fossil-fueled hazards pose the threat of a "new tyranny" pitting citizen rights to protect themselves, the environment, and their democratic institutions against oil, oligarchs and the tyranny of a deified market.

Among the untold stories of California's celebrated body of laws, the public interest lobby is an amorphous concept, frequently composed of community groups, environmental organizations, and many gatherings of people both formal and informal. It is a lobby whose advocates often possess little in the way of resources or political access based on financial might. Because the very concept of who precisely can claim to represent the public interest is subject to debate, defining the boundaries of the public interest lobby is a slippery endeavor. For many, the public interest lobby is more easily understood in terms of contrasting approaches adopted by its usual opponent – the corporate lobby and its reliance on so-called free markets.[21] In the following chapters, 'free markets' loom large as a guiding principle for the politically moderate and even for a number of large public advocacy organizations.[22]

Democracy and the Pivotal Role of Public Interest Advocates

A common mistake is classifying the actions of one group as representing truth and justice while the other is demonized as an evil force. When immersed in conflicting claims about protecting jobs or science or humanity, it is common for even the politically skilled to become confused about whose side they are on. The resolution of such differences is typically cast as a move beyond petty partisan bickering; suggesting that more level-headed people can reach compromises where each side achieves some benefit. The reality of democratic practice does not correspond so well with the popular portrayals, including easy compromises in the corridors of power. Whereas corporate lobbyist websites celebrate their ability to consistently win political battles, many public interest groups are portrayed as simply losing in a rigged game. The asymmetry between public and private interests, written about by numerous authors, has been perhaps best summarized by one of the most visible figures of American capitalism – Warren Buffett; "Actually, there's been class warfare going on for the last 20 years, and my class has won."[23]

Such broad characterizations, however, overlook the times and places where the seemingly powerless have overcome the powerful. A reversal of fortunes, where ordinary people triumph over money, is one of the more fascinating aspects of political work. Many insiders have witnessed the about-face achieved by public interest advocates representing the powerless, on numerous occasions. Less recognized still are the many instances in which public interest advocates have been on the cusp of moving California in even more progressive directions.

The election of Donald Trump as the 45th President of the United States appears as nothing short of a corporate coup d'état, threatening to overturn decades of public interest advocacy. Before even taking the office, president-elect Trump's earlier remarks on climate change as a hoax and his opposition to the Paris accords have been cemented with cabinet-level appointments of individuals dedicated to pursuing a major expansion of fossil fuel production while discouraging clean-energy innovations. Before completing his first 100 days in office, Trump advanced a budget to eliminate major programs relating to environmental protection, alternative energy, and climate change. As stories in this work reveal, California law poses a formidable challenge to such reversals. Whether President Trump, the Republican Congress and the corporate lobby can dismantle decades of public interest work is a question filled with uncertainty.

At first glance, the threat to California appears uniquely linked to the election of an unorthodox political maverick versus a left coast state whose voters delivered a majority of the popular vote to his opponent. With opposition to a federal dragnet of millions of Mexican Americans, the judicial defeat of efforts to seal the national borders from Muslims by a federal appellate court based in California and popular demonstrations across the state the gulf between the Golden State and Washington, D.C. deepens with each passing day. The notion of a "War on California" is only an appropriate description of our times.

Beyond today's noted headlines, the history surrounding the fossil-fueled crisis of the 21st century goes back many decades. If you speak with political veterans from inside California's capitol, you may unearth fascinating accounts about the nature of our current problems as well as what the public must do to address these crises. You are also likely to encounter untold stories centering not on political celebrities, but on a much larger cast of characters whose work is largely unknown outside the corridors of power, public interest advocates and activists.

The individuals recounted here, although lacking the typically recognized attributes of power, have frequently played pivotal roles in addressing the crises that are the heart of this story. A few of those I will feature include a young UC Berkeley professor from Chile with the audacity to challenge California's fossil-fuel laden agriculture, a young attorney from Ensenada serving in Governor Jerry Brown's first administration who mentors a generation of activists to join an international struggle for environmental rights, an irreverent lobbyist working on behalf of a water utility who initiates a highly successful fistfight with multinational corporations over a long-recognized hazard to public health, a droll and perceptive adviser to Wall Street who leaves the heady and highly lucrative world of corporate finance to advance projects including a plotted public take-over involving one of the nation's largest utilities.

Other activists who have clearly tilted the balance toward the public good in this struggle include a community activist from LA inspired by a cousin's participation in the Nicaraguan revolution and her own proximity to Hollywood to become a leading political strategist, a transplanted lobbyist from D.C. trained by Ralph Nader who is among the first to question the celebrated state solution to global warming, a quick witted attorney whose passion for environmental justice extends into multi-decade legal actions against major polluters, a noted pediatrician toiling in an obscure bureaucratic office with a preoccupation for eliminating threats to public health (instead of simply addressing the victims of a hazardous economy), a brash district attorney with a penchant for going after white-collar criminals, and a highly energetic second generation Filipina labor and community activist who seeks to forge a permanent coalition of nonprofit organizations working to foster a just economic transition away from the ultra-hazards of fossil fuels to clean energy alternatives for one of the largest economies in the world.

These stories of activists capture many key features of what it means to work politically. Beyond playing essential roles in California's capital, as a group, they have ushered many others into the noble pursuit of public interest advocacy. Their stories feature community organizers trying to alter local economies built on toxic wastes, and courageous public employees – all confronting daunting opponents who would subordinate democratic rule to market forces. In these myriad ways they represent in many respects the best of our democracy. Their stories are all the more significant due to the distorted view of that high profile political celebrities can fulfill the role of conducting themselves as public servants. The reality of democratic practice reveals that we are constantly served by countless individuals who remain largely invisible to the public. In cases extending from city hall to Congress, a multitude of public interest organizations have advanced rules relating to every imaginable topic, including laws governing land, air, water, public health, and environmental justice with a firm anchorage in local communities.

Another perspective gained from decades of work within the walls of the state capitol reveals a far more complex history surrounding many private-public conflicts. The narrative that flows from the works of public interest lobbyists disrupts the common conclusion that political conflicts are based on partisan battles. The reality is that in places such as California citizens can wield considerable political power, its demonstration contained in many untold political stories detailing what has become the focal point of political struggle in much of the world: a conflict between private and public interests.

The stories of public interest advocates are united by a central question confronting everyone: what is one to do in the face of the approaching storms? Lest readers think this refers solely to the Trump administration, many of our contemporary struggles have a much longer history, much of it reflecting private versus public interests. The conflicts between the public interest lobby and the corporate lobby places them at the heart of a central drama of our time: Will citizens confront the doomsday machine head-on, and decide on another path, or will fossil-fuels prevail as a force that threatens every civilization?

Perhaps the most vital lesson to offer from my long association within a narrative shaped around public interest advocates and activists is the positive contribution that these stories provide for the rest of us. In a time when the world appears overwhelmed by disasters seemingly beyond the power of average citizens, I purposely pursue a group of stories surrounding fossil-fueled crises to demonstrate that even complex, global crises must be subject to the power of citizens. Quite possibly the only viable alternative to the approaching apocalypse is for citizens to fully exercise our democratic rights to shape both how we are governed as well as forging an economy that will serve the public's interest. See end Serving the Public Interest: Profiles of Advocates, for more details on each of these individuals.

CHAPTER 1

Climate of Conflict

What "the [expletive deleted] is going on here?" The comment directed at me was delivered by one of California's state legislators serving on my Senate Environmental Quality Committee. Dashing back from another legislative meeting occurring simultaneously elsewhere in the capitol, the returning member was visibly stunned to find a fellow legislator's bill on the verge of death.[24] Returning my gaze, the legislator whose bill was near-death glared at me. Yet, for the audience of more than 100 people in the hearing room as well as countless others watching the closed circuit broadcast, it surely appeared as though the legislator and I were engaged in convivial conversation.

As a matter of practice, I regularly moved about the dais as legislators entered from other committee meetings to let them know what was going on in the hearing. This situation, however, was a distinctly unfriendly chat. Temperatures flared: and not simply owing to the capitol's unrelenting August heat. The hearing now took an unscripted turn. The legislator returning to the crowded room clearly thought his vote would be crucial to the passage of yet another piece of legislation sponsored by a group of industries. The measure before us, however, needed more than his vote. Placing my hand over the microphone, I provided a cursory review; "We are hearing Senator Calderon's bill at the moment. And, as you can see, the other members on the committee have serious questions regarding the merits of his bill." "Questions," vastly understated what everyone in the hearing room sensed: the author and his bill were in trouble. And by the look on Senator Calderon's face, he too recognized that his cherished bill balanced on the precipice of defeat.

The six other members of the legislative committee sitting on either side already recognized the questionable nature of the measure before us. While we were often engaged in clarifying recently enacted legislation, the committee members agreed with my written review: the bill before us was purposely designed to unravel legislation signed into law only a year before.[25] This recently enacted law established a new, more stringent California standard for lead in faucets - a hazardous material recognized for more than 2000 years. By further restricting lead, the new law promised to protect not only millions of Californians, but quite likely propel new national standards benefiting tens of millions of others.

Vigorously opposed by a group of multinational corporations, their corporate lobbyists actively pursued the reversal of a stringent California standard. The manufacturers were outraged when, during the previous year, their opposition to such a new limit had failed. They were now back in my committee, laboring to overturn the new, more restrictive standard. Sitting alongside the senator who was presenting their bill, the corporate lobbyists looked anxiously to the chair of the committee to save them from certain defeat.

Asking a group of legislators who had just last year instituted the new standard, to reverse themselves: struck many as a desperate act. Even though a group of global manufacturers stood behind Senator Calderon's proposed (reversal of an upgraded legal standard – heralded by advocates for children, environmental health and others hoping to eliminate another substance recognized as unsafe at any level – now captured the attention of everyone in the hearing room. As implausible as it appeared to outsiders, industry regularly demonstrated the sad truth for too many state legislatures across the nation. Given enough money, corporate lobbyists could package legislation extending the shelf-life of an inherently hazardous item as a compelling option. Generations of corporate lobbyists patiently explained to clients that they confronted a common and powerful obstacle in California's Legislature, the public interest lobby.

Senator Calderon, seeing that his bill was failing, quickly proposed an amendment that would establish an alternative standard, based on the review by an independent scientific body. Several members of the committee sought my thoughts on the proposed "independent body" offered by Senator Calderon. This body had been identified in academic literature as dominated by manufacturing firms, with little track record in achieving protections for public or worker health.[26] At this point a key member of the committee, who would soon assume the leadership of the Senate, shook his head in disappointment, concluding, "Well...I don't see how we can support this bill."

As the votes were recorded by the committee secretary, it was evident that the attempt to dismantle the new California lead standard was going to fail. During the shuffle of the next legislator coming forward to present her bill, Senator Calderon approached the dais, signaling that he wanted a private word with me. If it was not apparent to others in the audience, the bill's author bore no mistake about what had just happened. Standing across from me, he expressed his obvious displeasure in a somber tone, borrowed from the Godfather. "You killed my bill... I'm not going to forget what you've done." With that, he turned and walked out of the hearing room.[27] Much as I reveled in fights with those legislators who appeared to be serving as corporate handmaidens, the defeat of this bill had instead been largely brought about by a group of public interest lobbyists.

With multiple proposals to be heard, we turned to the next bill on the agenda. My colleagues on the committee faced me, awaiting my reaction to the disgruntled state senator. Nodding his way, I met the knowing gaze of one particular lobbyist, Randy Kanouse, who had largely orchestrated the defeat of this bill. For his part, Randy was always quick to assign such victories to the actions of many others, including two fellow advocates typically present at the capitol: Martha Argüello, with Physicians for Social Responsibility and Bill Magavern, then representing the Sierra Club. Other public interest advocates not present in the hearing room that day had engaged similar struggles, extending over many decades.

A fuller history surrounding this particular victory of the public over a group of multinational corporations would reflect the multiple generations of advocates who battled with lead. This additive was a kind of poster-child for its inherent hazards to human health. Over many years, public interest advocates had made the California Legislature increasingly hostile to the proposition that lead was a useful ingredient in anything. The reality that lead needed to be immediately removed from faucets had many helping hands. Among its chief advocates was Randy Kanouse, whose early career with the State Water Resources Control Board shifted when he was named chief lobbyist for the East Bay Municipal Utility District, one of the state's major metropolitan water districts.[28]

Early actions focused on the use of lead pipes and lead solders with a consensus among medical researchers that even infinitesimal exposures were a cause for concern. Attention grew to include water faucets that were previously regarded as a negligible source. With no hint of his usual element of whimsy, guided by his group of utility engineers, Randy Kanouse emphatically pressed this opportunity to eliminate a dangerous and unnecessary threat to public health. The political dynamic was similar to other poisons, be they pesticides, plastics or petroleum as pursued by Martha Argüello, Bill Magavern, and a supporting cast of thousands responsible for advancing dozens of laws over many decades. Anchored in the assurance that citizens had the right to place limits on corporate activities (whether involving hazardous products or money in politics) and reflecting the work of numerous public health professionals, legislators gradually learned to recognize the inherent peril of lead exposures; especially for children. The upshot was enactment of a law protecting numerous California households, to become a landmark standard for the entire nation.

For other advocates lacking the financial wherewithal, the engineering expertise, and a skilled coalition of talented advocates, such an effort might take years to reach even a muddled compromise. Randy's approach to lobbying was always impeccably professional. Outside of committee hearings, it was no surprise that among Randy's favorite venues was the middle of Market Street in San Francisco, marching at an annual gay pride parade – another team effort involving hundreds of thousands.

Kanouse gained the support of metal workers and smaller metal manufacturers to demonstrate that practical technologies were already in place to eliminate lead in faucets. The story surrounding the passage of the new California lead standard for faucets could fill a separate book. A group of faucet manufacturers operating globally with revenues in the billions of dollars, who naively underestimated their opponents, were furious with the new California standard. Its pivotal role in international commerce compelled a retool of their operations around the world. As was always the case in the Legislature, the art of the possible fueled corporate lobbyists with new energies to fight another day, even when public advocates had delivered their client[29] such a resounding defeat.

Corruption or Complacency?

From a staff perspective, legislators such as Calderon operated perilously close to the edge of potential indictments. The 'tells' included nuanced pay-to-play relationships with the corporate lobby. The interchange of business cards in the middle of a hearing, the stepping away from the dais to confer with lobbyists in corridors outside hearing rooms, the knowing smile from lobbyists, the ready response to confer with particular persons off the Senate floor, the meetings across the street at a less well known coffee shop or bar, the ease and familiarity of access for those with money who "helped" members to locate plum housing; to craft beneficial legislation; or to staff future re-election campaigns. While none such assistance was illegal, for certain legislators the question of whether they represented their constituents or the overall interests of amicable corporate clients became more muddled.

In 2014, the Federal Bureau of Investigation issued indictments against Ron Calderon for bribery and related violations of law.[30] The FBI indictment contained a description of the alleged wrongdoing in which a state senator " solicited and accepted approximately $100,000 in cash bribes—as well as plane trips, gourmet dinners, and trips to golf resorts—in exchange for official acts, such as supporting legislation that would favor those who paid the bribes and opposing legislation that would harm them."[31] The alleged violations filed against Calderon included nothing with regard to leaded faucets. Calderon's indictment for 'defrauding the public' was based on the exchange of money for a political favor. The ultimate stupidity involved in such a choice was that the Supreme Court had effectively legalized avenues for defrauding the public.

In a series of court cases known as Citizens United, opening a path for corporations to massively expand their financial influence in politics as protected speech. Traditional prohibition against taking bribes could now be accomplished just as effectively via massive campaign donations. Where elections are financed without any specific exchange, the result is a public defrauded in a more sweeping sense. Whereas bribes specifically attached to a particular political favor remain illegal, limitless corporate expenditures ensure that laws allowing for more lead in faucets are no more illegal than other laws fostering the continued exposure of farm workers to hazardous pesticides, or increasing release of fine particulate air pollution harming children with asthma, or allowing chemical contaminants to accumulate in the blood of the newborn.

The example of lead in water underscores what is common in the corridors of power; the struggle over rules increasingly pits a public interest against a private one. In a modern context, where corporations are regarded not simply as people, but afforded an over-sized voice in the political process, the opportunities for defrauding the public have blossomed in both number and scope. The struggle to remove lead from water becomes only a small illustration of a converging climate of hazards confronting a public operating with an antiquated notion of politics – built on narrative that follows epic fights between Democrats and Republicans.

Public hopelessness over politics is formed around anecdotes reinforcing the perception that many politicians are corrupt, accepting payoffs. A more accurate portrayal would begin by understanding that the modern political process is fundamentally dominated by corporate wealth. The conclusion that moneyed interests form an overwhelming force in politics, however, dismisses the many instances in which the public has prevailed over private interests.

The case of the battle over lead legislation was instructive in several ways. First, it provided a lesson that money was not always a guarantee for defeating the public interest. The Calderon bill was what insiders refer to as "wired" - meaning the bill reportedly had the agreement of political leaders that it would pass, nullifying the new lead standard enacted the year before. A group of public interest lobbyists had been told the day before the hearing that the Calderon bill had too much money behind it; they needed to come to grips with that reality and find some way to accommodate the demands of the corporate lobbyists.

Second, the public interest victory reflected not a chance occurrence but a concerted effort organized and sustained over many years. Among the essential characteristics of this victory was a broad coalition of groups. Whenever lobbying on lead, the many faces reflecting California's many communities reminded legislators that these public advocates looked like their constituents. Third, was how supporters held a hard and strongly defensible position. By marshalling scientific findings public advocates developed a powerful tool for establishing a common public interest by which to defeat spurious arguments by opponents. By the beginning of the century, no credible scientific argument could be conjured by corporate lobbyists to support the acceptability of lead in any amount.

Fourth, despite having dramatically fewer resources, the public interest lobby was united to overcome their corporate lobby opponents. During the 1980s, for example, the public interest lobby prevailed in enacting a series of legislative measures protecting farm workers, consumers, and communities from the multiple threats of pesticides in the workplace, food, air, and water. A fuller history of these struggles demonstrates that the principal legislative measures were orchestrated by a modestly financed legal services group, [32] the California Rural Legal Assistance Foundation, opposed by a collection of agribusinesses commanding vastly greater resources. As with lead faucets, a crucial element of success depended on mobilizing a coalition of public interest advocates.

A Convergence of Crises

A standard of political reporting treats the emergence of each crisis as largely isolated from any other: lead in faucets as unrelated to campaign finance; pesticides in foods as distinct from pesticides and farmworkers; home heating costs as separate from unregulated financial transactions, or the destruction of the planet as unconnected from a series of obscure state laws supported by unrecognized public interest groups. From the perspective of political struggle, however, these emerging crises share many common features.

Consider how lead emerged as an integral part of America's economic ascendancy. Yet, this substance appeared as an integral part of automobile manufacturing, along with other notorious contaminants, as would be revealed decades later by the massive poisoning of the entire community of Flint, Michigan. "GM [General Motor] plants literally covered the waterfront of "this automotive city." Into the Flint, as other rivers went the toxic wastes of factories large and small, which once supplied batteries, paints, solders, glass, fabrics, oils, lubricating fluids, and a multitude of other materials that made up the modern car. In these plants, stringing their production debris along the banks of the Flint and Saginaw rivers, lay the origins of the present public health emergency"[33] The linkage of lead to fossil fuels was deeply intertwined with a much broader public health disaster enveloping poorer neighborhoods across America.[34]

"In the 1920s, tetraethyl lead was introduced as an additive for gasoline. It was lauded at the time as a 'gift of God' by a representative of the Ethyl Corporation, a creation of GM, Standard Oil, and DuPont, as companies that invented, produced, and marketed the stuff. Despite warnings that this industrial toxin might pollute the planet, almost three-quarters of a century passed before it was removed from U. S. gasoline. In the following decades, lead idly spewed out of the tailpipes of hundreds of millions of cars and trucks. It tainted the soil that children played in and was tracked onto floors that toddlers touched. Banned from use in the 1980s, it still lurks in the environment today."[35]

Despite a contemporary public perception that the lead problem had been solved, the fact is that numerous battles continue to be fought in the enduring struggle by an array of public interest advocates across the country to rid lead from a variety of consumer products ranging from childrens' jewelry and toys, to food, light fixtures, medical devices, and yes, even faucets. Contemporary legal struggles between manufacturers of lead-containing products continue across California including the infamous Exide plant in Los Angeles as well as other cities with pending lawsuits.[36] For the parents of tens of thousands of children in California alone, the arguments about indemnification for damages seem like cold comfort regarding a practice that should have been brought to a halt in the last century.

As part of a shared artful dodge, manufacturer's first denied any linkage to public health problems, and then raised questions about the exact nature of these problems. Uncertainties bound to surround the evidence further delayed decisive action: who is to blame and to what degree? Manufacturers using lead in their products found comfort in delaying more decisive actions while substantial harms continued to damage children and others. Scholars comparing legal efforts to control both harms have drawn an even more direct linkage between lead and fossil fuels. A notable examination compares limiting lead to limiting greenhouse gases in air by means of the Clean Air Act. Despite the weight of accumulated evidence that greenhouse gas emissions present a much higher degree of multiple harms, public advocates as a tightly organized group who appear in common struggles, confront far greater delays to bring greenhouse gas emissions under control.[37]

The Architecture of Conflict

In order to appreciate the work of public interest advocates, it is helpful to better understand their workplace. Approaching the California state capitol via one of several bordering paths, you will find a classic domed rotunda with its large columned entrance and marble steps leads to a series of over-sized wooden doors. It is a reduced model of the U.S. capitol. There is nothing miniature: however, about the scale of state influence in the making of laws having a national, and at times even a global reach. Stepping inside the capitol, the theme of power shows: in subtle and explicit ways. Marbled and carpeted corridors march from a rotunda to the two major chambers where members of the Senate and the Assembly gather to debate and deliberate on the important matters of the day. On the first floor major hearing rooms are reserved to address "bills," or proposed laws. Walk into the hearing rooms during a meeting of the committees on rules, judiciary, or the environment and there is no mistaking that serious matters are being deliberated, with significant consequences for California – if not beyond. It is not uncommon for the public to find the whole place slightly intimidating.

Indeed, even new legislators looking across a sea of faces are struck that they are at the focal point where a collective force of lobbyists representing millions of people, some wielding hundreds of millions of dollars are jockeying to influence their decisions. Understandably, this once sleepy, valley town is now visited by the chief executives of multinational corporations, Hollywood celebrities, leaders from around the world, aspiring presidential candidates, and many others. The tens of thousands of laws produced by the California legislature over the past several decades appear to address every imaginable topic. The average person on the street gains the impression that this capitol building epitomizes a form of democracy which regulates every aspect of daily life.

This broad-brush impression of its Legislature misses a more careful examination of both what fuels the construction of these laws, and for what purposes? While such a walking tour conveys a certain sense of power, it is also deceptive. In any hearing room the architecture guides every view to the raised dais – prominent and august. The suites for the governor, elected representatives and other officials convey a uniform message: this is the place where decisions are made for one of the largest economies in the world. But is this where power resides? The grand finery of such public buildings does not reveal the power behind closed doors, especially the private domain of power in the many private suites in multi-storied buildings surrounding the capitol where an expanding army of corporate lobbyists enjoy a view from on-high.

The law books lining nearly every legislative office underscore the wide reach of public law. But open several tables of contents and you may begin to see another dimension of these years of accumulated work; the arenas where law does *not* exist. For many practiced hands, the absence of law is especially revealing about relationships between the powerful and the powerless. To state this a bit more precisely, the absence of public law does not mean the absence of rules, such as those defined by technology protocols, industrial practices, or financial standards.

Whereas laws are at least formally within the orbit of public control, corporations define the rules and their markets open a territory remote from the arena of democratic institutions and the rights of citizens.

Despite the portrayal of excessive public laws, the expansive gaps are most stunning to view are at the dawn of the 21st century. Among the most notable gaps is a categorical imperative for a comprehensive approach to address an increasingly disrupted climate already recognized as a problem of global scale: Creating law is but one chapter in a larger work involving deep and protracted conflicts. Other chapters might include a review of proposed laws that have been defeated or dramatically amended. These other chapters reveal the dialectic, where powerful interests prevail by constraining public representatives from even pursuing an alternative approach to a widely recognized problem.

For all the tens of thousands of laws passed by the California legislature over the past five decades, only a handful impinge on an economy built on fossil fuels. There are a multitude of laws pertaining to the commerce of fossil fuels (e.g., oil exploration, production, transport, refining, sales, taxation). Yet a careful recounting of their histories shows that many, indeed most were reached with the approval, even at the insistence of the fossil fuel industry. Close reading of statutory law in these instances reflects an effort to erect stable market shares and barriers to competition in contrast to the mock protest by oil companies of facing heavy burdens of regulation.[38]

Why has it taken so long to eliminate such 'bad actors'?

One popular response is that bad choices result from corrupt legislators. In observing hundreds of bills over many years, I am struck that outright political corruption is exceedingly rare. Those inside the process recognize, there are many more nuanced yet equally effective exchanges that did not require anything so obvious as to yield indictments. In place of private chats in smoke-filled rooms, corporations can now convey their vigorous support to anyone agreeing to promote free market approaches (e.g., removing strict regulation, as defined by law, and allowing a so-called 'independent group' to define acceptable standards).[39] Another explanation is that the simple matter of addressing a problem, such as public health, is never so simple.

The corporate lobby has become especially skilled with demands that 'sound science' requires exhaustive reviews regarding the time, place and circumstances surrounding potential hazards. Among the pivotal arguments supporting Randy's approach to remove lead from faucet manufacture was a demonstration by his public utility engineers that affordable lead-free faucets could be readily and affordably manufactured[40] As Randy testified on various occasions, the attempt to construct a scientific rationale for revising California's lead-free standard would only delay and muddle what could be readily achieved in law.

Can the same approach be adopted for dismantling fossil fuels? This account revolves around this question. More specifically, these stories focus on a group of public interest advocates' attempts to grapple with more systemic questions of how such interest rises to the fore. A detailed analysis of prominent environmental laws reveals a vast gathering of talented, energetic advocates who regularly represent a public interest in democratic fora ranging from city council meetings to demonstrations around the state capitol. This broad and increasingly racially and ethnically diverse group has crafted some of the most protective public health, workplace, consumer, and environmental laws in the world.

The very concept of a "public interest" begs the question about who precisely belongs in this category. Wearing my academic robe, the question is an important one, worthy of both quiet reflection and consideration. As described in the opening scenes of this chapter, the rough and tumble of politics often requires a quick determination. As this book will go on to show, simply following those holding a banner proclaiming to uphold the public interest can be deceptive. At the same time, as the scenes of this chapter also illustrate, distinguishing between public versus private interests is seemingly a stark one. In many dozens of meetings with deliberations on hundreds of bills, those assembled before us clearly state whose interest they are serving. Yet, even this easy self-identification can be a muddled one. As presented in later chapters, the insistence by several of state environmental leaders that they are representing the public's best interest by pursuing 'market mechanisms' as a solution to a climate crisis becomes increasingly challenged by community activists across the state.

Taking a not-so-random walk through one of the world's most important centers for the production of law, my purpose is to present a series of stories extending over many years, focusing on a topic that has become the most important issue of our day: fossil-fueled crises. The story in this opening episode, involving a victory over a well-recognized poison and its linkage to fossil fuels is only one in a long series of struggles taking place inside the corridors of power.

CHAPTER 2

Inside the Law Machine

We're "*not* going to do any fucking hobby farming bill!" I had just joined the California Legislature after being selected as a 'senate fellow' to work for a year with a state senator.[41] My real passion was teaching. Without any job prospects and our resources being largely nonexistent, my partner and I figured that a short stint working with the California Legislature would not necessarily hurt my academic resume. I wondered again about my choice.

"Fucking hobby farming?" I repeated to myself. Born and raised in Oakland and having worked my early years in college as a Teamster, I was not easily shocked. Still, I found the statement somewhat stunning, particularly given the source.[42] Just across the street from my cubicle in the California state capitol, stood a suite of offices maintained by the University of California. As we both took a seat at an intimate conference table, and I opened my file to discuss proposed legislation, a vice president for one of the largest national agricultural research programs leaned across the table, displaying undisguised contempt; "We're not going to do any fucking hobby farming bill!" The meeting ended as abruptly as his remarks.

One of the most globally recognized names in academia refused to even discuss the bill.[43] Crossing the street toward the major pedestrian walkway leading back to the capitol, I wondered again, "Is this how they make laws? Is this how laws *should* be made?" I found myself wrestling with this dilemma only because in late 1984 I landed an unusual temporary gig – working for one of the more powerful members in the

California Legislature, Senator Nicholas C. Petris, who represented a distinctive district oft-times known as the People's Republic of Berkeley. Though I had recently completed my doctorate in political science, I knew next to nothing about state politics. In truth, I regarded anything connected to American politics as a pursuit for the brain dead. My partner found it a constant source of amusement to now witness me deep in the belly of the beast.

Senator Petris, the elder statesman, with a mane of prematurely greying hair, was known for his oratorical flourishes. In the Senate chambers he would hold forth on many topics of the day, seeking to influence his colleagues about the right thing that must be done to protect poor communities and farm workers, to end the death penalty, and a myriad of causes - including lavishly providing for a premier institution of higher education, the University of California.

In a political career spanning four decades Senator Petris established a reputation for designing laws based on a dialogue about justice. During the 1960s, many of his peers characterized the Senator's skill for problem-solving as predicated on a deep and abiding respect for social justice; and on frequently honoring otherwise unheralded voices at the legislative table. While based on a complex exchange, the Senator's notion of justice contained two dominant strains: one a place, the other a principle. The first could be found when he was asked how he could author such an array of outrageous laws. He would quip: "the people of Berkeley made me do it!" Strangers might find such explanation off-putting, but staffers lauded his earnest belief in the virtues of democratic institutions and in decisions led by citizens.

This basic notion – that citizens and their government exercised control over private sector activities – characterized many California representatives, especially those who experienced World War II; government taking control of basic industries was simply a part of how things got done. It also explained a moment in the 1960s when the public was poised to turn a key fossil-fueled crisis in a wholly different direction. With major California metropolitan areas increasingly shrouded in smog, millions of constituents demanded to hear what elected leaders intended to do. A group of Southern California legislators responded by requiring Detroit to produce cleaner cars.[44] For a legislator representing the so-called People's Republic, the answer was clear, as Senator Petris proposed a measure to outlaw the internal combustion engine.

The proposal immediately outraged car manufacturers, the business community and the oil industry. The oil industry reaction, according to Petris, argued that no viable alternatives were readily available or affordable. Despite the aggressive push-back, the Senator's suggestion to ban the internal combustion engine mobilized others to prompt Congress to consider federal funding for research into electric vehicles. The oil industry actively opposed the entire concept on the grounds that needed research into alternatives was already underway.[45]

The push by Californians and their legislators set in motion a series of laws placing the state at odds with letting the market decide. "In 1961, the first automotive-control-technology in the United States was mandated by California to target hydrocarbon crankcase emissions. It went into effect in 1963 on all domestic passenger vehicles sold in California, which eventually meant everywhere, since California was, and remains, the biggest market for all new and used vehicle sales in the country. That was followed by tailpipe emission standards, established in 1966 – also the first in the nation....The Federal Air Quality Act of 1967 included a waiver for California to set and enforce its own more stringent emissions standards for new vehicles sold in the state."[46]

Years later fuller exploration would reveal that even as industry dismissed Petris' proposed ban, various oil companies gathered patents on technologies for reducing engine emissions. By 2016 a group of states' attorneys general filed a massive lawsuit against the oil industry for having perpetrated what might be considered the most massive fraud against humanity. Petroleum interests began mounting a decades-long campaign to perpetuate continued use of their lucrative product, despite their own recognition of the growing hazards associated with the burning of fossil fuels.[47]

By 1970, the state senator from Berkeley would be lauded as among a group of influential leaders who played a catalytic role in the passage of the Clean Air Act by Congress as well as the California Clean Air Act of 1988. Nicholas C. Petris, however, would dismiss the praise, citing his usual attribution that he was merely following the guidance provided by his constituents. His glib response did reflect a shared perspective among many of his colleagues; they too were not shy about placing citizen demands above that of corporate lobbyists.

The Linked Crises of Fossil Fuels

Nor were legislative conflicts limited to simply the burning of fuels for transportation. In the 1960s Nicholas C. Petris identified the plight of California's farm workers as a cause célébre, and for much of his career regularly pursued legislation surrounding the mistreatment of workers who were essential to producing food for California and the nation. He fought for decades to eliminate pesticides posing known health hazards to workplaces affecting hundreds of thousands of farm workers became a decades-long battle. Like many of his colleagues, my new found mentor felt that democratic practice meant to bring as many different kinds of people to the table to participate in the making of laws as possible, vesting them with broad latitude to guide the course of legislation. In my own case, this involved "carrying bills" - meaning his staff would be personally responsible, not simply following him around from committee to committee, but actively participating in the legislative process.

As someone who had fought for farmworker rights for so long, the University's role of simply fostering agricultural production struck the Senator as wholly inadequate. With so many pesticides with unknown effects being readily applied to such vast acreage, what responsibility did the University leaders have for an agricultural research system so apparently disinterested in the routine poisoning of many thousands of farmworkers? While some university leaders suggested that a solution would eventually emerge from the marketplace or agricultural innovations, as many in the public demanded immediate legislative action to address this social injustice, even if this meant venturing into the arenas of private property or the proprietary claims of multinational corporations.

Returning to the arid Central Valley and the capitol from the misty, coastal congestion of Berkeley, I was amazed by the temerity of university leaders who, after receiving enormous public resources for so many years, now responded to a legislative proposal to create a program on sustainable agricultural research with a "fuck you very much" reply. If this was the response of a public university to such a mild request from one of the most powerful legislative members: how in the world did genuinely adversarial parties manage negotiations, especially those lacking the manifest power, the hallowed-hall presence and public office?

In many important respects my academic training as a political scientist and my tutelage in California's capitol represented entirely different worlds of politics. Whereas the former was conducted largely in isolation for many years, the capitol environment demanded working in teams. Little did I know that, venturing into the seemingly innocuous world of sustainable agriculture, I had chosen to take on some of the largest forces in California politics. Agriculture represented much more than simple production of food, if indeed that could be regarded as simple. It rerouted water, with a byzantine politics much more complex than even the film China Town could convey, with layers of competing interests seeping into every facet.

Other corporate interests in agriculture included vast land holdings, machinery and equipment manufacturers, as well as shipping, rail transport, and trucking. Perhaps most important in all of this was an agrichemical complex, with relationships ranging from petroleum refiners and specialty chemicals, formulators of fertilizers, seed producers to the vast complex of finance. The "simple" notion of asking the University of California to provide a program on sustainable agriculture sparked the perfect opportunity to unite many of the state's most powerful forces against those least powerful.

Despite the asymmetry of power, public interest advocates pursued legislation to restructure California's agriculture for the simple reason that agribusiness no longer appeared invincible. The sustainable agriculture bill followed from a 1984 victory of what seemed revolutionary at the time: a state law requiring the testing of pesticide ingredients to determine the hazards to farmworkers and others. The Birth Defects Prevention Act represented the crowning achievement by a group of physicians, environmentalists and labor unions who, in one step, placed California in an equivalent role to federal government and its agencies ostensibly responsible for regulating pesticides.[48]

At the heart of the California campaign to aggressively identify and regulate pesticides were multiple groups working as teams. While representatives of the agribusiness lobby strolled the corridors of power self-assured in controlling the production of law, its hegemony was crumbling. Public interest advocates, in contrast, expanded their coalition of supporters on a seemingly daily basis. By the mid-1980s, farmworker activists joined labor organizers, public interest science and public health groups, consumer attorneys, environmental organizations, local governments and many others to lay the foundations.

The confrontations were telling. In hearing after hearing, the visuals juxtaposed very different constituencies. Growers and agribusinesses were typically represented by a group of too-well-fed, older white men defending their right to conduct farming however they saw fit, even if this resulted in exposing hundreds of thousands of workers annually to hazardous chemicals. Supporters of farmworkers' right to safe workplaces included organizations representing a broad sweep of faces every legislator recognized as a reflection of their district. As one public interest advocate of the time commented to me while observing a hearing, nodding in the direction of a well-known agribusiness lobbyist across the room, "The Dinosaurs don't get it, but their hold over the Legislature is disappearing."

Behind the various bills paving the way for a changed treatment of farmworkers was a young pediatrician, Dr. Richard Jackson, one of the central figures in the launch environmental health policies over many decades.[49] While Dr. Jackson would later serve as California's Public Health Officer and direct environmental health at the U.S. Centers for Disease Control and Prevention, in the 1980s Dick moved largely unrecognized among the world of political movers and shakers.

Dr. Jackson actively orchestrated the work of fellow advocates spanning a wide scope of public health issues. In the arena of toxic substances, he readily briefed newspaper reporters and journalists, foundation boards and officers, members of congress, state legislators, attorneys and legal activists, not to mention numerous community, state, and international groups. In addition to these extracurricular activities, Dr. Jackson and his colleagues gradually transformed an obscure post at the foot of the University of California's Berkeley campus into an internationally recognized office that assessed environmental health hazards.[50]

Despite efforts to remain anonymous, Dr. Jackson soon earned unending wrath from a variety of corporate entities. Beginning in the late

1980s the corporate lobby regularly advanced proposals for curtailing the budget, personnel, and work of Dr. Jackson and colleagues. Once, after a corporate lobbyist alerted a legislative ally to defeat a supplement to Jackson's budget (set to investigate endocrine disrupting chemicals that would become widespread contaminant in human blood) Senator Tom Hayden stepped out of the ongoing hearing to carry a message back, "This fight isn't over: we are going to get those bastards!" As Hayden well understood, it was going to be a long fight.

One dimension of the work on sustainable agriculture was anchored in research extending over many years confirming that the University of California, far from being some neutral agent, provided extensive support to uphold a kind of status quo for dominant industries. The vehement objection to "hobby farming" was for many an unconscious poker ploy, revealing what cards you are holding. Revealed in this case was that the University had no intention of undermining the fate of agribusiness, particularly with respect to the role of labor.

For Richard Jackson had just led the battle requiring testing and disclosure of damaging health effects posed by pesticides, as continued on various other fronts. Limitations on pesticides in water became a major victory during the 1980s, as did greater restrictions on pesticide toxins in air, schools, parks and other occupational settings.[51] Operating at a level of near invisibility for much of this time were teams of physicians, epidemiologists, toxicologists inspired, if not specifically guided by Dr. Jackson to provide a form of public interest science to support health protections for consumers, children, workers and others. The carte blanche that had been provided dysfunctional federal statutes was being revealed and displaced by new California law.

More than simply narrowly crafted legislation designed to lessen farmworker poisonings, coalitions questioned the larger structure of agriculture. The conditions of work, wage levels, children's health, nutrition, education, and housing all related to the enterprise of corporate agribusiness. The broad sweep of public interest activism paralleled the expansion of the citizen-led laws. It also set California apart from Congress in both the production of law and the direction of those laws.

Why the disparity between Congress and a state legislature?

In the 21st century, California is not simply an economic powerhouse; its Legislature occupies a global presence. Each legislative session, a period spanning two years, its bodies typically deliberate on around two thousand bills, often sending many hundreds to the Governor's desk each fall. Since the 1960s California has enacted tens of thousands of legislative measures.[52] While pundits annually make sport by commenting on the most absurd bills, they tend not to provide any useful analysis of the impact of hundreds of other noteworthy bills, signed into law.

Whereas most states and even Congress will gamely endeavor to conclude their work on a much smaller number of bills, California as an entrepreneurial force, crafts hundreds of laws spanning a range of topics.[53] To put the comparison in perspective, Ronald Reagan signed approximately twice as many bills into law during his eight years as California's governor (1981 to 1989) than all of the measures passed by Congress over the next twenty-five years (1990 to 2013).[54]

Congress, while seemingly working on larger scale issues: typically takes many years to reach something approaching a consensus among varied and numerous interests. Many of my counterparts in D.C. complain that even simple bills require meetings with several dozen lobbyists, jockeying between committee jurisdictions, orchestrating a blessing by the major party, the administration, or finding votes among vastly different constituencies for 535 members. The Congressional process is sufficiently cumbersome to provide an opportune field for opponents to stymie the progress of any proposal, reinforcing a business-as-usual approach. Negotiations on the same subject in Sacramento might entail no more than orchestrating a few meetings with a small group of legislative staff, a dozen lobbyists from two major perspectives (e.g., industry and environment), a half dozen representatives from the Governor's offices and finding 21 votes in the Senate and 41 votes in the Assembly.[55] Many lobbyists and professional staff working on a particular topic know one another, know their clients, and interests before ever entering a room to begin negotiations.

Whereas negotiations on a bill might easily require several years in D.C., negotiations in California frequently conclude within two years. Even gridlock in Congress is often attributed to partisan recalcitrance: those same divisions do not create a similar impasse in state policy-making efforts. What is more, California's work in many instances generates a cascade of similar laws enacted in other states that then combine to provide the force to establish a uniform Congressional act. And there is the significant fact that enacting a law in California has an immediate impact on one of the larger economies in the world.

Added to this calculus are the very different procedural rules for considering legislation. In D.C. many negotiations begin with a determination of whether a committee chair will entertain a bill on any given topic. The Congressional model means that no matter how meritorious or virtuous the law proposed, if the committee chair is not inclined toward the measure (or toward the author), then the matter will not progress. It is part of the reason why Congress may see numerous measures introduced each year, but only a fraction of those actually pass out of a committee hearing (something approaching no more than 5% of this number, according to various estimates.)[56]

As the chief of staff for a California legislator later elected to Congress stated, "How's Jack you ask? He is utterly bored.... He now realizes that two to three dozen bills that he would get signed into law each year will never happen during any year in Congress." After pausing for a moment, his former chief of staff reflects with a sad shake of his head. "Hell, the guy would probably be lucky to get a single bill passed with his name on it in the next five years."[57] Many California legislators are thus reluctant to move from their positions in Sacramento to D.C. Ironically, measures they have authored and seen signed into law as a California legislator may have greater national impact than those they are able to author as a member of Congress.

California's Legislature, although often characterized as hostile to business interests, offers the private sector a distinct set of advantages over

Congress. In addition to resolving issues much more quickly, California provides the classic 'laboratory' for testing legal approaches before launching similar approaches in other states, nationally or even internationally. Second, if a disastrous experiment ensues, the damage is at least limited, with a clear opportunity to promote alternatives in other states or federally. Third, contrary to the image of a business-hostile climate, Californians have invested substantial tax incentives for public research and infrastructure with publicly financed bonds to support entrepreneurial activities in technology, biotechnology, medical research and alternative energy.

Fourth, and probably least well recognized, business interests very frequently win in the California Legislature. This reality stands the portrayals of so many media heads, well... on their heads. Instead of generating too many laws and regulations that keep the economy from fully advancing - the California Legislature often operates according to an agenda defined and designed by a variety of corporate interests. One financial observer recounted a corporate president who boomed (when asked about competing for market share in the boardroom,) "For god's sakes man, we don't compete in this business, what do you think regulations are for?"

All of which still leaves one to wonder, what are the consequences for producing thousands of laws in this manner? It may be most instructive to focus on some of the state's most celebrated environmental laws. Who is actually winning in these conflicts? What constitutes winning in a world confronting a converging threat of fossil-fueled crises? Before addressing the current situation, it is useful to review a contentious effort to launch sustainable agriculture in California.

"So what happened to the farming bill?"

When a conference colleague familiar with various controversies involving the University of California, asked about the state's now long-forgotten entry into sustainable agriculture, I related how, for years, others had approached U.C. researchers with questions about soil health or the problematic interactions between bugs and different cropping patterns, or other approaches adopted in their own fields and found in response only puzzled looks from those extension staffers. Despite U. C.'s many objections over the years (including an argument that they were constitutionally exempted from the laws of the Legislature) a variety of meetings were held with stakeholders, especially conventional farmers and many U. C. researchers who insisted that our artfully amended and reposed alternatives bill had no meaning as such, since they were *already* engaged in sustainable agriculture. When organic farmers would meet with neighbors who used conventional methods, those conventional farmers too provided puzzled looks. The organic farmers who brought the sustainable idea to Senator Petris in the very beginning of my tenure thereby found the campus system's response both laughable and incredible.

One of the very sharpest divisions between conventional and alternative agrarian practices hinges on the use of pesticides. While many organic farmers struggled to find substitutes for pesticides in their fields, U. C. researchers and conventional farmers regarded such approaches with the same contempt expressed by U. C. leadership. Arguments became more intractable and bitter as the legislation moved ahead, with committees agreeing that the Senator's bill should progress as discussions continued. Many in U. C. leadership opposed this bill, but the Regents and others were loath to turn down such a seemingly simple request from a Senator who had delivered so much over so many years. The University's opposition was such that a Senate offer to divert millions of dollars from fees assessed on petroleum manufacturers towards University programs was rejected: reportedly with the statement that no amount of money would alter its' established agenda to support conventional agriculture.[58]

As a way to demonstrate the "fact" that the bill had no authentic support beyond the small band of hippie farmers engaged in "hobby farming," U. C. did agree to stage a number of community meetings up and down the state. Administrators expected no serious farmers to show up, nor would the public demonstrate any kind of support. The outcome was much different. In meeting after meeting numerous members of each community voiced enthusiastic approval. Farmers, including some of California's largest rice and grape growers showed up in surprising numbers to advance a new kind of agriculture. Perhaps even more surprising, a wide range of restaurant owners, elementary school teachers, organizers of farmers' markets, joined with other community members to vocalize their support.

One of the sharpest arguments arose as to whom, inside the University, would control the program? As the University prepared for the enactment of the bill, I recommended the Division of Biological Control at Berkeley as one of the most hospitable places for devising new practices. The Division possessed a strong reputation for advancing biological instead of synthetic chemical methods. Its faculty members, including Professors Van den Bosch, Don Dahlsten, and Miguel Altieri, were some of the most dependable critics of fossil-fuel intensive agriculture.[59] This long-standing critique of pesticide-intensive agriculture was too much! University representatives were not amused. They insisted on locating the program instead at the mothership for conventional agriculture: their campus at Davis.

On one level, when the bill was finally enacted, it evoked very little change across University campuses. Many went about business as usual; dusting off older grant proposals that included phrases like "sustainable practices" to adorn the same chemical intensive approach used for years. U. C. largely neglected the program, hoping for its quiet demise. What's more Senator Petris, termed out of office in 1996, witnessed little of what he most hoped for – a major effort that would promote the serious reduction of pesticides while fostering healthy workplaces and communities for farmworkers. In another regard, the organic farmers who first approached Senator Petris succeeded along with countless others across California in planting an idea that would gradually spread to niche markets: demonstrating a wealth of sustainable agriculture practices with the promise of moving more conventional growers away from energy-intensive, petrochemical-reliant model hazardous to consumers to workers and to the environment.

A thorough-going and critical review of California's agricultural production system, including its more glaring contradictions, has remained largely unaddressed by the state or the University. No less disturbing has been the inability of the University to come up with a serviceable solution to the enormous energy requirements surrounding the state's food production system. Even though the intent-language of the bill established a clear directive for research and required demonstrations to eliminate or reduce the state's dependence on pesticides and petrochemicals, with the quiet demise of earlier alternatives, little has been achieved in the subsequent decades since the passage of the Sustainable Agriculture Research and Education Program.[60]

Problems of a fossil-fuel intensive agriculture paralleled those of a transportation system founded on petroleum. Challenging the internal combustion engine and chemical-intensive agriculture meant redirecting the state's economic foundations in a very real sense. It would require a broadly based and sustained political campaign to subdue entrenched and powerful economic interests that were cradled by most conventional practices. The question of whether the public interest would prevail over private interests was about to enter a new phase.

CHAPTER 3

Taking the Initiative

We're "going to sue you personally as well as the Senate Office of Research!" The agribusiness lobbyists seated across from me, were familiar with my work. Only the year before another group of their colleagues had stormed onto the Senate floor, demanding my immediate firing.

On that occasion I had allegedly intimidated the newly installed political appointee and retired chemical company executive into handing over confidential documents on pesticides. But that was another story... This day's angry display resulted from my analysis of their statewide ballot initiative sponsored by a gathering of the state's largest agribusinesses. After they invested considerable sums of money to counteract popular proclivity to ban numerous pesticides outright, my less than encouraging assessment of their work yielded the predictable response: more unhappy corporate faces across the conference room table.

The director of the office, Elisabeth Kersten, joined the meeting. As a protégé of Speaker Willie Brown, Elizabeth was practiced in the lobbyists' bullying tactics. Even so, she later admitted that this more aggressive corporate tactic was something of a first – to reverse our typically sleepy analyses of statewide ballot propositions. The source of their anger over my analysis stemmed from two very different initiatives appearing in the forthcoming election. One, penned by state agribusiness interests was largely designed to counter a competing measure. "Big Green," an initiative supported by numerous public interest groups threatened, among other provisions, to simply eliminate numerous hazardous and cancer-causing pesticides from the marketplace. Agribusiness groups argued that, in an already over-regulated industry, Big Green would cause food prices to rise sharply.

To undercut the popular appeal of Big Green, the state's major agribusinesses offered "greater scrutiny" of potential pesticide hazards with their own, competing initiative, one many of us mockingly referred to as "Big Brown."[61] After reviewing the arguments presented by Big Brown's sponsors, I concluded that scant data existed as to the relationship between more restrictive pesticide regulations and higher food prices; such claims by agribusinesses appeared inconclusive, at best. The fuming lobbyists were not about to accept this conclusion by the California Senate's research office, thus resorting to a less publicly displayed method of influence peddling: intimidation and threats. After allowing the rant for several minutes, Elisabeth Kersten interrupted, asking if they had anything further to add to their complaint. Reacting to the abrupt dismissal, the still-outraged lobbyists charged out of our offices.

I, of course, wondered if my budding career with the California Legislature might be coming to an end. Elisabeth provided instant relief with a chuckle, "Well your dry, objective analysis of their ballot measure was apparently not to their liking." Turning serious, she counseled me to carefully review my work. As she retreated down the corridor, I could hear her laughing to herself, with the comment "This may be a first for the Office of Research, a threatened lawsuit for our analysis of a ballot measure....I wonder what will be next?"[62]

While corporate anger over my work blossomed into a career theme, it also involved a much larger group of people in a political conflict predating my entry. The conflict was steeped in what many in the corporate lobby viewed as public interest advocacy run amuck. Not only were public interest lobbyists winning decisive battles in the Legislature; they were now expanding their reach by devising ballot measures for voters to deliver even larger victories that could otherwise not be so easily achieved with a Republican Governor. The initiative process in various other western states had emerged during the Progressive era in response to overwhelming industry influence on state legislatures. By allowing voters to act directly on ballot measures, the hope was to snap the stranglehold over elected representatives held by rail and mining interests. Between 1911, when this process began, and 1989, some 680 initiative measures appeared in California.[63] Lately, ballot battles have surged in number.

Over the course of its first 70 years, the initiative statute presented issues ranging from limits on campaign contributions to limits on property taxes to bond measures and much more. Yet it was the 1980s when an explosion began. Between 1911 and 1990, fully 40% of initiatives appeared during the 1980s.[64] The context reflected several converging factors: one, linked to a former governor - Ronald Reagan, then serving as President of the United States, meant that the expansion of government came to a halt. Reductions in force, otherwise known as downsizing federal agencies became widespread.

In California, the political winds blew in the opposite direction. The simple political fact of the 1980s was that various industries still dominated Congress sufficiently to dramatically amend, if not defeat, a range of environmental bills. The enthusiasm surrounding a proliferation of federal environmental laws during the 1970s gave way to a growing impatience with outcomes where little was changing on the ground. As President Reagan undermined federal environmental programs, shifted staff and withheld funds, California's advocates pressed legislators to accomplish more than the floor of minimal protections provided by federal law. With the exception of judicial actions, the frustration experienced by a growing number of public interest organizations and directed toward Congress during the late 1970s and 1980s encouraged many an advocates' end-run on Washington D.C. while focusing their work on creating new state law.

Proposition 65: Citizen Enforcement of Laws

Among the most dramatic victories achieved by environmentalists in a statewide ballot initiative occurred on November 6, 1986, when California voters enacted what would become one of the most significant laws to regulate toxic substances in the 20th century - the Safe Drinking Water and Toxic Enforcement Act. By a margin of 62.5% to 37.43%, Proposition 65 was supported by a majority of voters in 45 of the state's 58 counties.[65]

Major provisions included a) prohibiting the release of substances known to cause cancer or reproductive damage caused by the state's drinking water sources; b) publishing and updating annually a list of such substances; c) requiring warnings and notice regarding exposures to listed substances; d) imposing civil penalties of $2500 per day per violation of the initiative's provisions; e) broadening the penalties for violation of certain state laws to as much as $250,000 per day and three years in jail; and, f) allowing citizens to initiate suits in the absence of enforcement by state and local authorities within a specified time, as well as the imposition of fines for violation of specific provisions.[66] It was especially the last provision - allowing for citizen suits, which many in industry called "the bounty-hunter provision" -- that would drive many in industry crazy with rage against the public's ability to directly craft law.

The corporate rage over Proposition 65 also stemmed from the fact that the public interest lobby was becoming much more-savvy in constructing what became known as "bullet-proof initiatives." In place of vague and broadly stated federal environmental statutes that left wide discretion to administrators, California's statutes were being constructed to survive a hostile political climate ranging from challenges in the courts to federal preemption. A budding generation of savvy public interest lawyers would meet regularly with legislators, professional staff: a cutting edge to California's legal activism.[67]

The California ballot measure ignited an intensifying debate over the adequacy of public health protections provided by federal agencies. Reports issued by the Congressional Office on Technology Assessment, the General Accounting Office, the National Academy of Sciences, and various Congressional committees cast growing doubt on the ability of federal agencies to identify and to control toxic substances, particularly with respect to preventing cancer and reproductive hazards. Prior to November 4, 1986 various industries spoke out, in anticipated that the passage of Proposition 65 would severely affect the state's economy:

> "A 'yes' vote cast will bring chaos to our state's court system, cripple our economy, and send California's technology and business

improvements back some 20 years."[68] – *California Grape and Tree Fruit League*

"Proposition 65, if passed: would have a sweeping and profoundly adverse effect on California agriculture."[69] – *Californians Against the Toxics Initiative*

Various industries also challenged the legal authority of California to require warnings on foods, drugs, cosmetics, and medical devices already within the jurisdiction of state or federal programs. Other industry association petitions argued that existing law already satisfied certain of Prop 65's provisions. Petitioners included the Pharmaceutical Manufacturers Association.[70] Finding no opportunity to overcome Proposition 65 in federal court, the Grocery Manufacturers Association joined with the National Food Processors Association in a petition submitted to the state's Health and Welfare Agency as well as the federal Food and Drug Administration to grant federal preemption from the initiative's warning requirements.

In the absence of a decision favoring the industry petition, on July 27, 1988 the White House Domestic Policy Council initiated study for an executive order to essentially preempt Proposition 65. The White House Policy Council, reportedly finding little basis for supporting federal preemption, concluded that the alleged burdens resulting from Proposition 65 were vastly overstated by industry representatives.[71] As industry licked its wounds from defeat at the polls in California, in the judiciary, and even among its allies in Washington, D.C., many corporate lobbyists remained smugly aloof from the ongoing drumbeat of scientists and their findings of the still mounting threat from toxics.

As aggressive as Proposition 65 was in pursuing approximately 200 to 300 substances recognized as causing cancer or reproductive damage at the time of the initiative's passage, there remained a universe of substances with unknown effects. While most scientists scrupulously avoided examining the larger social and environmental consequences of their work,[72] a number of their more audacious colleagues stepped forward to express dismay, including a statement delivered by Dr. Samuel Epstein to Congress following the passage of Proposition 65: "In the early 1940s annual U.S. production of synthetic organic chemicals was about one billion pounds. By the 1950s, this had reached 30 billion pounds, and by the 1980s over 400 billion pounds annually. The overwhelming majority of these industrial chemicals has never been adequately, if at all, tested for chronic toxic, carcinogenic, mutagenic and teratogenic effects, let alone for ecological effects, and much of the limitedly available industrial data is at best suspect."[73]

The debates surrounding the scientific basis for a variety of California rules governing production, use and disposal of toxic substances would continue for years to come. In many instances, the scientific debates themselves provided the excuse for corporate lobby's ongoing dismissal of rapidly evolving rules to address tens of thousands of chemicals used to manufacture a world of products. At legislative hearings on new laws, questions surfaced regarding the burden of proof of damaging effects for human health or the environment. The premise regularly advanced by the corporate lobby was that, absent demonstrable scientific certainty, the state was obligated by due process to allow private sector firms the right to continue their business activities as usual. An active agent recording them, however, would be reminded from time to time that the question of whether the public should carry the burden of demonstrating a scientific proof that would satisfy the manufacturers of chemicals was not the overriding issue.

Before the end of 1989, a district court judge severely rebuked the California governor, George Deukmejian, about his effort to undermine the implementation of Proposition 65 by erecting a more difficult scientific barrier for regulating chemicals. Judge P.J. Puglia reminded the Governor and others that the essential question turned not on scientific evidence, but in the imperative to ensure a public right to control their perceived safety:

> "Proposition 65 clearly reflects the result of public dissatisfaction with the state's efforts to protect the people and their water supply from exposure to hazardous chemicals. It is not our function to pass judgment on the propriety or soundness of [the Act]. In our democratic society, in the absence of some compelling, over-riding constitutional imperative, we should not prohibit the sovereign people from either expressing or implementing their own will on matters of such direct and immediate importance to them as their own perceived safety."[74]

Before the end of the decade, other initiative measures would shape the governance of fossil fuels. Indeed, by 1990 California voters received their first opportunity to address global warming on a comprehensive basis. As with so many Golden State laws, it was a political juncture that would cast a long shadow around the globe, for many years to come.

Big Green: The Public Interest and the Economy

'Big Green', known more formally as California Proposition 128 was prepared as a statewide initiative for voters to decide on during the November 6, 1990 general election. Big Green promisd significant changes to California's laws governing pesticides, food safety, air pollution emissions, old-growth redwood forest preservation, coastal protection, and the coordination and enforcement of state environmental laws.[75] The Environmental Protection initiative of 1990:

- Requires pesticide use regulation to protect food, agriculture, and worker safety.
- Phases out use on food of pesticides known to cause cancer or reproductive harm, chemicals that potentially deplete ozone layer.
- Requires reduced emissions of gases contributing to global warming.
- Limits oil, gas extraction within bay, estuarine and ocean waters.
- Requires oil spill prevention, contingency plans.
- Creates prevention, response fund from fees on oil deliveries.
- Establishes water quality criteria, monitoring plans.
- Creates elective office of Environmental Advocate.
- Appropriates $40,000,000 for environmental research.
- Authorizes $300,000,000 general obligation bonds for ancient redwoods acquisition.

The initiative was breath-taking in its reach; any one provision might well have constituted its own ballot measure. Together, the initiative suggested an approach designed to alter the content and direction of the state economy. The greenhouse gas reduction plan was especially striking, calling for a 20% reduction in CO_2 emissions between 1988 and 2000 along with an additional 20% reduction between 2000 and 2010. In response to opponents' claim that such reductions were impossible without sinking the state's economy: supporters argued that this initiative could achieve requirements by adopting a suite of regulatory measures, including:[76]

- Doubling the average fuel economy of new motor vehicles. [77]
- Planting trees and painting surfaces with lighter colors (16 percent).
- Improving lighting and appliance efficiency (12 percent).
- Increasing renewable resources for energy production (10 percent).
- Improving industrial efficiency (7 percent).
- Improving building efficiency standards (7 percent).
- Managing forest lands (7 percent).
- Improving mass transit programs (2 percent).

Central to the philosophy behind Big Green was the idea of catalyzing a system to propel a race to the top in terms of standards and the outcomes for environment and society. The objective would not be to perpetuate regulations, but rather to rapidly eliminate toxic products in the marketplace. Instead of an economy characterized by many as "a race to the bottom," the architects of Big Green hoped to spur industry competition to achieve constantly improved workplace protections, public health and environmental protections.

The Public Leading Its Leaders

The architects of Big Green next performed a political Jiu-Jitsu. Instead of waiting for endorsements to accumulate, they asked major candidates to adopt the wide ranging provisions as part of the platform of what they committed to do, once in office. Remarkably, John Van de Kamp announced his run for Governor with a statement signaling his support for Big Green along with two other ballot initiatives. Strategically combining the candidate with a specific platform for change presented a potentially new political dynamic in the electoral process. Not only might the initiative process again serve as a tool of populism; but it also now opened the door for merging candidates with progressive platforms.

Van de Kamp's prospects were made more difficult when Diane Feinstein joined the primary race for governor, a choice that certain observers inside the capitol viewed as stimulated by Van de Kamp's endorsement of Big Green; a political agenda too far for the moderate wing of the Democratic party and its many corporate sponsors. In addition to Big Green, Van de Kamp recalled that Willie Brown was not amused at a press conference he attended on the front steps of the capitol, when John announced that it was "time to drain the swamp," referring to the FBI sting operation resulting in the indictment of several legislators and staff.[78] Whatever the truth, Feinstein succeeded with besting Van de Kamp in the primary. The sweetest part of the victory for the corporate lobby occurred in November with the defeat of both-Big Green and Feinstein, a now term-limited legislature, and a newly elected Republican governor.

Attorney General Van de Kamp acknowledged that among the miscalculations of Big Green were including too many issues in a single initiative; an observation that many involved in the drafting would later concede. Others, engaged in a post mortem, noted that while the initiative energized environmentalists of every persuasion, it also galvanized a broad opposition by private sector interests.[79] The Big Green defeat stemmed, in no small part from its corporate opponents. "Over $13 million, 99.5 percent of the opponents' money, came from business interests led by three oil companies ...over $8 million came in contributions between $100,000 and $1,000,000 and more than half the opposition money, 55 percent, came from outside the state."[80] Even with supporters generating approximately $6 million for Big Green, the experience confirmed what many observers believed to be a fundamental asymmetry between "what it takes to defeat an initiative for change and what it takes to pass one."[81]

Big Green resulted in the creation of the California Environmental Protection Agency (Cal EPA), designed to bring together disparate state departments. Most pointedly, the state's pesticide regulatory body (previously located inside the Department of Food and Agriculture), was placed under the authority of Cal EPA. The agribusiness lobby repeated a vent of its anger at one individual in particular who it held responsible for disrupting its control over a captive regulatory body: Dr. Richard J. Jackson. According to a source who spoke with Jackson years later, a particular demand made by corporate lobbyists to Governor Wilson was that Dick would not be given any position of authority in Cal EPA. The demand, it turns out was granted. One odd twist on this piece of history was that a group of the Legislature's senior staff worked doggedly to create a super agency designed to address *environmental health.*

After various political battles of the 1980s, there was a strong sense that separating state environmental work from public health was nonsense. With many of the most important issues – pesticides, water pollution, toxic contaminants - it was essential for policies to consider public health. In these discussions, Dr. Jackson was the spiritual guide in our work.

After many years with influencing so much of California law, it was not surprising to find the corporate lobby spending precious political capital to keep Jackson away from any position of authority. Yet, he would quickly move to assume even greater authority: initially at the U.S. Centers for Disease Control and Prevention, later as California's Public Health Officer under Governor Schwarzenegger. When at CDC he instituted the national programs to bio-monitor chemical body burdens in the American people (e.g., lead, phthalates, Bisphenol A). In 2005 after California passed its own bio-monitoring law, chemical industry lobbyists, who clearly had not done their homework, appeared at the Health Department's front door attempting to convince Jackson that this impeccable body burden work was flawed and wasteful. After his odyssey, Dick had a good, private laugh, but refrained from defenestration. Such a luminary's exile would weaken the state position as an environmental and public health leader for years to come.

The Campaign of Deception

Years later the role of oil companies in defeating Big Green would expose an even darker side of a covert agenda to misdirect public action regarding climate change. More than a decade earlier, in July 1977, a chilling assessment was delivered to Exxon's corporate headquarters:

carbon dioxide from the global use of fossil fuels would warm the planet and could eventually endanger humanity. Exxon was warned again by the same top technical Research & Engineering division experts that a doubling of the carbon dioxide (CO_2) concentration in the atmosphere would increase average global temperatures 2 to 3 degrees Celsius (4 to 5 degrees Fahrenheit), and as much as 10 degrees Celsius (18 degrees Fahrenheit) at the poles. Rainfall might get heavier in some regions, and other places might turn to desert.[82] Confronting scientific evidence that its core business constituted a threat to the planet, Exxon initiated a scientific research team to investigate more fully the relationship of fossil fuel emissions and climate change.

Coinciding with Exxon's investigations into burning fossil fuels and climate change, a larger task force was formed by the American Petroleum Institute (API) enlisting scientists from major oil companies, including Exxon, Texaco, and Shell. In 1979, the task force was briefed by a Stanford University professor whose findings were even more startling than those presented to Exxon in 1977.[83] The presentation began by noting that the primary problems associated with threats to the climate stemmed from the burning of fossil fuels. The threat, moreover, was by no means trivial. His modeling concluded that the amount of CO_2 in the atmosphere would double by 2038, affecting "a 2.5 degrees Celsius rise in global average temperatures with "major economic consequences."[84] Suggesting even worse to come, "he then told the task force that models showed a 5 degrees Celsius rise by 2067, with catastrophic global effects."[85]

Exxon and API's own scientific reviews provided little comfort: they confirmed a rising tide of critical scientific studies. Original purposes for industry-sponsored investigations were subverted. "In the early 1980s, Exxon researchers often repeated that unbiased science would give it legitimacy in helping shape climate related laws that affect its profitability." Decade's later investigative journalists working with archived materials described this as a move from open scientific debate to an unrestrained effort to totally dominate decision-making:

> "They took the environmental unit and put it into the political department, which was primarily lobbyists...They weren't focused

> on doing research or improving the oil industry's impact on pollution. They were less interested in pushing the envelope of science and more interested in how to make it more advantageous politically or economically for the oil industry."[86]

Coinciding with the internal political calculus of the major oil corporations, a young regulatory scientist, James Hansen, told Congress in 1988 that there was enough warming to declare that the greenhouse effect had arrived. Also that year, the United Nations set up the Intergovernmental Panel on Climate Change (IPCC). It was a moment that Exxon's climate experts had been forecasting for a decade: as warming became unmistakable, governments would move to control it.[87] The IPCC, after intense deliberations, prescribed deep reductions in greenhouse gas emissions to stave off the looming crisis as but one precaution that is "certain".[88]

The pivot from impartial scientific fora, as described by the investigative journalists, marked the initiation of a project designed to dominate the public sphere. "Toward the end of the 1980s, Exxon curtailed its CO_2 research. In the decades that followed, Exxon worked instead at the forefront of climate denial. It put its muscle behind efforts to manufacture doubt about the reality of global warming its own scientists had once confirmed. It lobbied to block federal and international action to control greenhouse gas emissions. It helped to erect a vast edifice of misinformation that stands to this day."[89]

It is unclear to what extent Big Green sparked Exxon to move from a position of inquiry to covering up and denying the damaging consequences of fossil-fueled economies. What would become clear years later was that the leading global petroleum company had certain knowledge that its product represented a global danger that would persist for decades, if not centuries. In place of open exchange, Exxon and its allies worked to defeat a series of public efforts to address the doomsday machine that it was responsible for unleashing on the planet.

Downsizing Democracy

The defeat of Big Green in 1990 also coincided with another equally devastating change in California politics with the passage of term limits for elected legislators. Proposition 140 contained two principal components. The most prominent provision would limit members of the Legislature to three terms in the State Assembly and two terms in the State Senate. California voters were recruited to a popular impression, created by common analogies to "the swamp," of legislators as too entrenched and out of touch with the concerns of average Americans. California's term-limiting measure, however, contained a second, less recognized provision to cut the Legislature's budget by 40%. The clear and immediate effect was to dramatically downsize a key platform for California's progressive law machine: a large body of professional staff. Within a year of enactment, hundreds of Legislature's staff, including many of its most seasoned and talented professionals left the capitol.

A number of functions, including the Senate Office of Research and the Office of the Legislative Analyst, were reduced by something on the order of 30 to 50%.[90] Years later, after virtually all of the generation of legislators who had served before the onset of term limits were gone from the Legislature: the climate for professional staff had changed noticeably. At a superficial level, all of us who served as senior staff were indeed more powerful – as partly measured by the very few flanking a hearing room who knew the procedures, current law, past laws, institutional history and larger context surrounding a proposed law.

As senior advisers, we found ourselves increasingly in conflict with a newer generation of legislators who were often ill at ease. And with good cause! Even after several years, too many legislators were in an inferior position to staff who demonstrated a facility that many elected representatives lacked. Conflicts surfaced in decisions surrounding the passage of a bill when legislators on a committee might give greater weight to the analyses of professional staff than a committee chair's murkier basis for votes cast. Unlike earlier generation of relationships where a shared perspective on the law and the endgame of negotiations often existed – the modern Legislature increasingly operated in a world of friction with their staff. Yet, what was increasingly was a result of additional clashes between staff and corporate lobbyists.

On the positive side it was enormously refreshing to encounter committees no longer comprised solely of old white men. Faces reflecting California's diverse communities continued to grow in representation over the years. The blossoming of caucuses, both formal and informal, representing Latinos, women, Asian and Pacific Islanders, African Americans and others created an excitement that brought forth topics and issues too long ignored. Celebrations in the rotunda that now included mariachis conveyed a sense that the capitol was a much more welcoming place to many communities too long excluded. If the faces of elected representatives changed, there was a dearth of evidence that the mechanisms of power had been altered.

To be sure, corporate lobbyists complained that they now had to train a whole new group of legislators every two years. For many other entrepreneurial lobbyists, the constant new wave was simply an opportunity to expand client billing. To put it more bluntly, less stable political districts became ripe hunting grounds for corporations to recruit and nurture a new generation of moderates or *corporados* – who would proceed to shape both the content and the style.

For many professional staff, however, the entry of term-limited legislators constituted a stark change in negotiating almost every bill. If, prior to term limits, legislators were impervious to certain popular demands, it was also clear that the same applied to private demands. Prior to 1990, many of California's legislators were comfortable enough to tell a lobbyist where to stuff it when threatened by corporate dissatisfaction. The perception among many legislators of this earlier generation was recognition that no corporation or group of corporations was going to defeat them in a coming election. Following term limits, in too many situations it was evident that many term-limited legislators approached committee or floor sessions with trepidation about making a wrong move that would threaten their re-election.

Following the enactment of Proposition 140 and the de-professionalizing of the legislature, a pivotal change occurred with the loss of so many veteran staff. Whereas the prior work of Legislative professionals involved constructing new programs, procedures and approaches, the subsequent downsizing in the era of term limits ushered in many more staff whose time horizon focused on tracking legislation constructed by others, especially by professionals outside the capitol. Possessing a much broader and deeper experience that made them more audacious, veteran staff who had seen waves of members come and go, frequently expressed disappointment with legislators who lacked the courage to pursue ground-breaking proposals. Term limits, however, represented only the most overt part of an evolving campaign to bend California lawmakers, like other state legislators, to the will of a corporate lobby. A more elaborate plan took shape following the citizen enactment of Proposition 65.

The failure to reverse this Safe Drinking Water and Toxic Enforcement Act had extended from the Governor's Office to the U.S. Congress to the President of the United States - and ultimately led to a meeting convened at the Sacramento Convention Center circa 1998. A group of corporate attorneys provided a briefing to members of the corporate lobby regarding failures to deal with the fallout of the now notorious "toxics" initiative. As any savvy attorney might counsel his client, the question about "what to do" was not a rhetorical one. It was at this meeting that the first mention of "trade agreements" arose as a political tactic to address the problem of California's activist voters. Without divulging any specifics, several unidentified speakers suggested that their colleagues in the corporate lobby should contact their clients to aim new instruments at the problems posed by California's too progressive electorate. Trade agreements were presented as devices that could override "disobedient citizens," thereby providing a solution to not only to one initiative measure, but potentially to a much larger body of laws.

To compound the loss of many veteran legislators through term limits, their replacements held a much different disposition toward the role of specific corporate lobbyists as well as a much more positive disposition toward so-called free markets. With Republicans wresting control of the governor's office as well as the Legislature's lower house, a new state agenda was to lift burdensome regulations developed by an earlier generation of legislators. Among the many measures put forward was a particular bill introducing market mechanisms to the sale and transmission of energy. Celebrated as measure fostering a free-market for energy, within a few short years it would also turn out to be a center-piece in one of the first crises of the new century.

Big Green instead of addressing simply one policy silo (e.g., the damaging effects of pesticides), identified the combination of damages to both California's environment and economy from an economy run amuck. Another of its distinguishing traits was that it galvanized corporate opponents. The defeat of Big Green signaled a major reversal of public victories over the direction of the economy. California would revert to a political theme dominant in many states: dismantling regulatory controls placed on corporate activities. Among the most damaging consequences in defeat of Big Green was the lost opportunity to gradually exit fossil fuels while promoting alternative energy production.

By the time California revisited a comprehensive approach to address climate change, more than twenty-five years had passed. As would become evident, 21st century legislation would, in many crucial respects, represent a much weaker approach to questions concerning the combined negative effects of energy production, the promotion of alternatives to fossil fuels, and on who should control the state economy? The political context leading to the defeat of Big Green was not limited to a victory of corporate control by an older generation of elected officials in its own economic domain. Because an older generation was replaced, beginning in 1990, with a newer generation (who were immediately, recognizably fearful of the corporate lobby and insulated from the influence of private corporations) the skids were greased for a dormancy in California's law-making in support of lifting controls on the corporate sector.

And so, the new theme of deregulation would reverberate for years to come. A comments delivered by Exxon's chief executive challenged the idea that the planet was warming at all, despite the evidence cited by Exxon's own team of scientists.[91] No less revealing than the pivot away from scientific evidence was the founding of a political agenda on tactic successfully employed by the corporate lobby - to deny and delay the imposition of public controls. [92]

CHAPTER 4

So Far from California

What "were you thinking, *pobrecito*? First, telling a room that Mexico-California relations were vitally important, and then further asserting that California had a lot to learn from Mexico? Didn't you see the looks on their faces? They were outraged! It's a wonder you ever made it into the capitol, at all..." My career with California's Legislature began only because of my earliest political mentor Martha Valdez.

Among an elite group of Latinas selected by Governor Jerry Brown to serve at the top levels of state agencies, many in state government recognized Martha Valdez for her detailed knowledge of a broad sweep of of environmental law. At the conclusion of Jerry Brown's first term of office, Martha joined a group of Jerry's former political appointees, 'Brownies', who continued their public service to staff the Senate Office of Research. At once dignified and humble, Martha's counsel was eagerly sought by many legislators before they ventured into the growing thicket of finely detailed laws.

Also popular for guiding young Latinos working in the capitol, Martha had the cool bearing and utter decisiveness attributed to Iberian royalty. For me, Martha Valdez figured prominently as one of my earliest mentors, taking pity on me as someone obviously in need of guidance in the ways of working politically. Indeed, my selection as a Senate Fellow was due in no small part to Martha's advocacy on my behalf, arising from our shared interests: the converging politics of Mexico and California.

Over many years, we shared thoughts about the importance of Mexico when discussing California policies. One of our earliest conversations involved an agricultural project sponsored in Mexico by the Rockefeller Foundation in the early 1940s. It would become the cornerstone of an international effort to modernize agriculture around the world. Even among those familiar with Mexico in the 20th century, the story remains largely unknown, especially the fierce conflicts between a small band of U.S. scientists and Mexico's own professionals, who challenged the premises of a corporate-styled agriculture, which assist Mexico's most affluent and politically powerful farming interests while ignoring the vast number of subsistence farmers. With massive investments in export agriculture during the following decades, scant attention focused on the worsening conditions confronting millions of Mexico's small farmers.[93]

Fossil fuel intensity in agriculture became an integral part of the Mexico project, extending from engineered crops predicated on the extensive use of synthetic fertilizers, pesticides, the intensive energy required for mechanized planting and harvesting regimens, movement of irrigation waters, processing of grains, and a hugely expensive transport infrastructure. While the Rockefellers' so-called Green Revolution became an export model for modernizing agriculture around the globe, less publicized features included a host of negative consequences affecting rural households with increased unemployment, worsened nutrition, and damaged environments. In the following decades, the emergence of highly capitalized and petroleum-reliant agriculture fueled the mass migration of millions searching for jobs in California and beyond.

Growing up in Ensenada and later attending law school in San Diego, Martha was already familiar with the absurdity of blaming Mexican immigrants forced from their communities with the collapse of traditional agriculture. The agricultural modernization project orchestrated by U.S. scientists, as well as later trade policies, contributed to her caution: do not assume the consequences of modern technology are necessarily beneficial.[94]

Assessing Technologies

A less known Congressional advisory group, the Office of Technology Assessment (OTA) contributed importantly to Martha's work. The Office reviewed emerging technologies both to understand their consequences and to pose a question too often lost in the rush to craft legal solutions: Did the technological solution have anything to do with what caused the problem in the first place? OTA reviews countered the attraction of technological solutions among many in Congress, encouraging more thoughtful approaches. One favorite Valdez report focused on the out-of-control contamination resulting from hazardous wastes. Dismissing industry's preferred option of how to better manage hazardous wastes, OTA recommended Congress approach the origins of the problem: encourage the serious source reduction of hazardous materials. OTA recommendation offered both savings for industry as well as fewer costly damages, typically paid for by taxpayers.[95]

The Office of Technology Assessment won Martha over, and her closest colleagues followed. In place of traditional cost/benefit analyses or performance reviews of government programs, OTA's approach suggested a new path: how might the public encourage differing approaches to address problems rooted in the production practices of modern corporations? At the Senate Office of Research, Martha served as a state experts on hazardous wastes. With federal and state legislation initiated in the 1970s, hazardous wastes became a focal point for an industrial epidemic spreading across the country. By the 1980s, California hazardous waste sites numbered in the tens of thousands.

Like enhanced awareness of lead contaminants that had been ignored for too long, public awareness grew regarding the hazards emanating from abandoned industrial sites. Discussions in the state capitol frequently turned on how to manage industrial wastes, who would pay, and how clean was clean? The technical nature of such questions propelled a bevy of laws sharing a similar approach: how to "best manage" hazards? Lost was a more fundamental question: Did dominant industrial practices pose intrinsic hazards?

Martha Valdez recognized that the corporate lobby had succeeded in erecting a byzantine architecture of laws indecipherable to the general public. Lost in the minutia of legal provisions detailing management procedures was any thought for the archaic energy foundations of the state's economy – particularly the extracting, processing, disposing and burning of fossil fuels and the legacy of damages enveloping tens of thousands of sites, air basins, estuaries, rivers and communities. For Martha and her colleagues, the subversion of law by the corporate lobby arose with the push for treatment technologies as a status quo option, undermining an obvious alternative: to aggressively curtail fossil fuels while mandating safer alternatives.

Martha Valdez, for one, recognized how this question of alternatives opened a much more ambitious political project. If society were to avoid the worst kinds of private sector damages, then democratic institutions must surely have authoritative wherewithal to direct the course of markets. It was a matter she discussed from time to time with amused wonder. How was it that so many in the United States denigrated Mexico as less developed when Mexico already embraced what so many in the U.S. aspired to attain: markets virtually unrestrained by citizens and their political institutions? For Martha, many disasters of modern Mexico were inextricably linked to the savagery of unrestrained 'free' markets.

One of the consequences of Martha Valdez' work in California (and that of her counterparts in Washington, D.C.) emerged with the larger efforts to dismantle both the Senate Office of Research as well as the Office of Technology Assessment. To be sure, the eventual elimination of these research groups would spring from a multiplicity of factors. The shared trait of questioning private sector business practices earned both offices an enduring enmity within the corporate lobby on both coasts. Perhaps only in retrospect did it become clear that open challenges to the corporate lobby in the late 1980s meant the effective elimination of the Senate Office of Research (a topic receiving further attention in the next chapter.)

500 Years of 'Free' Markets

Years after first meeting in the capitol, Martha and I departed the California Legislature at the same time in 1990, each of us electing (in a circuitous way) to return to work involving both Mexico and California. For Martha, this meant joining friends in a well-known community-based group, the San Diego Environmental Health Coalition. For my part, it involved pursuing another study in Mexico, this time scrutinizing the newly proposed North American Free Trade Agreement or NAFTA.[96]

After arriving in Mexico, I was introduced to a group of talented professionals at the ministry of agriculture who were transcribing large swaths of U.S. federal regulatory law and placing the same language in Mexican law. When I asked about it, a common reply suggested a simple task, "We are modernizing Mexico by harmonizing our standards to conform with those of the United States:" For many Mexican academics the process of "harmonization" begged scrutiny of an unexamined premise: What problem was NAFTA designed to solve? The purpose of the proposed trade agreement would not be discovered in the dreary corridors of Mexico's bureaucracies.

Many premier Mexican universities engaged in more penetrating examination of NAFTA than asking what problem it was established to solve, and its potential consequences. Indeed, investigations stretching over many years indicated that the trade agreements provisions would, in all likelihood, accelerate the depopulation of the countryside: pushing additional millions of small family farmers off their lands. The supposed benefits of the free market now threatened to place subsistence farmers as competitors against highly capitalized and politically-powerful agribusinesses. The outcome held no mystery for anyone familiar with Mexican agriculture. The only absence of certainty appeared on the U.S. side of the border where a complacent press served as a conduit among corporations already celebrating the spread of free markets.

U.S. enchantment with free markets left many observers with little doubt as to the outcome of the proposed NAFTA Treaty. Even though the Mexican academic community provided stunningly detailed and brilliantly argued papers against it, the conferences seemed like a sideshow. Professors and their entourage would present important papers, include critical perspectives delivered by U.S. and Canadian farmers, announce their findings, and return to the obscurity of campus offices. Even so, many younger scholars privately vented their frustration that evidence-based arguments held a very marginal role among North American trade delegations.

Leaving behind Mexico City's many conferences, I noted NAFTA seemed remote from everyday life in Morelos, Guanajuato, Oaxaca,

Puebla, Vera Cruz, Jalapa, Merida and other locations as I conducted my investigation. All of that changed when I arrived in Chiapas. During my visit years earlier to a specific region of Chiapas, San Cristóbal de las Casas appeared like a forgotten village - remote and disconnected from the rest of Mexico. By 1991 San Cristóbal appeared as only a slightly more active and traveled place.

My visits to surrounding villages and conversations with locals reflected a subterranean activity, including a tension not unlike the unrest more common to rural parts of Guerrero or Michoacan. While I did not know enough about the indigenous culture or history to discern much, my visit centered on a figure frequently mentioned in Mexico City newspapers, Archbishop Samuel Ruiz. The Archbishop received press scrutiny as a reflection of ongoing battles within the Catholic Church, specifically his controversial role in liberation theology. Samuel Ruiz was notable in Mexico as staunch in supporting the role of priests who understood their service to the Church as protecting the poor in this world.

On a Saturday morning, I joined a long line of parishioners extending outside of the cathedral doors. Standing in line among others facing evident hardships, I wondered about my audacity in traveling to this hub to ask abstract research questions about a topic seemingly so distant from this plaza. When I finally took my turn to speak a few words, the Archbishop graciously welcomed my question, "Can you please share your thoughts regarding the proposed trade agreement?" His pause in response made me reflect that only someone as naive as a young Californian could dare to barge into an audience with one of Latin America's most highly respected priests, ask such a fuzzy question, and expect a serious response. To my surprise: the Archbishop launched into a topic that was clearly a very familiar part of his own considerations.

While noting that the proposed treaty promising "free trade" delivered nothing new for his parishioners, he further detailed how the proposed trade treaty continued a dark legend of oppression in the Americas; "Chiapas and Mexico have suffered the consequences of free trade for more than 500 years." The consequences were likely to be little different now than those of the period following the Spanish conquest. In only the last few days, he stated, a group of *hacendados,* large landholders, had used helicopters and trucks equipped with weapons in order to dislodge peasants from their occupation of ancestral lands not far from San Cristóbal.

The free trade proposal only exacerbated the plight of Mexico's poor in terms of basic conflicts over the control of property and the exercise of democratic rights. The Archbishop concluded his brief commentary with a question of his own, "What is there in the nature of the free trade agreement that will change the problems faced by people in Chiapas or elsewhere in Mexico?"

Over the next two years, the specific provisions of NAFTA took shape. While much of the critical attention in Mexico focused on agriculture, other provisions of the trade agreement would set in motion equally dubious, but less recognized impacts. With respect to energy, for example, NAFTA explicitly exempted oil and gas exploration and development subsidies from challenges, while leaving solar and wind subsidies subject to dismantle as posing unfair obstacles to trade.[97]

Another, less recognized change accompanied finalized negotiations advancing free trade: a growing antipathy spreading across Mexico. On a January morning in 1994, the world awoke to discover that the deceptively quiet and remote town of San Cristóbal de las Casas had suddenly become the center of a revolution. The Zapatistas, now recognized as a movement initiated largely by the indigenous people of Chiapas, would challenge some of the basic political and economic relationships in Mexico - including the belief that a free market, dominant for the past 500 years, represents a good thing for the people of Mexico.

As the Zapatista revolution expanded in the coming days, the world would also learn that Archbishop Ruiz was serving not simply as a protector of the indigenous people of Chiapas, but for the Zapatistas as well. The Archbishop would play a pivotal role, by inserting his Church into the middle of an unfolding revolution. In months following the public emergence of Zapatistas, the major U.S. environmental organizations based in D.C. helped achieve Congressional approval of NAFTA. Sensing a close vote, President Clinton launched a savvy campaign to win support from the environmental community, gradually gaining backing from Conservation International, the Environmental Defense Fund, the National Audubon Society, the National Wildlife Federation, the Natural Resources Defense Council, and the World Wildlife Fund. In exchange, these same groups dropped an initial demand to create a commission empowered to subpoena documents and issue sanctions against violators of the environmental standards spelled out in the side agreement.[98]

The conflicts between free markets and democratic rights identified by Archbishop Ruiz would continue to emerge. Within twenty-five years Pope Francis broadened arguments raised that the free trade regimes of the 21st century threatened not only the poor, but the survival of the planet. The Pope's encyclicals on these topics, as later chapters explore, would include critical discussions exchanged with California's governor and the state's use of markets as a solution to a worsening global climate.

The Past as Prologue

By the mid-1990s, Martha Valdez immersed herself once again in the topic of hazardous wastes. Only now she provided guidance to activists in both Mexico and California, addressing the never-ending problems of toxics generated and disposed in both countries. Following retirement from the Legislature, Martha joined a well-respected group of public interest advocates near to where she had attended law school: the San Diego Environmental Health Coalition. Among Martha's many admirable qualities was the ease with which she moved from counseling the state's most recognized political leaders to sharing ideas about political tactics and strategy with ordinary citizens. Unlike those seeking revolving doors toward more pay and power, Martha Valdez refreshingly pursued work without a focus on her own status or self.

We met again at a meeting in El Paso designed to further collaborations between citizen activists working on either side of the border. Following a signature approach developed by San Diego's Environmental Health Coalition, a basic organizing tactic typically involved a series of meetings on topics such as how to replace household toxics with safer alternatives. As organizers explained an agenda built around the topic of toxics, they also emphasized that the immediate objective was to include a fiesta. Simply lecturing folks, even your neighbors, on the hazards of toxics was not seen as especially inviting: whereas, a fiesta at the end was something everyone could look forward to.

The organizing also possessed a deeper genius. At the end of the conversations, neighbors inevitably called organizers with unrelated questions: about problems at school, issues involving work, concerns about crime… As time went on, the organizers realized that the numerous other emergent issues not only were not a distraction, but in fact marked what everyone should agree was success. Their objective should build a political movement that would expand and deepen the community's collective linkage to others, beyond local or even regional boundaries. We spoke during a recess in the binational meeting. "You can't believe how satisfying this is....instead of sitting for hours negotiating with a bunch of corporate suits on some arcane provision of hazardous waste law, I now spend my days directly with people who are such a pleasure to work with. I only regret that I did not leave Sacramento sooner!"

The artful simplicity of expanding a political base at the neighborhood level at the San Diego Coalition to address multiple concerns felt by everybody's household reminded me of organizational efforts to address a common set of problems that appear on both sides of the border. In the coming years, a common strategy began with not simply occupying a single seat at a negotiating table dominated by powerful interests, but with establishing many other tables -- to determine what must be done with respect to property and unrestrained choices by private interests for both Zapatistas and community-based coalitions in California.

Among the most intriguing was the expression by Archbishop Ruiz that the problems confronting folks in Chiapas, Oaxaca, and beyond shared a common denominator to those confronting their counterparts in San Pedro, El Centro, Compton, Richmond, Barrio Logan, and other communities across California. The link is located in commerce dominated by powerful economic interests that also control political institutions. The question was how to unite community activists and public interest advocates into a larger community?

Pre-empting State and Local Laws

In one of our final meetings, Martha counseled me that more was contained in the NAFTA agreement than evident at first glance. Embedded in the passages of the trade agreement were provisions allowing for companies to effectively hold the public liable for laws dampening even *potential* corporate profits. The early reactions, "what in the world did this mean?" became manifest in the late 1990s in one of the earliest suits brought against a U.S. law; it was a California executive order and regulations addressing what would become an infamous gasoline additive: MTBE. Initially added to reduce the carbon intensity of gasoline, health scientists quickly recognized its hazard to human health.

Once revealed, California was equally prompt to reverse its mandate for such uses, moving to phase-out application expeditiously without disrupting the supply of fuels. Methanex, the Canadian manufacturer of the additive seized upon NAFTA provisions designed to protect corporations from the loss of profits and filed a suit against the state of California. The case eventually found in favor of the United States and against the Canadian manufacturer, Methanex. The impact, however, reverberated across California.

How could state laws protecting public health and the environment be vitiated by an unelected panel of judges having no accountability relative to its voters, the U.S. Constitution or the laws of the land? Despite the fact that California's program for regulating fuels remained intact, the episode served as a warning regarding the potential threat of trade treaties for undermining any law. A frequent refrain of Martha's mentoring over the years pointed both to obstacles and opportunities that state and federal laws provided for public interest advocates. As a result, the notion that the force of all of these laws might be swept away as a result of unelected tribunals struck her as not simply absurd, but dangerous. We readily agreed that the erosion of citizens' rights by so-called trade treaties marked a dangerous turn in politics.

Martha made this observation in one of our last conversations playing on an iconic Mexican saying, "*Pobre* California, so close to corporate interests, so far from God."[99] In years to follow, activists of all stripes would reflect on Martha's encouragement to examine larger issues embedded in California laws, including their impacts elsewhere in the world.

CHAPTER 5

The Path Not Taken

Just as everyone else in the capitol called it a day, the most challenging part of my workday was only beginning. I saw that the late afternoon sky was ominous. The start of the legislative year in early January, typically a time of optimism, was anything but – in the new year of 2001.

California's system of electrical production and distribution verged on collapse. One of three major stste utilities neared bankruptcy; the state entity for coordinating energy sales and distribution warned that citizens faced many days to weeks of rolling blackouts; Governor Davis was preparing to declare a state of emergency; and, Californians were paying exponentially increased amounts, in energy bills. At this rate, it was unclear how much longer households or businesses – could keep their lights on.[100] My job was to find out precisely what was broken, and to propose a remedy for fixing it. As usual, I reached for the most dependable research tool on my desk, dialing a private number in Boston.

"Casey, you're familiar with what's happening with energy prices in California, yes? What's your advice?" My brother responded with unusual wry humor given the even later time on the East coast. I could picture his eyes twinkling behind thick horned rims - "Simple… Eat or be eaten." His characteristic bluntness captured his sharp-edged reputation in the world of finance.

In 1985 Casey Jennings was the consummate economics gear-head. A graduate of UC Berkeley specializing in quantitative economics, he was immediately fascinated with designing financial deals, just so long as it had nothing to do with academia. Instantly bored in the classroom, Casey was most comfortable challenged with seemingly insurmountable problems. Early on, he found the practice of economics in the real world provided an opportunity to freely move with little supervision as well as substantial rewards. Before reaching middle age, he was among a small cadre of financial wizards constructing deals around the globe. Working for one or another multinational banking or finance firm, my brother was definitely recognized in terms of his value to corporate America. The head of a Fortune 100 corporation provided a memorable summary of my brother's work, "Casey Jennings? Oh yeah, he's the guy who makes us a shitload of money."

Over the years, we conversed more and more on a variety of topics, but mainly developed a kind of tutorial where Casey would reveal the world of finance and I would compare the practice of politics, at least my version from inside the state capitol. We both found that even though our worlds were separated in many ways, politics and finance shared common attributes. Our conversations were a kind of parry, engaged since childhood. One version was to demonstrate that each of us occupied the crazier and more corrupted place on the planet; a competition pitting the world of financial irrationality against the insanity of government. The new legislative session in January 2001 began with a chaos that promised a rich landscape for this competition.

Beginning in April of 2000, by the close of the year California had witnessed an 88% increase in the wholesale price of electricity.[101] Combined with staggering prices charged to households and businesses, the state experienced rolling blackouts. By all outward signs, the spike in energy prices caught the Governor and his advisors wholly unprepared. Gray Davis later offered a demonstration of extreme political understatement, "I knew nothing about electricity."[102]

The prelude to California's energy debacle included a variety of sources, but especially in the popularized sentiment that government had grown too big. According to corporate lobbyists and their allies, the solution emerging with a vengeance in the 1990s was a simple one.

The push for deregulation reflected a carefully planned and orchestrated agenda. "By the mid-1990s, pro-deregulation forces were organizing. Large industrial customers that had threatened to leave the state formed Californians for Competitive Electricity (CCE), composed of the California Manufacturers Association...the California Large Energy Consumers Association...the California League of Food Processors... California Independent Energy Producers, they represented big bucks (with the Manufacturers Association alone dropping $1.7 million in lobbying dollars in the state capitol in 1995 and 1996)....California's three large utility companies spent $69 million between 1994 and 2000 on political lobbying, most of that on promoting deregulation, both to get the law passed and to keep it in force."[103]

During one of the few episodes when Republicans gained control of both the governorship and the lower house in the legislature, the deregulation experiment targeted California. Signed into law by Governor Pete Wilson on September 23, 1996, the Electric Utility Industry Restructuring Act (Assembly Bill 1890) moved the State process of purchasing and transferring from a world strictly regulating public utilities to the" wonderful" world of free markets.

As a State Historian would later describe it, the legislation seemingly held something for everyone: "The big-ticket industries wanted the right to buy wholesale from non-regulated energy companies. They got it. The regulated public utilities wanted the right to recover some of the billions of dollars spent on nuclear plants and federally mandated alternative energy programs, even if it meant selling assets (including generation plants) to nonregulated wholesalers. They got it. Environmentalists wanted some $450 million for research into and construction of renewable and alternative energy projects. They got it. Large-scale users such as BART [the Bay Area Rapid Transit], the University of California, and agribusiness wanted some $200 million in price breaks in the new system. They got it. Labor wanted a multi-million dollar program to retrain workers for the new system. They got it. Municipally owned utilities wanted to preserve their independence in the new order. They got it. Residential and small business users wanted a 10 percent rate cut for four years. They got it."[104] It was a classic "Christmas tree" approach of hanging as many goodies as necessary to cobble together the necessary votes.

As described in later revelations, "...[T]he sheer complexity of the rules governing deregulation seemed to make them exploitable...Clever [energy] traders could find loopholes in the thousand or so pages of rules and game the system...."[105] With the dawning of the twenty-first century, it was quickly becoming evident that the wild world of free markets had captured California's energy sector. Did anyone genuinely understand the broader implications of moving from a largely publicly controlled regulatory system to a system of market controls? For one veteran energy lobbyist, the answer could be found in who authored the original legislation: "The bill [AB 1890] was clearly not written by anyone inside the building [the state capitol]."[106] The consequences of moving toward a market-defined solution would become painfully apparent.

With the implementation of the Electric Utility Industry Restructuring Act in March of 1998, stability of California energy pricing rapidly began to unravel. Following the new authorization of the bill, California's major utilities immediately began selling-off their electric-generating plants. The buyers included a number of energy trading companies; "..led by Enron, [the energy trading firms] had become uninterested in serving the small-time California consumer at rates capped by the PUC (Public Utilities Commission) when they could be getting into the much more profitable business of buying the generators that would soon allow them to corner the California market."[107]

The Western Energy Crisis

By the first week of January, 2001, the outward quiet pervading the capitol's corridors disguised legislators who, behind closed doors, displayed the poise of residents occupying a burning building. An earlier petition to the Federal Energy Regulatory Commission (FERC) requesting a wholesale rate price cap on December 15, 2000 was rejected, providing instead a "flexible cap" plan of $150 per megawatt-hour. On that same day, California was paying wholesale prices of over $1400 per megawatt-hour, compared to the $45 per megawatt-hour average that had prevailed one year earlier.[108]

As a means of getting through what was seen by some as a limited scare, Governor Davis gave the go-ahead for the state to subsidize the purchase of energy. But even these early remedies faced long-term liabilities. In the final months of 1999, Californians were paying billions of additional dollars to keep the lights on in homes and businesses. In 2000 and 2001, the electric bill for *each year* amounted to approximately $27 billion, as compared to an average of $19 billion just a few years earlier.[109] Following a Monday morning session, the Assembly leader called for a meeting including about a dozen legislators who chaired committees having jurisdiction over the issue, as well as three or four professional staff. The purpose was to get some sense of how Assembly leadership could manage this issue.

The ornate room, located directly off the Assembly floor was only rarely used when the full Assembly was convened. This was a rare occasion. Even among a group practiced in the art of devising unscripted solutions, the meeting was one of barely contained chaos. The very large table was being ignored, members and staff preferring instead to stand and caucus in twos and threes, trying to figure out what was happening in the unfolding crisis, who was responsible, and what should the Legislature be doing?

Assembly member Carole Migden, one of the Legislature's most outspokenly aggressive members, turned to the legislators present, and asked more in the tone of a threat, "What's the plan? Who has an idea of what we need to do to respond to the crisis?" After some hesitation, several members cautiously offered a dodge – the Governor's office was undoubtedly acting to address the issue. Other legislators followed with a scatter-shot of hearings, proposed laws, and resolutions to Congress. But, all recommendations came to a halt as Carole turned to one of the professional staff who "whispered," in a stage voice, what only a few members heard, "What, what did you say?" demanded Assemblywoman Migden with a barely concealed hostility, based on an unspoken premise that it was those legislators present who should be answering.

"I merely stated," replied the committee staff director "that we need to begin this conversation with someone who actually knows something about the topic. I don't think we have the facts in front of us about what is broken." All heads now turned back to Carole, awaiting her judgement. "And who the hell are you?" Migden demanded to know

"I'm the guy in the room who raises these kinds of troubling questions" replied the staffer unabashedly. Migden, for once, had nothing to say. The meeting soon adjourned, but with an unspoken directive to the smartass committee staffer from the committee chair: If you're so smart: go find someone who can explain to us what's broken and what needs to be done to fix it.

For outsiders, the plaintive complaint about "de-professionalizing" the Legislature sounded like so much whining by a body they already held in low regard. If a term-limited Legislature meant fewer staff would be handmaidens to many legislators, so much the better! Capitol insiders, however, were gaining a new appreciation that term limits represented a different facet of the minimal governance concept, deregulation, and the growth of market forces. The fact of the matter is that few legislators even remembered the bill carried by a Democrat, in 1996. To "deregulate" electricity, for the state's Republican governor, constituted a no-brainer. It resonated as precisely the kind of bill designed to match the new era of limited government; representing the next wave of California's model for the nation.

Deregulation also dovetailed with term limits in a more nuanced way. During the hearings on energy deregulation, the Legislature's professional staff who might otherwise have informed deliberations on its darker repercussions was largely gone. As one Senator later remarked, "...[the] electricity deregulation scheme, passed with hardly any debate by legislators, who had virtually no idea what was in it." The same legislator would recall this as a striking "advertisement of why term limits were a bad idea."[110]

Eat or Be Eaten

As some of the staffers present set out to define the problem and pose solutions following the ad hoc meeting with legislators, they initiated the usual kind of sophisticated research methodology that is not typically a part of graduate courses in public administration, but which commonly characterizes the California Legislature - a series of phone calls to different parts of the world, to Congressional staff, academic experts, lobbyists in Sacramento and beyond. The most insight came from a private sector acquaintance with a deep and comprehensive knowledge of corporate behavior, including a variety of the world's largest corporate and financial groups. That call was with my brother.

"So eat or be eaten. It's a nice sound bite....can you elaborate?"

"Look, if this were occurring in the private sector – and these kinds of events happen with regularity in the private sector – California has the choice of either allowing energy companies to savage them until everyone in the state is bleeding out of all orifices at once or.....California takes control of one or more of those who are participating in the savaging of the taxpayers and ratepayers. Any corporation in the same situation would do the same: you eat those who are savaging you or they eat you." Pausing to catch his breath, he concluded our discussion, "What else did you want to talk about?"

Within a week, the committee staff had identified and dragged to Sacramento a young and savvy economist from UC Berkeley who was among a rare breed of economists – possessing both a practical and academic knowledge about energy and its markets. A smaller group of legislators were reassembled in a cramped room on the third floor above the Assembly chambers. Typically such review, which originally had provided for an hour briefing, was finally scheduled with a bare twenty minutes before Legislators had to retreat back to the Assembly floor for another session. And true to a form that always brings a smile to the faces of non-academics, the economist launched into a presentation which anticipated a quiescent and captive audience, willing to sit and take notes for at least an hour.

After a couple of minutes, the young professor was prompted to tie up his presentation, with maybe five minutes remaining. After a moment of visible shock, he recovered nicely, spelling out (in only slightly altered academese) the mechanics of how California was likely being gamed by artificial rises in prices – beyond what one would expect in any "free market." Others would later describe, in excruciating detail that, among the provisions: deregulating utilities were forced "to sell off their generating facilities. They were forbidden from entering into long-term contracts and instead had to purchase power in the spot market *every day*."[111]

His audience, already on their feet and preparing to exit the room in a call to the floor session heard the young professor gamely provide a closing message, "So... the state really only has one viable option: it must act decisively to control power generators or it will continue to face astronomical charges." One of the assembled legislators coughed out, "What in the hell does that mean?" "It means, sir that the state of California needs to take control of the energy market!"

More than one legislator muttered a similar sentiment as he exited the room, "Did I just hear a socialist proposal for the state to take over energy producers? Is this what we were brought together to hear?" The logical conclusion to such a heated demand followed, encapsulated by one legislator's comment, "This is absurd and I've got better things to do with my time than entertain some ivory tower theories about what's wrong and what's to be done. I'm outta here!" Except for one or two who remained silent and attentive to the young academic and the committee staff, none of the assembled legislators seemed at all pleased. Later in the afternoon, while passing the still-assembled stragglers who remained locked in a debate about who was to blame for the energy debacle threatening California, Assembly member Alan Lowenthal pulled the committee staff aside.

"Okay, several of us have been talking over this morning's presentation. What's your idea about what needs to be done? Can you put together a proposal on how California would "take control" of its energy market?"

Taking Public Control of Energy

During the next six months, a small group of staff devised several options to address the still-unfolding energy crisis. The group was convened by the Speaker Pro Tem of the Assembly, Fred Keeley, whose leadership provided the essential backing to devise what would become the most audacious, inspired and politically risky plan for addressing California's energy crisis.[112] From the start, Fred Keeley was given broad latitude to forge a solution to the state's energy problem by virtue of his prowess. Unlike many of his peers for whom statewide policy was a foreign concept, Fred came to the California Legislature already experienced with such matters.

On Martin Luther King Day in 2001, Fred Keeley joined a select group of legislators visiting first the parent company executives for

Edison International and later in the day at a parallel meeting with PG & E. Both companies conveyed the same message: we are paying more for wholesale prices than we are able to charge for retail prices. While the outcome facing both was largely the same – 'we will soon be bankrupt' - PG&E faced more dire circumstances. The request was also largely similar: 'grant us a rate increase or devise a way to bail us out!'

Fred Keeley, in what his fellow legislators referred to as 'a work-out, not a bail-out', arrived at these meetings prepared to assist the public utilities, but only in manner benefitting the public interest. In exchange for any state assistance, Keeley's sine qua non was for the public to gain control over the environmental assets. While Edison International possessed little in the way of such resources, PG&E watersheds, forests, and hydro facilities were expansive. Part of Keeley's intent was to ensure that should PG&E go broke its assets would not simply be privatized.

Solving a private sector problem by granting the public control over private sector assets was an inspired approach that would remain invisible within a few short years during the worst financial disaster in nearly a century. While PG&E executives did not reject the proposal neither were they racing to embrace the rescue plan. From Fred Keeley's vantage, the houses of the Legislature held two distinct perspectives on the energy crisis. Virtually no member of the Assembly by 2001 had held office during the agreements forged by Governor Wilson and Steve Peace. But most members of the Senate had been party to the deregulation of utilities and energy producers. As a consequence, the two were not agreed on a common problem-solving approach. Amidst the chaos, Fred Keeley orchestrated yet another path for resolving the state energy crisis.

The plan was eloquent, simple and decisive: The State of California would buy Pacific Gas & Electric (PG&E), one of the largest energy entities in the nation. At first glance, the state utility would appear to be an unlikely place to begin California's recapture of its floundering energy market – as it was being driven into bankruptcy by the same energy traders who were gaming California. Yet, as both Casey and the U.C. economist endeavored to explain, California had to begin somewhere to claw back its control over energy producers. And PG&E represented a high mark political profile to demonstrate California's aggressive stance; now responding to a market in which ever expanding numbers of citizens were heading toward bankruptcy.

Over the next two months a central task for the workgroup in the capitol was to identify a source and potential partner to purchase the energy company. The experience was eye-opening. Among a large group of private sector contacts who regularly facilitated business transactions across the globe, Casey found a newly discovered reluctance among bankers and others to pursue this deal. Once the nature of the deal was mentioned, the excuses would immediately follow: "Oh, I see.... [extended pause] Well, you know, my firm has many links to PG&E, so I'm afraid this deal might not be right for us." "And why is that?" Casey responded. "Let me get this straight. When we last concluded a deal, I thought you said that you were in it for the fee? If this provides you with the same fee, which it would, what's your hesitancy?"

At first, it appeared that precisely the kind of takeover that was the rage among many investment bankers was seen as toxic when the people of California wanted to buy a bankrupt company in order to stabilize their energy prices and staunch the hemorrhage of public subsidies and debt. While the plan did not deal directly with a state gamed by energy traders, the plan initiated a bold move for the state to control the generation and transmission of energy. After an exhaustive search, Casey did, however, find a willing financier for the deal. The European banker, eager to gain a foothold in the U. S., saw the prospective deal as one that was part of its job in global finance projects. And, of course, the fact that the banker operated in nations where the public typically owned a variety of enterprises, including energy producers, struck a perfectly acceptable chord.

The outline of the proposal essentially provided for a joint purchase of PG&E in which virtually all of the California-based assets, including energy production and vast land holdings, would become the property of California. The parent company assets would go to the European banker. The purchase price for California would be somewhere in the ballpark of $5 billion, with perhaps a significant portion provided by the sales of bonds to finance the deal. There were, however, two primary stumbling blocks before the deal could go forward. First, how would the private sector react to such a proposal? Would it be labeled a communist plot and a threat to America's free enterprise? And, would the Governor support such an effort, arranged behind the scenes by members?

To test the waters among the business community, a meeting representing a large and diverse number of firms was arranged in Los Angeles.[113] In truth, legislative staff had serious doubts about letting the "cat out of the bag" before a group that might well take up an immediate campaign to upend the proposal. Nevertheless, staff presented the plan's essential elements was made in about an hour. In the first few minutes of silence, one after another of the business leaders around the table endorsed the idea [!]. The legislative consultants were querulous, having prepared for a lengthy argument in which lines would be drawn and perhaps only a minority of businesses would agree that it was a necessary step. Instead, the business community expressed relief that finally a real plan might back off the ever-increasing prices driving their companies into the ground. There was one catch. Not one wanted to be identified. Recognizing that there might well be considerable vengeance on any business that sided with the people of California, they asked that the Governor take the first step. They would then mount a quiet campaign to support California's takeover of the energy behemoth.

The next meeting was the nitty-gritty. In a quiet conference room outside of the capitol, the proposal was presented to a small group of principals representing the primary energy-related agencies. Also in attendance was a representative from the Governor's office, who pointedly informed those present that everyone should understand that he was never present for the discussion. That favorable convergence of the stars was not to align. The record was never official and there are no minutes to review, especially as regards the common rumor at the time that the Governor was essentially catatonic regarding important decisions.

On May 15, 2001, S. David Freeman, who had been appointed by the Governor as chair of the California Power Authority, testified before the Subcommittee on Consumer Affairs, Foreign Commerce and Tourism of the Senate Committee on Commerce, Science, and Transportation, making the following statement: "There is one fundamental lesson we must learn from this experience: electricity is really different from everything else. It cannot be stored, it cannot be seen, and we cannot do without it, which makes opportunities to take advantage of a deregulated market endless. It is a public good that must be protected from private abuse. If Murphy's Law were written for a market approach to electricity, then the law would state 'any system that can be gamed, will be gamed, and at the worst possible time.' And a market approach for electricity is inherently game-able. Never again can we allow private interests to create artificial or even real shortages and to be in control."[114]

By the summer of 2001, the forecast given by the Berkeley economist in January unfolded as:

> "...a drought in the northwest states reduced the amount of hydroelectric power available to California. Though at no point during the crisis was California's sum of actual electric-generating capacity less than demand, California's energy reserves were low enough that during peak hours the private industry which owned power-generating plants could effectively hold the State hostage by shutting down their plants for 'maintenance,' in order to manipulate supply and demand. These critical shutdowns often occurred for no other reason than to force California's electricity grid managers to purchase electricity on the 'spot market,' where private generators could charge astronomical rates."[115]

The larger truth is that virtually everyone involved in Sacramento felt they were in uncharted waters when it came to the state taking over a private entity. Despite fact that such transactions were occurring with regularity in the private sector, the notion that a similar activity might be taken on behalf of the people of California seemed utterly unfathomable from the start: Except, of course for those persons who were most intimately familiar with the free market.

"It's as though the public takeover of a bankrupt company is a violation of some natural law," Casey puzzled. " I don't get it. The people of California and their elected representatives find it more acceptable to be savaged by private sector companies than to provide a signal that they will not tolerate such behavior?"

A veteran of the Legislature replied, "No, you don't understand. For all of the talk about the excesses of government, the intrusion of government over businesses, the excesses of regulation - there are only a tiny group of people in this town who understand economics, finance, or business. And if you try to identify anyone in government who understands all of the issues you know from a private sector perspective, as someone who actually knows how to protect yourself from being eaten alive in the free market - well there really is not anyone."

"It's ironic, isn't it? California is seen as this outrageous outpost of progressivism, where the state is almighty, but the idea that the people of California might make a profit is seen as fundamental violation. There is a clearer line between church and state than between the state and the free market." Casey replied with some weariness, "Yes: and all the more so given that both the church and the free market are largely faith-based systems."

Reverberations

The saga surrounding the public control of energy would remain unresolved for years to come. Among the little reported facets of the state's energy debacle, not only did energy prices rocket out of control, the cost for sourcing of energy in future contracts also spiraled. A review conducted by a small group of insiders revealed that the forward contracts laid the basis for effectively stalling the use of renewable energy sources for years to come. Contracts that would have effectively anchored the state to fossil-fuel sources were unwound, both as a means of addressing price gouging as well as opening a state path to more vigorously pursue renewable energy production. [116]

A year later, Casey found himself en route to yet another business meeting, hopping off one plane and sipping a coffee before moving across the concourse to another leg of his flight. From across the way he is hailed by one of his numerous business associates from across the globe: a European banker who had worked so hard to bring the PG&E purchase to fruition.

"It's a shame," the banker spoke over the din of the airport: "How's that? You mean to find yourself in Chicago and reconciling the need to eat something and having America's bountiful airport harvest in front of you?"

"Nope," replies the banker, "I'm referring to the California deal. I was talking to one of our colleagues in Paris last week." He then recalled a quick back of the envelope calculation that if California had purchased PG&E, "the state would be about $20 billion ahead."

"Yes," Casey related his response "...or just about enough to cover all of the energy contracts that the people of California had to pay out to Enron and company."

In the spring of 2005, capitol staff received notice of a free film showing at the nearby theater highlighted with ornate velvety scrolls. Although free movies regularly drew a considerable crowd, the many empty seats suggested a special night for capitol wonks: Enron: the Smartest Guys in the Room. The story was already familiar to a few hangers-on since Steve Peace orchestrated California's deregulation of the electric industry in the 1990s. Insights on the inner-workings of one of the nation's larger companies silenced the usually talkative audience.

As we stopped around the corner at a popular brew pub, Mike, who also worked in the capitol, started the film review. "Look, I get the part about the corruption by Lay, Skiling, Fastow, and Pai. That part of the story is hardly news. But the scale is breathtaking. Besides casting thousands of Enron's employees under the bus, their 401ks destroyed – how's that for predatory capitalism?" Another movie-goer wistfully envied a scene from our counterparts in D.C. "How come we missed having a hearing like Barbara Boxer's? Imagine how great it would have been to replay the tape before a packed hearing where an Enron executive is reassuring investors that all is okay, while selling his own stock in the company?"

"Yes," Mike's colleague replied, "it was a great show and my hat goes off to Boxer. But, of course, in this Republican Congress, what is she supposed to do about the more destructive part of the story - our inability to come to grips with the larger theme: corporate malfeasance on a much grander scale? Quite frankly, I find the movie depressing because it demonstrates to me that we don't fully comprehend what's going on in the private sector, until after the body counts come in." In the coming years we would reflect on increasingly unregulated utilities that actively undermined community-controlled power generation, distributed solar energy generation, and an adequate oversight and control of potential surrounding underground pipelines.

Community Choice Aggregation

Less than a decade after the Western Energy Crisis, the state would once again confront a renewed case of manipulated energy markets. This time, the Federal Energy Regulatory Commission (FERC) would intercede before too much damage had been done, imposing an initial fine estimated at $1billion in 2013, on J.P. Morgan for allegedly manipulating energy markets in California and the Midwest.[117] The episode went largely without notice in Sacramento, perhaps owing to circumstance: that most elected officials who had witnessed the earlier energy crisis were no longer present.

By 2016, California was still unraveling the damage wrought by unprecedented manipulation of energy markets some fifteen years after the Western Energy Crisis. One of the last businesses charged with market manipulation in a case pending before the Federal Commission, faced a proposed fine in the hundreds of millions of dollars to compensate a public defrauded by market traders who joked about their activities at the time. "I don't know how honest that is, but we are not in the honesty game, are we?"[118] The energy trading group, a division of Shell, was among the last in a line of other companies accused of "unjustly profiting from the long-term contracts having paid settlements to California worth a total of $7.7 billion."[119]

The political control of energy markets would continue to be an active part of political conflict in the 21st century. As discussions regarding California's energy future frequently turned to the innovative role played by publicly owned utilities, the 2010 election included a substantial effort to erect barriers against local governments as part of a community choice aggregation (CCA) project. CCA's represented a cornerstone for many public utilities for entering or expanding their place in retail energy sales. Based on a 2002 law, local governments were authorized to purchase power to sell to residents and to construct municipal electricity generation facilities. It was, in short, an open door for local governments to compete with private utilities. The irony was that in place of deregulation, at least one of the state's largest utilities pursued a kind of selective regulation to defend its monopoly status.

Private energy companies banded together to form Proposition 16 as a remedy to the "problem" of competition, to be presented to the voters. The ballot measure promised a new set of conditions including a new two-thirds voting requirement before either a CCA or new public utility would be allowed. And just in case the merits of the Proposition were not readily apparent, the Pacific Gas and Electric Company contributed approximately $46 million to advance the ballot measure while opponents mustered less than $100,000. Despite the lopsided expenditures by the utility company, California's voters soundly rejected the measure. Decisions about energy production were best left to private interests.

Casey later reflected that the lesson of California's energy crisis was quickly lost on the many who simply assigned the blame to a small group of Enron traders. "Oh it was certainly a chapter regarding the excesses of an out-of-control corporation resulting from deregulation. But it was also a prelude to what was yet to come: a financial melt-down on a global scale," he forecast with fair certainty. In this sense there was a clear irony. "One of the reasons why things did not go much worse during the energy crisis was that the state possessed at least some minimal architecture to control energy production and prices," was his conclusion. In 2007 the public was on the verge of an even larger crisis – about to learn the price of an unregulated financial sector.

CHAPTER 6

A Tale of Two Lobbies

This "place always reminds me of my early days at the Pacific Coast Stock Exchange ....except you all trade in legal futures instead of pork bellies, right?" My brother is standing just outside of my office, in a recessed mezzanine with a view from inside the capitol's rotunda, as Lobbyists dash back and forth. And his observation fits. During peak times, the foyer leading to the Legislative chambers certainly reminds one of commodity trading floors. In place of copper futures, lobbyists trade in what can be an even more valuable activity: the making of law. As we walk out of the capitol, Casey initiates a now-familiar discussion.

"Is lobbying the rough and tumble of competing interest groups? Or are the evil alien overlords merely engaged in yet another form of domination?" Lunchtime conversation compares our two worlds: his world of making money for what he calls 'the Great Satan' versus my typical day of devising laws to trip the corporate forces of darkness. We generally agree that while everyone has an opinion about what's wrong with politics and politicians, so few understands what goes on, particularly inside the esoteric arena of corporate finance. California may be on the edge of two possible, and radically divergent, futures in fossil-fueled conflict. The fault line wavers between corporate and environmental lobbies and the disparate paths each actively promotes.

Returning from lunch, Casey and I pass along corridors with iconic reminders of the state's history. Portraits of past governors, sweeping stair cases, stately hearing rooms and chambers mark the arena where

Californian legislators have received Hollywood celebrities, world leaders and throngs of school children. Amidst all the murals, paintings and grandeur, I am struck that the capitol's interior does not reveal many of its secrets to the hundreds, sometimes thousands of visitors passing through the building each day.

As if channeling my thoughts, Casey goes on to explain "Look, I think the problem is that the public doesn't have much of a clue about what goes on in here. Those guys over there..." his nod indicates a group of lobbyists whom I recognize as the hired guns for several corporations, sharing a joke. "The public is seriously mistaken if they think these folks have horns or are identifiable by black hats. As you've told me many times, California's corporate lobby includes many generous, kind, affable people...or, at least I'll take your word on that."

Casey then recounts that for one of his multinational employers, their D.C. office expanded from perhaps 100 to more than a thousand lobbyists in the span of a decade during the 1990s. "What the public misses is that the personal traits of individual lobbyists don't much matter. The essential characteristic of the army of people we employed in D.C.," Casey continues, "is that they received a consistent message from people in my world - the financial masters of the universe – on a daily basis: 'make more money,' 'increase my market share,' or 'dig a deeper moat around my monopoly!'"

Turning to the two public interest lobbyists, Martha Dina Argüello and Bill Magavern,[120] who I wave to as they pass beneath us toward the governor's office, Casey gives another nod in their direction... "Versus those two who just passed, whose marching orders are probably scattered and disorganized: 'protect us from global warming,' or 'pass a water bond,' or 'support some obscure regulation.'" Casey recaps as we turn away from rotunda and back to my office, "the difference between the two is that the public interest crowd doesn't have a clue that the corporate folks are not just eating their lunch, but their children as well." I find it curious that while many inside the Legislature automatically respect the perspective of small businesses, few are familiar with the vast gulf between Main Street and Wall Street. When I mention this to Casey, he displays a well-practiced contempt for those confusing one for the other.

"'Small business interests'? You tell me when you last encountered anyone representing small businesses in this place...and don't give that Chamber of Commerce crap. In my world small businesses are road kill, the shock troops don't recognize that the Fortune 100 could care less whether they live or die." Casey's experience with a number of major player corporate insiders is captured by a pithy characterization: "They are sociopaths."

While I might discount his take on corporate America, I acknowledge that no one inside the Legislature or even most of California government possesses Casey's experience, years of working in the top echelons of global corporate finance. I am more sobered by his finance-world perspective on the asymmetric warfare between the public interest versus corporate lobby. Even though this categorization of lobbying groups suggests too hegemonic an image of black or white, I take his point that the corporate lobby possesses a cohesive singularity of purpose that the public interest groups lack.

Even though there are occasional conflicts between warring corporate factions, such divisions are overshadowed by unity among corporate lobbyists. In the world of D.C. politics, the dynamic has been described by scholars as America's "elite," while not always winning their favorite law, exercise a decisive veto over Congressional actions that they dislike.[121] From my desk inside California's capitol, our main divergence from D.C. is the less decisive political power wielded by the corporate lobby in conflicts with the public; it is a difference largely the result of a much more active group of citizens and their other full-time representatives: the public interest advocates.

In the world of California's public interest advocates, Bill Magavern and Martha Dina Argüello are but two among a small and exclusive group of Californian veterans lobbying on behalf of the environment.[122] Each one has steadily worked on projects ranging from community and regional efforts to statewide and national projects. Both are very practiced in lobbying before the California Legislature. Even though millions of Californians regularly rank the environment as among the most important issues facing the state, most people have virtually no idea about their advocates' day job in the capitol.

Martha and Bill blend very different backgrounds and perspectives, reflecting what some call a "new wave" of environmentalism separating California environmentalists from many of their brethren in Washington, D.C.[123] Whereas various organizations anchored in the nation's capital project a hierarchical and clubby atmosphere dominated by dower white men rooted in preserving the natural environment, California's environmental lobby is increasingly defined by the urban environment, especially the disproportionate impact of toxics affecting low-income communities of color. California's environmental advocates are frequently characterized as a scrappy and adversarial group with a knack for adopting creative political tactics. Some of the state's most notable public interest groups combine community-based allies from more edgy neighborhoods with savvy attorneys to forge campaigns bent on challenging the corporate status quo. Many of their works center on toxic substances, climate change, and social justice.

Epitomizing this characterization perfectly, Martha is highly-dedicated, constantly cheerful, and be careful if you cross her! Highly regarded for her political skills, Martha is equally comfortable with testifying before legislators in the state capitol or listening to neighborhood activists in the non-tourist zones of Los Angeles. Bill, for his part, projects a quiet confidence that has earned him respect across the capitol. Among his professional traits is a straight forward tenacity, not unlike what one sees in U.S. Senator Elizabeth Warren, reflecting his early and successful lobbying career under the mentoring of Ralph Nader. As impressive as each of them are for their respective organizations, their persuasiveness is especially formidable when joined with others. Martha can readily identify which issues are most valued by the state's varied constituencies, seemingly performing this task on a neighborhood by neighborhood basis: Bill is able to deliver succinct summaries about the virtues and vices for a range of legislative proposals.

While both advocates are deferential and humble, it is also an effective disguise. Bill is among the most-savvy of environmental attorneys in a state possessing a wealth of environmental lawyers. Among distinguishing traits not generally part of law school curriculum, Bill knows how to listen to others. Martha is a political organizer who continually impresses California's multitude of political organizers. Like Magavern, one of Argüello's valuable skills includes building political strategy by listening and being guided by ordinary people; often times an essential skill when demonstrating to a legislator that you know their district.

Bill's well-respected reputation in legislative policy began with work in D.C. politics in the 1980s, contributing to a nationally recognized legal team fighting on behalf of consumers, citizens and the environment. Typically understated, he explains, "As the director of lobbying for US PIRG [public interest research group], I wasn't formally a member of Public Citizen's legal team.... working in the same building where Ralph's offices were located meant I regularly walked across the hall to join him on meetings at Public Citizen... Ralph occasionally invited me to travel to meetings across the country during my years in D.C."[124] And do, with his arrival in Sacramento, Bill quickly recognized as among an annual listing of the 100 most powerful political figures in Sacramento.[125]

While both Martha and Bill are consummate representatives for public interest advocacy and have each worked successfully in persuading numerous legislators to their views on legislation, I hesitate to calling either of them "political insiders;" probably because the notion too often calls to mind a private political broking occurring behind closed doors. Both Bill and Martha are often at their best negotiating in an open, public forum. They display what appears at times to be a lost art: giving voice to a public perspective in a democratic forum as the basis for shaping laws.

Representing her community in a familiar routine, over the years Martha has commuted to Sacramento. She starts her Sunday morning flying from her home in Los Angeles to Sacramento. She misses the usual Monday morning crowd of legislators she might otherwise schmooze on their flights to the capitol. To start her weekday early, with a series of meetings, she catches the shuttle to Burbank for an afternoon flight. After covering the details for local organizing events Martha Dina Argüello has thus resumed her travel loop with another shuttle to her destination from downtown Sacramento.

Argüello checks into the three-story hotel; a place not among the locations frequented by those with ample expense accounts, but at least it is a relatively short walk to the capitol and saves on cabs or car rentals. It is a routine similar to many community-based groups who don't have the funds for stylish accommodations. Sunday evening she calls and emails various people she has arranged to meet with during her four-day visit. This particular week combines testifying on bills important to a coalition of community groups, meetings with agency personnel on pending regulations, planning meetings with lawyers litigating on behalf of several chemically-exposed communities, and filling her spare time in meetings with legislative staff.

Since Argüello's other colleagues don't arrive until late Sunday evening, she gets on her laptop to stay current on the constant changes occurring on a daily basis across the United States. Although Martha has no office in Sacramento, colleagues in the environmental community allow her "squatter" space, to store her briefcase and computer throughout her typically hectic day.

Magavern has the convenience of a quick bike ride from his home in downtown Sacramento. Bill's easy proximity to the capitol seemingly a blessing of convenience also entails his frequently being called on by friends and allies to constantly attend impromptu regulatory, legislative or other meetings across Sacramento. Bill is absolutely tenacious, both about what initially might appear to others as a "small" detail in law: a word, a cross reference, subordinate paragraph or some other feature that might utterly change the content of proposed legislation.

Like so many of his colleagues, one of the most demanding parts of his job requires thinking, acting and speaking in real-time, including face-to-face exchanges with adversaries. Martha and Bill are practiced with navigating the capitol's corridors, juggling an agenda of staff briefings, testimony on bills, and keeping their members updated on the latest news. Tracking the tsunami of bills flooding the capitol is made more complex by the ever-changing language of legislation. While the process for committee hearings formally requires pre-printing, 30 days before a hearing, the dance of legislation inside the capitol translates to the constant negotiation and movement of language. It is part of the reason why committee hearings on a bill can be situations in which Bill and Martha's skills are tested by their agility to address the sharp turn of proposed amendments, counter the arguments of opponents, or offer compelling testimony.

Team Work

Martha, Bill and their compatriots regularly introduce a younger generation of activists to the intricacies of lobbying. Over the years, Martha's ability to recruit hundreds of young women and get them involved in the lawmaking process has been awe-inspiring. She often begins by explaining that initiating legislation in Sacramento is relatively straightforward. For the most part, any legislator's staff can be approached with a simple statement that begins with a description of a problem, a proposed solution, and a sketch of who might support or oppose, and an outline of the proposed law. Ushering a bill proposal through even a quick nine-month legislative journey is fraught with many perils.

The intensity and complexity of orchestrating even a modest lobbying effort demands considerable resources. While Bill and Martha have usually worked with solidly supported organizations, many of their public interest allies operate with minimal funds. It is not uncommon for community-based organizations to share space with others, moving constantly in a search for inexpensive rents. Many Magavern and Argüello colleagues from across the state are not typically available at a moment's notice. The logistics of organizing a variety of coalitions across disparate groups can be time-consuming and arduous.

Martha and Bill's adversaries, by contrast, start with fixed offices with complete law libraries, and access to electronic resources for legal research, can constantly communicate with their clients across California and the nation. The difference is not just resources: Perhaps most crucially, too many public interest groups lack the experience in the use of legal tactics to advance. Perhaps most crucially, the corporate lobby's objectives are readily agreed upon as they possess extensive training, and intensive backing, to leverage the position of dominant market forces. Having described lobbyists characterizing two of the better known faces among California public-interest advocates, who are their opponents? Selecting one person is difficult, yet one of the best representatives as someone possessing comparable regard for excellence in lobbying skills is a person also unlike many of her peers, Laurie Nelson. She is not old, white, over-bearing or content in working with a group of dinosaurs, sharing old stories about ancient clients or victories from another era.

One of my first impressions of Laurie was in her immersion and commitment to lobby persuasively on behalf of her clients. With a history of serving as professional staff in Alaska's Legislature, Laurie began in California in 1985, where she is clearly at home working among and between many familiar legislative offices and readily welcomed.[126] One amusing reaction of those with a preconceived antipathy to those representing corporate America is how charmed they are by not just Laurie, but by many of her colleagues. I have often observed members of the public who seem surprised to find that Laurie does not sport a cigar in the side of her mouth or a briefcase, bulging money! The fact is that many community members probably know less about Laurie's lobbying activities and more about her public role as the Board President of the Sacramento Philharmonic & Opera.

Two things stand out in Laurie's work in the capitol. The first is her persona. Laurie is someone who legislators like; who nearly everyone looks forward to seeing in the course of a complex day. Gently sardonic yet empathetic about the struggles of daily life, Laurie has mastered a combination of being personally charming while unyielding when negotiating on behalf of her clients. Unlike the stereotypic face of the corporate lobbyist - the suits - who are self-possessed and self-important, Laurie's capacity to walk into a legislator's office and instantly convey the very strong message that, aside from presenting her clients, she is also personally invested in that legislator, makes her a success. She often reminds me of two professors at a well-known environmental law clinic who would invite lobbyists sharing Laurie's approach as a simple demonstration that your opponents may have a much more persuasive bearing. Working for Satan does not mean your opponent isn't more attractive than you!

Laurie is frequently tasked in committee hearings with not just opposing environmental measures, but with persuading legislators that such opposition is only reasonable. Unlike many of her predecessors, who thought of their job as simply one of voicing the displeasure of powerful corporations, she masterfully meets and discusses any range of possible amendments to make a legislative proposal more acceptable to both sides of a debate: This orientation alone frequently wins legislators to her position. They, too, feel that their job mirrors what Laurie presents as a common objective: fashioning a compromise.

Laurie Nelson's disposition to fashion compromises is like that of so many of her corporate colleagues: pragmatic to a fault. After many years of working across from one another, I recognize that her pragmatism is guided by what she would probably term a healthy distrust of government combined with an elevated respect for the free market. This positive element of advocacy - promoting a free market unencumbered by *unnecessary* law - is a defining characteristic shared among corporate lobbyists. Their differences about which laws are necessary is, on occasion, controversial; especially during times when corporations fight and weaker lobbyists look for opportunities to find a space between combatting giants to advance a public interest. Such conflicts, however, are uncommon. The corporate lobby has a ready unity that gives them the advantage. Typically, corporate interests line up, and the times when corporate interests ally themselves with a public interest are even more rare.

The Never-ending Cycle of Fund-raising

For all of their skill and savvy, Bill and Martha's ability to defeat the corporate lobby is challenged by an obvious presence permeating the capitol. It is clear that even when their compatriots are able to mobilize the public to persuade legislators about the crafting of law, the role of money provides a more insidious advantage within democratic institutions. The public typically misunderstands how money works within the system, as though bags of greenbacks are being secretly passed from corporations to legislators.

Fundraising for the next election is an odious necessity for most legislators, it requires nearly daily attention. Every legislator's schedule includes time outside the walls of the capitol, to work the phones with those who can fuel the next election. The role of money is simultaneously transparent and opaque. The transparency requires reporting, tracking and disclosures largely nonexistent prior to the 1960s. Even with the ability to monitor money in politics, no longer is anyone surprised by reports that a typical campaign costing more than $1 million.[127] During the two-year period of roughly 2013 to 2014, for example, the members of California's Legislature raised, on average, about $1,000 a day to cover election expenses. Some observers note how such activities detracted from a focus on actual legislation.

The opaque dimension of money in politics is that fundraising has merged with decision-making. At a practical level, legislative deliberations often reflect the ever-present role of cash. Virtually all legislators spend many hours a week dialing for dollars outside the capitol. When a contributing lobbyist testifies before a committee, his financial affability not only greases the skids for a favorable passage, the very exchange may also influence expenditures either for or against that legislator, now sitting in judgment. Not all lobbyists have access to the additional money doled-out by individuals or the even larger unreported sums of political groups not controlled by an individual candidate. In conflicts between public and private interests, the resource divide is often a decisive one.

Public interest lobbyists may survive for a decade on meager salaries, while their adversaries in the corporate lobby frequently are drawn from groups of former legislators and professional staff who have many years of experience inside the Legislature before they continue long careers on behalf of corporate clients. The sheer length of experience shared by members of the corporate lobby, involving deep contacts across government, often carries a breadth of exposure in the making of law and policy that public interest advocates do not possess.

Money also serves as a cohesive force binding together the corporate lobby with a common objective as they go about conducting a seemingly highly positive agenda. The 'yes we can' image of many corporate lobbyists often contrasts sharply with a public interest message too often based on one all-too-common theme: a "toll of doom". The dynamic of new legislation is often cast as a group of citizens complaining about some particular transgression (e.g., a polluted water body, factory smog). They then sit across the table from facile negotiators such as Ms. Nelson, who offer various avenues for addressing the problem. Typically nimble enough to entertain a proposal which, at most, only involves some minute adjustment to an existing law, is it little surprise that Laurie Nelson is highly regarded by her clients?

Bill and Martha readily acknowledge that lobbying in the California Legislature typically runs on money, something in vanishingly short supply among public interest groups. At a gross level, the statistics for 2011 reveal that businesses, unions, and others spent in excess of $285 million, a new record over the nearly $282 million spent in 2008.[128] Yet, even the aggregate numbers disguise the dynamics of a contest between private versus public interests. The corporate lobby's very focused, positive images of a free market compares to the environmental lobby's defensive and complaining posture that more efforts must be taken to protect ancient forests, remote wilderness areas, or species lacking any of the charisma of polar bears or butterflies. The divide between rich and poor public interest advocates has been further exploited by corporate interests who have seeded further confusion within the environmental community by drawing its wealthier members into the orbit of compromises based on market mechanisms, regulatory flexibility, or financial instrumental design in the private sector.

California's environmental lobby contains many historic and deep divisions both among its own advocates and with its allies. A specific group organized to protect endangered species cannot necessarily be relied upon to defend farmworkers from pesticide hazards. Or those interested in parklands may be absent when removal of hazardous wastes from inner city neighborhoods looks for broader support. Finding revenues for water bonds might well exclude even minor assistance for beleaguered communities of immigrant and poor households in the central valley.[129] The absence of a shared agenda among public interest groups has too often resulted in the absence of a larger, strategic vision.

Though the larger national organizations endeavor to set an agenda that includes states as a subset, California's environmental lobby regularly rejects this orientation. Part of the rejection reflects caution in following a national leadership dominated by organizations having the ample representation of moneyed interests among its board and staff.[130] Despite typically commanding greater resources, national environmental organizations frequently lack an essential stance possessed by many of California's community-based groups: the willingness to wage protracted campaigns inside the political boundaries of office holders. Ironically, it is precisely this level of political combat so often deployed by large corporate interests when laws or elected leaders do not go their way.

There is also a cultural clash. In many instances, national groups struggle to negotiate laws by reaching a lowest common denominator in order to gain acceptance across fifty states. California's environmental campaigns are often anchored in two of the nation's most progressive metropolis: Los Angeles and the San Francisco Bay Area. When both national and California-centric environmental organizations appear together in the capitol, there is frequently a kind of schism between the two. In recent years especially, community-based environmental organizations have expressed hostility toward national environmental groups as not only too readily engaging in compromises, but supporting unacceptable proposals from the start: an experience frequently referred to as "being thrown under the bus."

The perceived need for bigger offices, fancier websites, and a larger advertising budgets impacts the political posture of the national environmental lobbies as well. Many of the larger national groups have made an uneasy peace with donor-sponsored campaigns and operations, often inviting corporate participation on their boards of directors. The self-imposed austerity of community-based and environmental justice groups is both a reflection of their constituents as a basis for avoiding the intrusion of corporate interests accompanied by a weakening commitment to ferociously pursue the public interest.

The Political Overlords

Many academics have written on the role of interest groups in U.S. politics. One of the most graphic portrayals throughout the year is found in legislative hearing rooms where the fine details of public laws are crafted, by the dozens, on a weekly basis. In many of the most important committees (e.g., agriculture, business and professions, revenue and taxation, judiciary, banking and finance, environment, labor), private sector lobbyists no longer operate "in house," employed by a specific firm to track law on behalf of a unique client, such as a regional bank. In the modern era, single-issue private sector lobbyists have been replaced by larger, even global multi-purpose firms, whose proactive safeguarding offers an expansive reach into the democratic process.[131]

The political dynamic surrounding public versus private interest lobbying is striking. As my brother Casey explains it, "there are innumerable disagreements within corporate America about how to get there - but 24/7 there is only a single destination: the 'so-called' free market: where everyone gets a pony, too!" By comparison, those lobbyists registered with environmental groups display very different numbers relative to their corporate opponents. The environmental lobbyists permanently located in Sacramento consist of roughly two dozen advocates. Corporate operations consist of many times that number, with registered lobbyists reaching into the hundreds. More telling is the commonplace: and similar asymmetry I observe while attending meetings to negotiate legislative language.

The mischaracterization of politics as defined by partisan gridlock disguises a more far-reaching warfare between the corporate and public interest lobbies. Despite an astonishing mismatch of resources, public interest groups have tallied many notable victories across a range of laws. The corporate lobby, in turn, has assembled an increasingly sophisticated political machine, with the capacity to shape the larger arena of political choice via political action committees, advertising groups, social media, trade associations, university labs, foundation programs, private sector facilities, factories, and franchises with jobs present in every corner of an electoral district. While Bill and Martha place a premium on transparency, announcing their intentions to citizens and supporters, law sponsored by the corporate lobby might be best described as opaque and deceptive. Even professional legislative staff members find it daunting to discern what is going on in a variety of corporate sponsored changes to the law.

Among the various corruptive influences, one of the most direct is simply using one's legislative office to act as a handmaiden for the corporate lobby. An obvious tell is the legislator who cannot even explain their bill in the midst of deliberations. During a hearing of the Senate Environmental Quality Committee in the mid-2000s, a bill was presented by a relatively new member of the Assembly. The corporate handlers included two well-recognized lobbyists. Both had served as senior advisers to powerful legislators, prior to being recruited into lucrative positions working on behalf of a member company of the Fortune 500.[132] The bill was especially contentious with discussion and debate extending for nearly an hour. The Committee Chair, a professor from Stanford Law School, engaged in a prolonged debate with the two lobbyists, touching on finer points of law, historic aspects of the state's Environmental Quality Act, contract law, and the duties and responsibilities of cities' and counties' public utilities relative to arrangements with private companies.[133]

Afforded an opportunity to summarize and respond to the debate on his bill, the legislator author struggled mightily to demonstrate that he had even followed the discussion. Many in the hearing room came away with an impression that the corporate sponsors were wholly in control of the legislation, if not the legislator as well. To be sure, various Committee chairs mature to gain a legal knowledge that exceeds the command of those newly elected. The crafting of law, and the weaknesses of that process: point to troubling trends. First, the limited terms for legislators mean that more of those involved in these processes are amateurs, as the role of committee consultants with technical legal knowledge and a sense of institutional history is diminished. [134] Lost too is their capacity to reveal agendas that are not readily visible. Beyond a vanishing cadre of public interest attorneys, only a small group of seasoned legislators and practiced committee consultants are able to comprehend the significance or consequences of legislation sponsored by an army of corporate lobbyists.

Winning at Everything

The dominance of lobbying in the capitol by a complex of corporate groups creates another advantage. The ability of talent to go to work for environmental, labor, public health or other such groups is generally limited by a simple absence of jobs. On the corporate side young people, particularly those with an inclination toward compromises favoring the private sector, find a welcoming corporate lobby. Veteran committee consultants may reach a stage of life where paying for college or taking care of aging parents make the lure of corporate offers irresistible. Consequently, those with legislative training and skills move inexorably toward the corporate side of the street. The corporate lobby's siren song subtly seduces certain legislators, certain of whom lose their interest in public service long before ever exchanging anything of value with the corporate lobby.

For both Bill and Martha, and indeed, most everyone in the capitol, the ever-present question - "Where's the money?" - permeates too many transactions. To cap this description of the very different worlds of public interest advocates and the corporate lobby, consider two prominent lobbying groups: Kahl Pownall (KP) Public Affairs and the Sierra Club California. Each known well and regarded for their work in the California Legislature, the KP website is impressive, starting with the home page's glowing self-portrayal: "Experts at Winning."

Paging through the website reveals *individual* corporate clients with a financial wherewithal that can rarely be matched, even by coalitions of environmental and consumer groups. KP places individual corporate clients in a network with the promise of not simply lobbying for a particular bill but a comprehensive political strategy that involves drafting legislation, providing testimony, and monitoring regulations. Public relations campaigns feature ongoing counsel and response to changed circumstances with new tactics. More fundamentally, it means recruiting allies and building coalitions through grassroots organizing. This includes reaching deep into communities, from church groups to local civic organizations, to professional associations, to embed their proposals. The website proudly notes, "KP's experienced professionals have helped to organize some of the largest coalitions in California history."[135]

Behind all of these activities stands a group of professionals in finance, medicine, labor, public health and the environment. Such coverage means that clients are offered more than a narrow realm of expertise, but a special kind of synergy. Solving a client's environmental problem in siting a facility or introducing a new product can mean everything from arranging public financing bond offerings to encouraging the preemption of a state law to facilitating support among scientific bodies to the mining of social media... to generate seemingly spontaneous public expressions of support.

The image of a well-attired lobbyist entering a smoke filled room with promise of a payoff for arranging sleazy political deals is archaic;

it misses just how KP's comprehensive political strategy ensures that its clients prevail. The strategy is to orchestrate active public support. From the perspective of modern-era corporate lobbying firms, getting *caught* making a deal is simply stupid. As KP puts it, "we also understand that sometimes the best media relations involve keeping our clients' names out of the news."[136] A common political maxim in California's capitol reflects much the same sentiment: the most important exercises in power are most often invisible. For well-orchestrated campaigns, success is often characterized by the absence of debate. As one corporate lobbyist informed me early in my career, "things are working best when I don't have to even appear in the capitol."[137]

The Sierra Club California website, by comparison, displays precisely what many in the capitol see as a wearied Don Quixote tilting at windmills, engaged in the noble and virtuous fight. Those pictured on the Club website show a happy lot; yet, the tone of their website is often more reactive than proactive: And with good reason. With only a handful of paid staff, it is a marvel that the Sierra Club prevails in any legislative battles against such well-financed adversaries. The website intones many virtuous and noble causes: saving the oceans, reducing greenhouse gas emissions, preserving natural lands, and fighting against fracking. Even this celebrated environmental organization does not possess the brawn to match the winning track record that KP promises to their clients. A comparison of pictures suggests the Sierra Club has recruited a wonderfully talented group, prepared to win a debate - but who fail to comprehend that their opponents have arrived fully equipped for a knife fight.

Closely resembling a parallel government, corporate lobbying complexes in Sacramento have become experts at the entire machinery of producing law. Their expertise takes on many of the attributes that are familiar to Casey from his world of corporate finance, including directing public resources toward private ends as a principal goal. My brother's question hangs in the air; "Is the place simply ruled by our alien overlords?" I am persuaded, at times that such knowledge of corporate America, provides much more of an insight about the nature of politics. The mismatch between public versus private might suggest that Bill and Martha's fate is sealed. Yet, the asymmetry of resources commanded by the "alien overlords" overlooks a basic source of Martha and Bill's optimism. Beyond the small circle of public interest advocates serving as registered lobbyists are vast numbers of community groups, nonprofit organizations, and just maybe...tens of millions of citizens prepared to launch a changed political climate.

CHAPTER 7

Market Solutions for Market Failures

Today, "California will be a leader in the fight against global warming... I say the debate is over. We know the science, we see the threat and we know the time for action is now."[138] The statement, issued by one of California's governors, suggested a bold plan to address a steadily advancing crisis - climate change.

Serving as a primary leader for state Republicans, this popular governor immediately placed himself at odds with President George Bush, who steadfastly avoided the issue, including his refusal to join 150-plus nations from around the globe in that eras effort to devise an international accord -- the Kyoto Protocols. Governor Arnold Schwarzenegger was delivering his plan to address global warming to open a United Nations World Environment Day Conference in San Francisco.

In making his announcement, Schwarzenegger issued an executive order directing the secretary of California's Environmental Protection Agency to reduce the state's emissions of greenhouse gases to 2000 levels by 2010; 1990 levels by 2020; and 80 percent below 1990 levels by 2050,[139] as the outline of a long-term program. Despite a mountain of scientific studies documenting a disrupted climate, the main directive from President Bush was to undermine California's recently enacted law to lessen engine emissions. The question of whether such a program would require too little escaped notice: It would be progress, seemingly, to launch *any* plan. However, in a setting where words and details mattered, the Governor's plan was about to hit a speed bump.

Gut and Amend

Within weeks of Governor Schwarzenegger's launched project to address global warming, an attempt was made to introduce a legislative proposal mirroring the broad strokes of the Governor's executive order. A member of the Assembly came to the Senate with a reputed agreement that the Governor would sign global warming legislation into law. The catch, typical to agreements reached late in the session, necessitated the Legislature to agree to a kind of blank check, largely circumventing reviews by policy committees...and the public. Last minute agreements of this sort often employed a technique known as 'gut and amend' taking legislation introduced earlier in the legislative session on one topic, later inserting entirely new language.

Few involved, if anyone, had the opportunity to analyze and reflect on the consequences of a proposed 'gut' or change. In certain instances, such as after a natural disaster, gut and amend served a valuable purpose: to act with the utmost urgency in the event of a crisis. Unfortunately, gut and amends too often were invented crises employed by powerful lobbyists as a device for circumventing more intensive public scrutiny. Whereas Congress and even many states passed measures without the benefit of even allowing sufficient time for representatives to read measures requiring their vote, California's Legislature exercised a very strong tradition based on an extensive review by professional staff as well as allowing for public review and comment.

Behind the Governor's directive to urgently address global warming lurked a more devilish question: who was responsible for setting the earth on fire in the first place? On this point, the Governor seemed to suggest that we all shared a responsibility for fixing the problem. The tension for many veterans of the Legislature involved their belief that a key ingredient in crafting 'good' law required everyone – especially the general public – time to digest what a legal proposal meant. Leaving vital details solely in the hands any governor was an approach many professional staff referred to by the simple and pejorative shorthand: faith-based governing.

Nearing the close of the 2005 legislative session, I was asked to join a meeting of the chair of my committee along with two other legislators to discuss a possible gut-and-amend. In the absence of any written draft, the proposal was presented as a broadly conceptual one: allowing a bill broadly encapsulating Governor Schwarzenegger's executive order on global warming to advance through the Senate's Environmental Quality Committee. The assembly member was emphatic in her presentation; here was a golden and urgent opportunity for the Legislature to act, we should not pass up this matter of crucial importance to the public. Almost as an afterthought, the anxious legislator mentioned a minor caveat: since the specific language was still being finalized by the Governor's people, the Committee would only be able to vote on the broad generalities of the bill.

In the closed-door meeting with the three legislators, the chair then turned to me, asking for my perspective on the proposed hearing for what was the Governor's bill on climate change. I began by noting that awaiting Congressional action had only presented us with a worsening crisis. In contrast to several previous governors, largely ignorant about global warming, the opportunity to work with one who acknowledged the crisis was significant. It was also clear from the look on the face of the legislator seated across from me that the opportunity to author a bill on the premier 'hot topic' of the new century was too good to pass up. After my many years in the Legislature, however, I was accustomed to passing up deals that were too good.

Facing the three legislators, I argued that giving any governor a blank check to address a problem was a bad idea, even more so given the gravity of this issue. "Look," I offered, "this is a complex, multi-faceted problem that is going to be with us for decades. The most important consideration is that we start off in the right direction, with a carefully crafted proposal. Without a draft, we have no idea if we even agree with the governor's basic formulation of the problem…" The other two of the Legislature's most-savvy lawmakers wanted to help their colleague with this bill, but also understood the enormous risks with endorsing a vaguely worded measure that left broad latitude to the mercurial

Governor regarding the specifics of how to design a program addressing global climate change. The meeting ended with the committee chair offering every-assistance to the Assembly member ...during the next legislative session. For the moment, however, the chair joined with me in stating that the committee had a duty to allow his fellow senators as well as the public a fuller opportunity to review and consider the specifics of the gubernatorial proposal.

The prospective author left, more than a little perturbed at a lost opportunity. In an increasingly common role, I was the recipient of that day's 'evil eye' award for splashing cold legislative water on another wonderful legislative proposal. I left the meeting wondering if some of the materials I had used a few years earlier with groups of students at UC Berkeley might have prompted a more fulsome legislative discussion. A particularly thoughtful author, prominent in my syllabus, argued that solving global warming involved more than simply a re-jiggering of technologies to capture fugitive gases. Instead, the task required more fundamental changes.

> "If greenhouse theory is correct, and the preponderance of evidence indicates that it is correct, humanity must drastically reduce its use not only of methane and CFCs (greenhouse gases), but of coal and oil as well, even though such a reduction means that the entire planetary economy must be re-structured – to a degree that implies a fundamental break with the energy economy that has underlain capitalism from its earliest days. This is not a matter of a few technical fixes, of isolated reforms to an economy that can remain essentially unaltered."[140]

Within weeks of that closed-door meeting with legislators, I began designing a climate change bill going well beyond a vaguely worded executive order issued by the Governor. My mentors, including legislators from an earlier era, taught me that unless I was prepared to ask for the sky, we would likely achieve only a partially poisoned atmosphere. The short-list of items contained in this draft package included policies to aggressively accelerate energy conservation, steeply graduated fees on the largest carbon emitters, triggers imposing even greater restrictions on emissions in the event of federal backsliding, and a massive increase in state resources dedicated to alternative energy projects, infrastructure and jobs. The time had come for California to decisively move its economy beyond fossil fuels. This grand plan, however, suddenly confronted an altered political reality.

During fall 2005, the chairmanship of the Senate Environmental Quality Committee changed. The change in committee chairs scuttled a number of staff projects, including my preliminary drafting of an aggressive 'Marshall Plan' for global climate change. The new chairman also dramatically altered the standing of corporate lobby's influence in shaping environmental policy. The usual briefing on substantive issues likely to appear before the committee during the coming months was eliminated as well as the invitation by the previous chair to attend any and all appointments by legislators and lobbyists discussing anything pertaining to committee. Instead I was asked to respond to a flurry of complaints that I was not adequately cooperating with the corporate lobby. My personal response was something less than diplomatic.

"Well...my door is always open...but I confess that I can no more provide a sympathetic forum for stupid arguments presented by the corporate gang than I would for anyone else." The sour look on the new chair's face foretold that it was going to be a *long* legislative session. Equally evident was a new hierarchy. Corporate lobbyists were welcomed to bypass the committee's troublesome professional staff and arrange meetings directly with the new chair.

California's Global Warming Solutions Act

"What's that?" I queried of my companion as we emerged from yet another meeting, as a van adjacent to the capitol's south entrance deposited a bulky item on the well-manicured grounds.

"It's the governor's podium," my colleague responded. "See the guv's seal on the front?"

"Yes, I see the podium, but what's he carrying in his other hand?"

Approaching the curb, we looked more closely. "It's his platform!" she responded to my puzzled expression. "You know: the wooden box he stands on to appear larger than life when towering behind the podium."

"You have got to be kidding me!"

"Come on Bruce, it's a Hollywood thing. For Schwarzenegger, this is all political theater." As we entered the marbled halls, we were laughing. "Oh it's theater alright: theater of the absurd."

Within days my attention turned to the first in a series of broadly outlined discussions about what might appear in the proposal being finalized for hearing before my committee. The bill, eventually celebrated as one of California's premiere environmental laws – the Global Warming Solutions Act, popularly known as AB 32 advanced a program supporters referred to as "cap-and-trade;" something that its detractors would later refer to with as California's pollution trading scheme.[141] The basic architecture required regulatory agencies, including the California Air Resources Board to set limits on the largest emitters of greenhouse gases combined with a vaguely stated trading program.

This bill would contain an essential flexibility for these large emitters that made AB 32 very different from a classic California regulatory approach. Beginning with a benchmark of total greenhouse gas emissions, a declining cap for these emissions would be imposed on the largest emission sources - designed to decrease total emissions to an earlier baseline - in this case, the earlier and lower 1990 measurement of total statewide emissions. Large emission sources, facilities such as refineries or energy plants owned by very large corporations, would be allowed to trade emission credits in an auction with other facilities not utilizing *all* their own credits. The concept held that as the cap on emissions decreased over time, credits would become more expensive, driving up the price of greenhouse gas pollutants. Companies would have various avenues to figure out how to deal with pollution, but eventually all emitters would be compelled to utilize less costly and less polluting alternatives.

From the start I found the bill title misleading, given that an array of California laws already addressed various facets of global warming.[142] With the availability of plentiful regulatory mechanisms, why was these members of the Assembly so enchanted with trading mechanisms as a means for addressing the climate crisis? I would slowly awaken as to why the bill's emphasis on a trading mechanism continually nagged at me. We would soon learn about a central feature that made this approach so distinctive.

During an early meeting with supporters, tentative language circulated for a bill being drafted by the Legislature's attorneys that appeared to be suspiciously like the work of the larger environmental groups in Washington, D.C. (and quite unlike the product of California's environmental advocates).[143] One telltale characteristic was that language crafted by many California environmental attorneys typically reflected an obsession with fine details, whereas proposals from inside the Beltway as well in Congress often proceeded with broad provisions. For many of us inside California's capitol, the Congressional model of drafting overly broad provisions in law only invited challenges and delays by powerful opposing interests.

Before launching legislation in D.C., one could first road test it in a state legislature. The main advocates in D.C. were laying the groundwork in California for a piece to follow as the national model: based on what they hoped would be the California law. A centerpiece of the bill used "market mechanisms" to define how global warming would be addressed, with the use of a trading scheme. Although trading had been used at that time in a program in Southern California, AB 32 advocates argued that theirs was a distinctive architecture.

At this point, as typical when working in the arena of concepts without benefit of actual language or empirical data, I resorted to a sophisticated technology honed by staff over many years. I picked up the phone to survey my ever-expanding universe of informal advisors stretching from journalists and physicians to regulatory scientists and activists in Los Angeles to gain from their deep knowledge. I was especially interested in the perspective of one who, over many years, was among the elite wizards responsible for pumping up the quarterly statements of major global firms through use of financial instruments. The source, of course, was my brother.

Trading and Politics

"Casey, I've got a question." It was another of what became more frequent calls to sound-out a private sector perspective on my political crisis du jour.

"Go ahead" Casey answered, "What's the latest from the temple of doom?"

I explained the outlines of the global warming bill, ending with a question about market mechanisms: "What do you make of the use of such an approach, especially emissions trading, since this seems to be where the bill is headed?"

"Bruce, Bruce, Bruce.....what's the matter? Haven't you given yourself over to the market? It is a wonderful faith-based system and it makes it easier for you to sleep at night." Casey then walked through how some of his financial wizardry, conducted on behalf of major corporations, typically relied on a contract to specify the obligations and responsibilities for both parties.

"So let me get this straight; you're saying this is a perfectly acceptable way to construct a program for reducing greenhouse gases, yet...?" Before I completed the question Casey interrupted, "No, I said that in corporate-land I have helped to define the financial terms for contracts. But in many instances the contract has followed a prime directive: if things turn sour, make certain that the other party is screwed to the wall. One of the wonderful parts of financial engineering is that virtually no one understands how any of this works. So my question to you is a simple one: who in the Legislature understands trading? Or better yet, ask the legislators and their supporters if they can explain it to you in more than a couple of sound bites." Casey was saving the best for last.

"...Oh, and there is the second part of working with contracts. For all of the contracts that I have been party to, we would typically write up something about 1,000 pages long, just to make certain that we have a very thorough understanding of where this agreement will take us and, most especially, a very clear statement about when the contract has not been fulfilled, how it will be enforced and, most especially, what we get when the contract doesn't have the outcome that we have agreed on."

"...So, you've got to ask some additional questions" continued Casey. "First, what does trading mean in this bill? Second, what happens when greenhouse gases aren't reduced over some period of time? And third, how extensive is the contract language?" "Well," I responded, "the bill does not have any specific contract language as such. It is simply a vague statement regarding the use of market mechanisms to achieve a reduction in greenhouse gases."

"Well, 'whoopee!' is all I can say," Casey laughed. "I know which side of that deal I want to be on....and it certainly isn't backing the people of California! ...By the way, let me know when this bill is going to the Governor so I can start shorting the state.[144] Remember when Enron's traders giggled as California's bureaucrats came to the floor to make energy contract purchases? This will be even better!"

Dealing with Uncertainties

One of the virtues of having two houses of a legislature is the opportunity to fine-tune legislative proposals into more precise, clearly stated law.[145] Ambiguous or confusing language conflicting with other state or federal law can invite legal challenges resulting in delays while courts, subsequent legislatures or governors try to decipher the meaning of the original legislation. After passing the Assembly and arriving to the Senate, AB 32 shrouded a variety of mysteries.

The Global Warming Solutions Act (AB 32) arrived in the Senate Committee on Environmental Quality setting-out to address an already widely and long-recognized problem. Unlike their counterparts in Congress, California's legislators were largely agreed on the scientific basis of human contributions to global warming. In Governor Schwarzenegger's words, "the debate was over." AB 32 was excitedly anticipated proposal, finally responding to the overwhelming evidence collected by an impressive gathering of scientists from around the world. It was all the more striking that the calls for immediate and urgent action arose from *scientists* who typically requested nothing more than modest funding for additional research.

Modeled loosely after the cap-and-trade program operating among a group of eastern states, the basic concept was to provide flexibility for industry to select the most desirable path to reduce its emissions, based on the trading of carbon credits. Many legislators were instantly drawn to any compromise solution that promised agreement between industry and environmental groups. While the Solutions Act garnered many supporters, its origins were still cloaked in vagary. Others would later credit the Environmental Defense Fund (EDF) for unabashedly promoting cap-and-trade as a virtuous, free market solution; "..[P]rojects that were employing practices that claimed to be keeping carbon out of the atmosphere – whether by planting trees that sequester carbon, or by producing low carbon energy, or by upgrading a dirty factory to lower its emissions – could qualify for carbon credits. These credits could be purchased by polluters and used to offset their own emissions."[146]

Cap-and-Trade: Theory and Practice

After many weeks of delay, the much anticipated global warming act finally arrived for my review. The bill authorized California, as the first state in the nation, to initiate a comprehensive program to address global warming drawing mainly on two approaches: one regulatory, the other an emissions program, otherwise known as cap-and-trade, to control greenhouse gases, GHGs.[147]

While emissions trading lacked a clear legal definition, the authors' staff explained the workings by resorting to illustrations of how cap-and-trade would work. As an example, if the cap were 100 million tons of carbon dioxide emissions, the law would create 100 million allowances, each equal to one ton of emissions. For a specified group of emitters (e.g., facilities), the program would distribute allowances equal to their total emissions for a set period of time. By establishing a market for pollution credits within the context of decreasing credits, the intended consequence is that a scarcity of credits, resulting from a declining cap, would provide the necessary incentive for facilities to reduce emissions to a targeted level.[148] Policy wonks spoke glowingly of cap-and-trade as a path that provided businesses with the flexibility to determine whether the best approach involved the purchase of new equipment, substituting fuels, altering chemical processes, or myriad modes that regulators could not easily or expeditiously consider according to old command-and-control regulations.

The impulse for unseasoned legislators to seize upon bills with novel concepts in law often produced a phenomenon that a group of my female colleagues likened to children opening presents: "Look! It's a shiny object: A bright, shiny object!" Information surrounding the practical operation and potential consequences of this new toy - emissions trading - was scarce among the bill's sponsors. In a memorable conversation with a well-known figure belonging to one of the largest national environmental organizations, I wondered about what was actually being required: "Are the goal emission reductions for businesses, too underwhelming?"

The response was dismissive. I narrowed the question to next ask how the bill's required reductions differed from a scenario based on contemporary regulatory requirements (existing in the Clean Air Act).[149] The response was that "no empirical evidence could be provided," but I should rest assured that such "reductions would be significantly greater than 'business as usual.'" I was not assured.[150]

The question of whether the Solutions Act called for too little reflected a tension common to many proposed laws. Whenever industry was held responsible to address a problem of their making, a common response was one of incredible outrage: "What are you trying to do? Kill us?" Counter-proposals were then presented by corporate lobbyists, often including an explosion of details that would later be used to blame an overly zealous and burdensome government. Over time, we would discover that the "onerous rules and regulations" advanced by industry were much too lax.[151] In the absence of specific provisions measuring outcomes the results might not just miss the mark, but be utter failures.

Pollution trading raised another obvious question: how would the proposed law affect the health and environment of those living and working in the shadow of refineries, power plants, cement plants, and other large emission sources? For well over a decade scholars and activists noted the discriminatory quality of 'solutions' to environmental problems; "In the United States, to be poor, to be working-class, to be female, or to be a member of a minority groups often means being subjected to a disproportionately large share of the country's environmental problems. Frequently, environmental disparities are merely another form of institutional discrimination."[152] Within a decade, the question would prove to be one of the more crucial issues concerning the politics of pollution trading. Beyond the bureaucratic cost of administering a trading program, impacts on corporate bottom lines, or even decreasing dangerous gases was the question about "externalities" - the broader social, economic and political consequences of providing flexibility to fossil fuel interests.

As one way of revisiting whether too little was being required by AB 32, I recommended the use of "triggers" or legal provisions that would automatically come into force if events (e.g., empiric thresholds such as carbon levels, regional ecological impacts, full analysis of costly externalities) showed that the Solutions Act was falling short in reducing dangerous emissions or even causing other problems. The suggestion was less of a critique than acknowledgement of the uncertainty that so often surrounded this type of proposal. As Martha Valdez had counseled me years earlier, it was frequently vital to have a backup provision when "things didn't work out as intended."

Another question regarding the draft legislation was whether it contained an adequate definition for greenhouse gases. In meetings preceding the hearing on the bill, a senior Congressional adviser who had worked extensively on the Clean Air Act recommended what he regarded as an essential provision: to not simply limit the emissions of carbon dioxide, but to include other gases as well. At the time, these other gases, sometimes referred to as "contributory" or "super" pollutants, were estimated to make up over one-half of the global warming problem. During an initial meeting with one of the authors, I was assured that these contributory pollutants would be included in the bill *if the scientific basis exists to make the case for their inclusion.* The list of items I was supposed to be assured about was growing longer with each meeting.

My most basic misgiving was a sense that few, if any, in the Legislature had a practical understanding about emissions trading. A surprising number of private sector firms entered my office, many of them expressing confusion and concern about what the law meant for them. Even among certain larger firms, responses included comments such as, "Look, I am a successful manufacturer. I understand how to work with regulations and have done so for many years. But trading? Does this law now require me to hire a bunch of people to engage in emissions trading? What in the hell is that...?"

Another of my questions centered on the body of work by academic colleagues in public health and the environmental sciences, who noted that the disruptions in biological systems were both more insidious and more pervasive than commonly appreciated by the public, citing not just lead and tobacco, but many thousands of substances. California's experience with "permitting" pollutants, such as air toxics or water contaminants appeared to be something of a slow-motion disaster in which advancing scientific reviews often revealed that assumptions of so-called "safe" or "acceptable" levels were seriously flawed.

If cap-and-trade facilitated the continued use of fossil fuels, did it not also undermine a more expeditious transition to an economy based on alternative fuels? As a long-term farm worker advocate and industrial hygienist reflected, "Would emissions trading provide a legal defense for polluting industries to release 'acceptable' levels of tradable pollutants, undermining existing laws that simply prohibited those emissions?"[153] Coinciding with these concerns was a more general anxiety, as expressed by many public-interest advocates throughout the process: the entire emissions trading proposal was cloaked in mystery. Despite the cheers among supporters for cap-and-trade, many community activists recognized that for all of its weaknesses, a regulatory program already existed and held much less mystery and greater promise to achieve the obvious objective: the dismantling of fossil fuels.

And time was of the essence. In 2005, prominent climate scientists had already concluded that wasting time would only worsen the impending crises. As much as everyone recognized the urgency of taking action on global warming, veteran political workers understood that if California initiated a wrong-headed approach - it might take many years to undo the damage. In a series of conversations with the authors' staff, I explored a variety of add-ons to their bill: a plan to finance energy conservation coupled with the promotion of alternatives, a steeply graduated schedule of expansive regulatory fees levied on the major energy companies, triggers to address federal government refusals to grant California waivers to achieve more restrictive regulations, metropolitan alternative energy program assistance, enhanced enforcement against violations of clean air laws (including releases of GHGs), and so on. I explained that if nothing else, these approaches could provide the basis for negotiating stronger provisions with the Governor's office. The measure's authors gave the very strong impression that the negotiations were only one way, nothing was being asked of the Governor.

Trading: Law for Schemes

I confess it: I was finally at a loss for words. My discussions with sponsors, supporters and staff representing the two legislators who authored the bill managed mainly feeble responses to questions regarding the mechanics of pollution trading, its impacts on communities of color, its consequences for existing law, not to mention the variety of issues arising from poorly drafted provisions. The parade of people informing me about the wonderful world of emissions trading possessed the same response given to me a year earlier by the prospective Assembly author: you should trust that the Governor will implement a good and virtuous climate program. Collective endorsements of the California Global Warming Solutions Act were clearly intended to sweep away any remaining doubts as an act of faith. All of which prompted me to ask at the close of nearly every meeting, "How can one reasonably expect a law based on free market approaches to solve a problem initially unleashed by the free market?"

The unfolding evidence indicting carbon dioxide as destructive to the earth's climate represented only a part of the larger story as to the wholly inadequate regulation of fossil fuels. In my tenure with the California Legislature there were numerous, compelling examples of substantial and ongoing damages resulting from largely unregulated chemicals. By the early 21st century, extensive contaminants affected the nation's air, water and soils with tens of thousands of chemicals. The entire petrochemical complex was responsible. And now lobbyists, including major environmental groups from D.C., called for us to grant petrochemicals *great flexibility*?

The steadfast response from the authors' representatives was that any of the changes I recommended would jeopardize the passage of the bill. Unlike a prior group of longer-term legislators, practiced with mounting a multi-year campaign to achieve fundamental changes, younger staff and legislators were regularly extorted by a governor's staff to not make changes beyond pre-approved agreements. The result, too often, was what professional staff regarded as 'press release bills'- designed to display grand achievements, but lacking real substance. The impulse for the unseasoned was to seize upon this "bright, shiny object!"

The most important source for understanding the potential impacts of cap-and-trade were not to be found in any of the packets of information or briefings delivered by the authors of the measure or their supporters. In place of assurances of positive outcomes and economists testifying about the efficiencies to be achieved by businesses were the disappointing results on the ground (and above it) with one of the oldest pollution-trading schemes operating inside of California's largest metropolitan area.

The rising alarm surrounding air pollution during the 1960s, lead to the passage of the Clean Air Act in 1970. The essential mechanism of the Act was to establish limits on the release of harmful air pollutants, which principally affected auto manufacturers, refineries, and heavy industries.[154] The regulatory requirements of the Clean Air Act were largely aimed at technological changes, including filters to remove recognized pollutants and meet air quality standards. "By 1991, however, the EPA had succumbed to the pressure of lobbyists demanding lax enforcement of the Act's regulations associated with expensive emissions equipment. EPA targeted Southern California to test a plan that would potentially increase healthy air while reducing emissions by offsetting the cost of pollution controls ....The pilot project, called Regional Clean Air Incentives Market (RECLAIM) established a system for trading 'credits' among polluters."[155]

While the authors of AB 32 pointed to an East coast emissions trading program to limit CO2 emissions (RGGI) as an illustration of how cap and trade might operate, RECLAIM was a much closer approximation to the broad contours of the Solution Act.[156] It is likely that the sponsors of AB 32 did not want to point to RECLAIM for one simple reason: it was "widely regarded as a failure due to the issuance of too many emission credits, resulting in weak prices."[157] Initiated as one of the earliest programs for emissions trading, RECLAIM faced challenges from the start. "Companies had an incentive to achieve escape routes (e.g., variances granted by local air districts) from caps placed on emissions." [158]

RECLAIM readily confronted intensive scrutiny from community-based organizations. Communities were already suspect of the basic premise that pollution trading from oil refineries, rail traffic, and other industrial facilities would not impose an even greater threat to their well-being. Various community groups viewed the entire premise of providing regulatory flexibility to the private sector with a blunt skepticism, particularly regarding the benefits of a pollution-trading scheme designed by those working from office towers in New York, Washington, D.C., or San Francisco. The suggestion that they should join with national environmental groups who had designed AB 32 yielded open hostility among a large number of community-based groups in Los Angeles, "This wouldn't be the first time that they threw us under the bus!"[159]

Another controversy enveloping the proposed trading scheme related to what many public health officials referred to as 'old science' vs. 'new science'. Early schemes to RECLAIM emerged during an era when trading was founded on an already dated characterization of 'pollutants' as chemical hazards posing principally short-term harms. By the beginning of the 21st century, newly emerging scientific findings included a much broader array of harms, reflected in an expanded set of statutory terms (e.g., neurotoxins, micro-particulates, endocrine disruption). Because the harms recognized latent effects impacting multiple generations, sometimes at exceedingly small exposures or other times based only the timing of exposures (i.e., first trimester for reproductive effects) legislative discussions moved from how to manage chemical exposures to a more pointed effort simply to eliminate the commercial production or release of substances posing inherent hazards.

Whereas various federal laws were firmly planted in an older model allowing private sector firms to release uncharacterized chemicals into the environment, public health officials and others conversant with these new scientific findings advanced precautionary approaches in law. By the early 2000s precautionary legislation became especially popular in California, with many calling for the rapid phase-out of various products containing bio-accumulative, biologically disruptive, and other such substances (e.g., mercury, lead, PBDEs). The operating premise for a variety of these laws was to prohibit the production, use and sale of substances posing inherent hazards. Lacking this preventative premise, the framing of the Global Warming Solutions Act was instantly contentious.

A fundamental question confronting the Legislature turned on how to construct AB 32 within the framework of existing laws, and pointed to very divergent paths. Inside the Legislature, the question pivoted on whether to incrementally manage the release in a calculus of what was most efficient for business. The new research emerging was predicated on the urgency to eliminate these substances posing known and dramatic threats to human life and civilization extending for centuries into the future.

The Hearing from Hell

"Bruce, why don't you start with your questions..."

The committee chair was late to the hearing. With one of the legislators who authored seated before the Senate Committee on Environmental Quality, my former committee chair asked me to begin questioning the author. It was more than simply an unprecedented way to begin a hearing; for both myself and the stunned audience in the hearing room: it was an unheard of. As neither the chair was present nor had the committee been officially brought to order, calling on me to initiate the committee hearing indicated that at least the former committee chair was interested in publicly airing my critical review of the Solutions Act.

Assembly member Pavley appeared mortified when she saw that it was I who turned on the dais welcoming her to the committee hearing. Sensing that this exchange was clearly ill-fated, another legislator quickly intervened, stating that we needed to await the arrival of the chair. Pavley was visibly relieved when the committee chair arrived a few minutes later to begin a much kinder hearing on her bill in which she summarily rejected the extensive recommendations for amending AB 32 contained in my analysis.

Among the first in a long line of advocates, Bill Magavern delivered his support for AB 32 on behalf of the Sierra Club, but with the proviso that the important issues raised in the committee analysis should be considered by the authors. The short rendition was typical of Mr. Magavern's lobbying style, as well as his never passing on the opportunity to strengthen legislative proposals.

The vocal support by advocates of my recommendations for amendments was by this time in my career a regular feature of most committee hearings. And so, Bill was quite taken aback to be immediately confronted upon his return to the rear of the hearing room when a representative from Assembly member Pavley's office asked with considerable agitation, "Why are you opposing our bill?" Bill was astonished that, by voicing problems in the proposed law he had effectively placed himself in the *enemy* camp.

Days before a coalition of environmental justice communities had approached me, stating that they would take an 'oppose unless amended' position at the committee hearing. Recognizing that the authors were increasingly resistant to any changes, I counseled the coalition to adopt a different approach; "You might want to phrase your letter as 'support, but with amendments', and argue that certain additions are crucial to maintaining your backing for the bill. Otherwise, I suspect you will simply be locked out of the room to negotiate any additional changes to the bill.

The authors are now operating with something of a siege mentality. And believe me this bill is on its way to the Governor." The coalition of environmental groups eventually succeeded in crafting a series of significant provisions in the Solutions Act, raising both the role of environmental justice as well as significantly expanding the resources available to communities of color and impoverished people across the state.[160] While enabling the advance community-based claims on resources, certain environmental justice advocates remained sceptical about utilizing emissions trading revenues, arguing that the pollution trading scheme paved the way for continued community exposures to co-pollutants while giving corporations a rationale for perpetuating the use of fossil fuels.

After too many years in the Legislature, my skin had only grown thicker. I reflected that if I was the only one in the room who remained critical of the pollution trading scheme, perhaps I was simply obsessing over minutia while overlooking the larger achievements of the bill? Or, as one colleague stated, "It wouldn't be the first time some committee consultant got twisted about, over a tempest in a teapot." As the bill passed out of committee, I had other, more immediate tasks, including convening a meeting of staff from several committees to scan final legislative attempts by the corporate lobby to sneak bad bills through the Legislature, a practice we called "The Sleaze Patrol."

Within weeks the Global Warming Solutions Act passed both houses of the Legislature and was sent to Governor Schwarzenegger for his signature. I looked forward to returning to a desk filled with other issues demanding my attention: water quality and the mapping of toxic plumes, occupational health and the flaws of risk assessment, budgets for environmental health research, attacks on academic freedom for researchers, the expansion of regulatory fees to address broader externalities of uncharacterized chemicals, plastics and ocean pollution, protocols for endocrine disruptors, pesticides and bee colony collapse, as well as the perennial search to support the circuit prosecutors project, the Office of Environmental Health Hazard Assessment and so on.

Also high on the list were proposals for addressing geothermal wastes at renewable energy facilities, the prospective preemption of California regulatory approaches to nanotechnology, bio-monitoring and the analysis of cord blood, reassessing vapor emissions at brownfield sites, protocols for analyzing large groups of uncharacterized chemicals, the analysis of genetically modified organisms and evidence of pesticide resistance, wage levels and the retention of state scientists, and incorporating regulated toxics by reference to other authoritative listings. And these were only my prioritized listing of issues needing early attention. The list of calls I had not been able to return grew with each passing week.

My inbox was overflowing. As a practical matter, I simply did not have time to reflect on what happened a week past. I was fully immersed with constituents, advocates, and organizations, outside my door in a seemingly endless line, hoping to get five minutes to discuss the next crisis du jour. Despite continued misgivings, who was I to put aside their demands in order to fight some lost battle? Whatever my misgivings, I was pressed to move on to the other issues. Still, I recognized so many of the pressing issues of the day that fell into isolated policy silos, obscured the linkage to larger, common themes involving conflicts between public and private interests, democracy versus capitalism, and the fossil fueled crises of the 21st century.

Who Killed the Alternatives to Emissions Trading?

Later that same fall I was visited by an even more stark reflection on the State's newly enacted solution to global warming. After the usual clean-up of the mess that enveloped my office, I found time to finally see the documentary, "Who Killed the Electric Car?" Among the collection of Hollywood stars who told a story of company collusion to achieve this end was a former chair on my committee, Senator Alan Lowenthal.

The 1990 California law for advancing electric cars was scuttled in the early 2000s. The film was a painful reminder that had California maintained its mandate increasing zero-emission vehicles, by the time that AB 32 appeared, the state might be well on its way toward addressing a transit system reliant on fossil fuels. Killing California's nascent electric car mandate did not simply set-back a strategic means to address a primary source of global emissions, it ironically advanced the industry position that 'failure' of a public law *proved* it was better to leave such choices to the private sector.

However outrageous the proposition by my original mentor to outlaw the internal combustion engine seemed in the 1960s, by the 21st century, many were beginning to understand that the conflicts over fossil fuels required something more than granting the largest sources a greater flexibility to release some of the most dangerous gases on the planet. The battles waged by community-based advocates were being joined by thousands of scientists around the globe to achieve a more decisive objective: to urgently and aggressively end fossil-fuel emissions.

Many in California and beyond were holding their breath.

CHAPTER 8

The Climate of Subversion

In moments the rumor spread across the capitol like hot campaign money. A very vocal shouting match just occurred outside the Assembly chambers. Unlike the sometimes acrimonious exchanges between legislators, this was a unique event: one of the Senate's senior advisers shouting at the leader of the Assembly.

The Senate leader's senior staff director for environmental policy, Kip Lipper, walked toward the Speaker of the Assembly's office to discuss the necessary amendments before the full Senate held a final vote on the Global Warming Solutions Act. Noting that the Assembly was still in session, Kip Lipper waited outside the chambers, near a doorway that opened to one of the Speaker's conference rooms. Peering inside, Kip overheard conversation between Governor Schwarzenegger's staff and the Speaker's staff.

Within moments, it was evident that these were final negotiations - and that any prospective Senate amendments would be rejected, as agreed to by staff representing Speaker Núñez, Assembly member Pavley and Schwarzenegger's chief of staff, Susan Kennedy. Turning away from the conference room door, Kip was clearly furious. At that same moment, Speaker Núñez beckoned him from the entry to the Assembly chambers:

Núñez: "Are we done yet?"
Lipper: "Oh yeah, WE'RE DONE!
Núñez: "What's the problem?"

Lipper: "How about we start with the fact that your disingenuous staff are meeting secretly with the Governor's office? Oh yeah: we're done!"

The Speaker shouted a vehement response that did not reach Kip as he moved swiftly down the corridor, back to the Senate. Within a few minutes, Kip had briefed President Pro Tem of the Senate Don Perata about the apparent plot to have the Solutions Act moved out of the Senate with only the Governor's privately negotiated amendments. Having already briefed the Senate leader about numerous unaddressed problems in the bill, Perata delivered his message to the Assembly leader: "We are holding that fucking bill until this gets fixed!"[161]

Returning to his office, Kip drafted a set of amendments addressing a range of problems, centering on the proposed trading program. Despite Núñez and Pavley's refusal to accept any further amendments,[162] the Perata edict ensured that the final Senate version contained language crafted by Kip Lipper. While Speaker Núñez and Assembly member Pavley fumed over the Senate rewrite of a bill largely guided by the Governor's office, their decision was simple. Either they wanted a bill addressing global warming or not. In fairness to the authors, and despite his own serious misgivings, Kip delivered a bill retaining the essence of what the sponsors sought: an emissions trading scheme. Even so, the final bill contained two important caveats: California climate programs would emphasize regulatory measures and only initiate emissions trading after demonstrating the feasibility and value of proposed market mechanisms.

Despite its later portrayal as a measure based on extensive compromises, the Governor's office threatened that any changes might unravel their careful negotiations conducted behind the scenes. Kip and his professional colleagues were stepping into a highly charged atmosphere. Governor Schwarzenegger would later attest to his personal efforts designed to win business community approval. While couching his negotiations as based on creating a "whole new clean-tech industry that would create jobs, develop cutting-edge technology, and become a model for the rest of the country and the world,"[163]

Schwarzenegger's immediate objective aimed at defusing concerns that the bill threatened the corporate world. Accordingly, "We talked to carmakers, energy giants, utilities, growers, and transportation companies. While we were working on the climate change act, I went to the heads of Chevron, Occidental and BP because I wanted to assure them that this was not an attack on *them*."[164] With late amended language imposed by the Senate, a question now turned on whether Schwarzenegger would move decisively to impose aggressive regulations on ultra-hazardous emissions or would he move California's Solution Act toward a more business-friendly posture?

On September 27, 2006 Governor Arnold Schwarzenegger signed the California Global Warming Solutions Act into law, to impose a graduated cap on emissions of specific greenhouse gases; and, to allow those facilities responsible for such emissions to utilize market mechanisms to achieve the required reductions. Despite the Legislature's extensive, time-honored tradition of crafting laws where words had specific meanings, the Solutions Act left considerable uncertainty as to the degree to which California's climate change policy would be governed by regulatory controls that typically spelled-out who was responsible for reducing toxic emissions, in what amounts, the penalties for failures, and enforcement actions to including citizen ability to file legal actions against corporations… all versus market mechanisms.

At a time when climate scientists increasingly insisted that everyone needed to move decisively to quell the fossil-fueled storms of the 21st century, California was embarking on an uncertain path. Amidst celebrations by the state's actor-governor, Hollywood stars and politicians proclaiming California's new law, many public interest advocates wondered how many of the same corporations that had for so long been responsible for the largest market failure in history, were now going to be a part of a market "solution" to global climate change? Community activists in Los Angeles described the recent history of emissions trading as a disaster where public health was sacrificed amidst supposed benefits, far outside their neighborhoods. In places such as Wilmington, California, with its prominent oil refinery, activists wondered about the consequences for their community when Shell began trading emissions credits. In addition to concerns about greenhouse gases, they asked, how could emissions trading curb the use of other pollutants affecting the health of nearby communities?

Assessing the 'trading' provision of cap-and-trade in the Solutions Act struck many as theater of the absurd. Regulators, business owners, community activists, environmental lawyers, and private sector financial analysts were openly skeptical about the state's entry into the world of emissions trading. Even though traditional command-and-control regulatory laws had many flaws, as businesses often complained about regulatory paperwork, many noted that AB 32 now required them to be savvy traders in a new commodity market. The relationship between the Solutions Act and other California law was by no means a trivial matter. The Golden State had already enacted a multiplicity of laws and regulations severely restricting the release of toxic chemicals into the air, and a larger array of laws placed California on a path toward eliminating fossil fuels as a source of energy in the 21st century. Kip Lipper had frequently served as a key architect in both the design and success of these laws. The potential for AB 32 to undermine California's other laws might well explain why Kip was the central character in a shouting match with the Speaker of the California Assembly. To all appearances the authors of the Solutions Act, Assembly member Fran Pavley and Assembly Speaker Fabian Núñez, saw their bill breeze through the requisite policy committee.

Without any substantive amendments, the problem they didn't anticipate was Kip Lipper finding their bill to have numerous glitches. And central to these was the combined push from author Pavley and Speaker Núñez that California would now accept some ill-defined approach whereby many of the same corporations responsible for emitting hazardous substances into the air should then benefit by credits for reducing emissions elsewhere. Over the previous two decades many activists had played a central role in advancing a series of laws placing California, not simply at the forefront of clean air legislation, but more important, placing significant restrictions on the use of fossil fuels in the state energy supply. Were these hard-earned gains to be undone?

As later reported by Catherine Witherspoon, the executive officer for the California Air Resources Board, Governor Schwarzenegger's political leanings were clear before AB 32 was even signed into law:

> "Governor Schwarzenegger and his staff were intent on delaying substantive work on climate mitigation until the U.S. Congress (which they mistakenly believed would happen before 2012 [the effective date of AB 32]. Their goal was to protect California industry - major Republican Party donors - from any competitive disadvantage. Schwarzenegger wanted it both ways: to be a climate hero and to avoid alienating the business community. Likewise, the Administration made strenuous efforts to steer the draft legislation away from regulation and toward market trading. That put him in direct conflict with Democratic leaders who insisted on 'early action measures' and who strongly preferred direct emission controls. The latter is precisely why the Air Board was given the lead implementation role: it was world renown for adopting ambitious, technology forcing rules. The Administration's counter proposal for a squishy, non-accountable, multi-agency implementation body was soundly rebuffed. The conflict boiled over once the bill was enacted."[165]

Wedge Issues

From a solely pragmatic perspective there was much to support the sentiment that just initiating *any* program to address climate change would be an important step. Among the influential materials circulated during deliberations on AB 32 was a chart identifying various "wedges" of actions to be taken, as devised by Professor Robert Socolow who became instantly popular among policy wonks, providing a rough guide for work for limiting greenhouse gas emissions.

The striking part of Dr. Socolow's argument was that we already possessed "the fundamental scientific, technical, and industrial know-how to solve the carbon and climate problem for the next half-century. A portfolio of technologies now exists to meet world energy needs over the next 50 years and limit atmospheric CO2 to a trajectory that avoids a doubling of preindustrial concentration." Many involved in the battle over AB 32 received Socolow's work as crystal clear: unless government intervened (to decisively and immediately alter the fossil-fueled economy), the excesses of free markets combined with a corporate lobby status quo mentality on greenhouse gas emissions would spell disaster.

When asked about the practicality of various targets to reduce greenhouse emissions Socolow responded that the question itself was wrong, "These things can all be done." His professional warnings would reverberate for years to come. His perspective on the essential problem was to not be one limited by science, technology or know-how. "So we may now look at this and say, 'we are tampering with the earth...It is clear from the record that it [the earth] does things that we don't fully understand: And we're not going to understand them in the time period we have to make these decisions'. We just know they're there. We may say "we just don't want to do this to ourselves. If it's a problem like that, then asking whether it's practical or not is really not going to help very much. Whether it's practical depends on how much we give a damn."

At first glance Socolow's work appeared agnostic on the question of cap-and-trade versus command-and-control regulatory approaches. Yet his insistence, mirroring that of most climate scientists, regarding the urgency of taking action posed a problem for cap-and-trade – the information about whether California's complex emissions trading would function as hoped or how long it would take to achieve called for reductions was largely unknown.

The prospect of using market mechanisms versus command and control created a distinct uneasiness among the capitol's professional staff within the environment committees. While not exactly proponents of regulations as a wonderful tool, analysts commended California's decades-long use of regulatory law to address a range of health and environmental problems. Strict laws on air pollutants held a proven track record. The dramatic reduction of LA's chronic smog, for example, followed strict and detailed regulatory law. Energy conservation, cited by Sokolow as the easiest wedge for reducing emissions, also responded to a set of laws. In the early 2000s California's law set forth a renewable portfolio standard for utilities, reducing emissions of engines, contributory contaminants, and largely prohibiting the entry of coal generated energy into the electrical grid - all fashioned by strict regulations.

The claim that businesses knew better where and how to achieve changes in their production processes than regulatory agencies, at first glance, seemed indisputable. Could regulatory staff, no matter how well versed and trained, rival the knowledge of those who designed refineries, boilers, cement kilns, and other facilities? Yet, public experience over many decades frequently demonstrated a steadfast refusal by corporations to address obvious problems affecting workers, surrounding communities, and the environment. Inside the capitol the *petroleros* and their allies were recognized for their fierce resistance to even acknowledge a problem. How the Governor would implement Global Warming Solutions Act now brought these issues front and center.

Even before the Governor signed AB 32 into law, Kip Lipper drafted a letter arguing that newly enacted regulatory provisions needed immediate and aggressive implementation. Later, in another letter co-authored by the leaders of the Assembly and the Senate, Dr. Robert Sawyer, was asked, as lead administrator of the Air and Resource Board, what he needed to expedite actions on the large group of contributory pollutants[166] threatening both the global climate as well as local neighborhoods. A crucial subtext discussion among leadership and staff brooked no excuse for delay. Statutory authority and programs already existed to reduce the larger group of contributory pollutants.[167] Whatever Dr. Sawyer thought was required, he would soon learn that moving - even slowly - to implement AB 32 was a risky venture.

In October, Governor Schwarzenegger issued an executive order to implement AB 32 that even the Assembly Speaker called "totally inconsistent with the intent of that law and with the way that it is written."[168] In essence, the executive order initiated market-based mechanisms *concurrent* with regulatory measures. From the perspective of the Senate, the clear purpose of the amendments had been to place primacy on regulatory reductions of emissions allowing for market mechanisms only after extensive evaluation, Air Board determinations, and a public process. On October 23, President Pro Tempore Don Perata sent a letter to the Governor, recommending that he rescind his executive order and "implement the law that was enacted." Perata concluded the letter, "Please be assured that the Senate will ensure faithful adherence to the law through its actions in the policy, budget, and confirmation processes," as a thinly veiled threat.[169] The victory the Legislature had achieved in forcing the Governor to conform to the actual language of AB 32 was still in flux. The question remained: whose agenda would prevail and what direction would California's solution take?

Fossil Fuels: Decisive Actions or Not?

The Governor was surrounded by a group strongly bent on promoting market-mechanisms as a foundation. To negate any impacts on the major emission sources in transportation, utilities, agriculture, cement and other industries, even while a business-as-usual agenda was pressing inside the Governor's office, found one of the Governor's closest advisers urging a much different approach. Among his closest aides, Schwarzenegger selected a personal friend from Los Angeles, Terry Tamminen, as both his head advisor on environmental issues as well as his appointee to lead the California Environmental Protection Agency (Cal EPA). Following the Governor's signing AB 32 into law, Tamminen authored what would become the major advocacy work of his career: Lives Per Gallon: the True Cost of Our Oil Addiction.[170]

If AB 32 captured the essence of a political compromise that would not threaten business as usual, Lives Per Gallon was its political opposite, stating starkly that America is addicted to oil. The book jacket summarized a case that left no doubt about the role of oil as a fundamental obstacle to dealing with a nest of problems: "Tamminen reveals oil's more insidious costs: tens of billions spent annually to secure 'our' global supply; crops ruined by petroleum pollution; cancer, asthma, and birth defects caused by car exhaust, and the list goes on. Tamminen proposes collecting damages and investing in clean technologies."[171] Unresolved conflicts within AB 32 were just emerging inside the California capitol, however.

While some in the Legislature held out hope that Tamminen's influence might encourage the Governor to act decisively on the petroleum industry, one of my colleagues witnessed another of the executive's cigar moments as a more telling thematic, while looking down on the Governor's interior courtyard: "He's just blowing smoke." The Schwarzenegger administration busied itself in the meantime with budgets and more senior political appointments to promote its work on climate change. Dr. Robert Sawyer's appointment to head the Air Resources Board, oversee regulations, and make crucial policy choices at the close of 2005 so lacked controversy that it barely merited notice by any media outlet. With a long, distinguished tenure in the University system, Professor Sawyer was a choice that no one could object to....or so it appeared.

During the next year and a half, Dr. Sawyer and many of his colleagues from various agencies worked steadily to devise procedures and rules to implement the Solutions Act. Their numerous meetings clarified many ill-defined and potential conflicting areas. While the architecture of emissions trading was assembled, Sawyer headed an agency expected to implement regulations, including adopting what were termed "early action measures," intended to expeditiously address some of the most easily available steps to limit sources of damaging emissions. As written, AB 32 detailed taking such actions as essential first steps, per the recommendations of scientific advisors. More than a hundred recommendations for California to pursue addressed the early action measures or "low-hanging fruit," were advanced with arguably limited cost and controversy.[172] Or at least, that was the impression from outside the Air Board.

On Thursday, July 28, 2007 the public learned that Dr. Sawyer had been fired from his job by Governor Schwarzenegger and his executive officer, Catherine Witherspoon forced out of her position as well. The removal of Sawyer and Witherspoon was a direct result of having moved too swiftly to adopt additional regulatory measures to address global warming.[173] The official story provided by Schwarzenegger's staff differed sharply with the account provided by Dr. Sawyer in which, according to the phone transcript, the Governor's office objected to the esteemed professor acting on his own to take additional actions that had not been fully vetted.[174] 'Fully vetted' for many inside the capitol was code for Sawyer and Witherspoon having acted too expeditiously against private sector interests having influence with Schwarzenegger. As later explained by Catherine Witherspoon, the line she and Sawyer had crossed was well recognized; "...The Governor's office ordered the Air Board to 'stand down'. Specifically the Air Board was instructed to ignore the new legal mandate for adopting near term mitigation measures. When the Air Board pushed back the Governor's office grudgingly authorized the board to proceed provided no more than three early action measures were considered. When the Chairman and the Governing Board ultimately said no...the Governor's office fired Chairman Sawyer instead and threatened the remaining board members with dismissal if they failed to fall in line."[175]

This firing conveyed an ominous message to everyone working inside California's agencies. Despite the best efforts by Kip Lipper and others to establish a clear legal directive to dispatch restrictions of dangerous emissions and immediately act on well-recognized hazards, the Governor prioritized market mechanisms, principally built on emission trading. Angela Johnson Meszaros, who co-chaired the state's high profile Global Warming Environmental Justice Advisory Committee (EJAC) as well counseling various community-based groups, noted that Sawyer's firing was not simply a minor dispute about implementing AB 32. It also involved a larger argument about the degree to which the recently enacted law would adhere to a vital provision added during final deliberations on the bill: to ensure that the law did not operate to the detriment of communities of color.[176]

Angela Johnson Meszaros' name is practically synonymous with environmental justice causes, her having also worked with the California Environmental Rights Alliance, and being among the most savvy of California's community of activist lawyers, She wrote that the California Air Resources Board (CARB) had many additional early action items that were now in doubt with Sawyer's removal. "We submitted 31, and they received 96 overall that were outlined in their report. We were trying to look for things the state could do right now to have the most benefit, not just for climate change, but for co-pollutants."[177]

The Environmental Justice Advisory Committee was especially concerned about poorly crafted actions that could harm low-income communities of color, and so recommended against the Low Carbon Fuel Standard, one of the three measures advanced by Schwarzenegger's team. EJAC cited "serious unanswered questions about the possibility of increasing co-pollutants, the threat of increased pollution due to biofuel production, as well as increasing food insecurity."[178] Officials who viewed Angela's objections as a matter of regulatory fine-tuning overlooked a larger and growing question about AB 32's adjacent potential effects on inner city populations and about sources including not only refineries, utilities, and manufacturing facilities, but also the epidemic level of asthma cases linked to busy roadways.[179]

In response to Dr. Sawyer's dismissal by Governor Schwarzenegger, Assembly member Loni Hancock, Chair of the Committee on Natural Resources convened a hearing on the high-level firing of a person who was among the most qualified scientists to address climate issues in the Schwarzenegger administration. Dr. Sawyer and his chief deputy, Catherine Witherspoon, both provided testimony explaining the problems they confronted implementing the law, particularly those involving interference from the Governor's office. Schwarzenegger's inner circle refused to even attend or testify. By all outward appearances, the principal authors of the Global Warming Solutions Act, Fabio Núñez and Fran Pavley, did nothing to press Schwarzenegger regarding his demonstrated refusal to advance the legal requirements of the enacted legislation.

The hearing underscored a number of problems surrounding the implementation of the AB 32 law, including the effect of inverting the statutory directive: the priority of imposing immediate regulatory actions. In the absence of a clear and aggressive stance by the bill's authors, the hearing provided little impetus to challenge the Governor. To many in the capitol, a not-so-subtle message was conveyed to the Governor: go ahead and implement AB 32 as you see fit.

The Governor swiftly named Mary Nichols as Dr. Sawyer's replacement. As a former chair of CARB during Governor Jerry Brown's first term, as well as having held a high level position with Clinton's Environmental Protection Agency, Nichols was readily approved by the Senate Rules Committee. Others, however, were less than thrilled with her resume, which included her backing of emissions trading at US EPA. Nichols' husband also represented the oil giant in the infamous Exxon Valdez oil spill case. One observer at the beginning of her nomination hearing pointed to a large impasse about her new post, "The question will be how she balances her instinct to compromise with the urgent need of greenhouse gas reduction."[180]

During Nichol's tenure at US EPA she reportedly played a pivotal role in cutting a deal with Detroit car makers to overriding the auto emission levels proposed by 13 eastern states aspiring to emulate strict California clean air standards. Various journalists noted how many economists and business development specialists believed that 14 states mandating such high standards would have created sufficient demand for electric cars to stimulate a booming new industry for America! Instead, the plan adopted provided tax incentives and pollution dispensation for planting trees; a plan that one Sierra Club spokesperson noted could have been produced by George Bush.[181] The impacts of market mechanisms appeared further tilted against poor people and communities of color.

In December 2007, Kip Lipper requested that each of the agencies charged with implementing AB 32 to provide a briefing on their accomplishments at a closed-door session in the capitol. The request reflected the still-simmering conflict embedded in the statute: if the Governor continued emphasis on market mechanisms over regulatory controls, how were greenhouse gases and practices actually to be reduced? A day-long meeting, convened in the Senate's conference room on the first floor of the capitol, contained presentations by representatives from the California Environmental Protection Agency, the Resources Agency, the Public Utilities and California Energy Commissions, and a variety of departmental and program units within these agencies.

Slicing through the prepared statements, Kip headed every presentation with a simple question: "What can you document that your agency/department/program has already achieved to reduce greenhouse gases?" At the conclusion of the day, virtually none of the agencies could present evidence of any reduction achieved. Governor Schwarzenegger's implementation of the Global Warming Solutions Act provided a clear picture to Kip and his colleagues in the Legislature.

While meetings, discussions, and budgets were organized to advance emission trading schemes, a host of potential regulatory approaches were ignored, and existing regulatory approaches left to languish. Despite the legislative mandate of the bill requiring the immediate adoption of regulatory programs to reduce greenhouse gases and ensuing examination of options evincing the value and feasibility of market mechanisms, the Governor's directives to his administrators turned the priorities of the statute completely upside down.

Market Mechanisms for Market Failures?

On October 6, 2006, less than thirty days after the Governor signed AB 32 into law, among the first comprehensive assessments of global warming by an economist published the Stern Review on the Economics of Climate Change. Undertaken at the request of the government of Great Britain, it analyzed the effect of global warming on the global economy. Among its major findings; unless actions were rapidly put in place, the overall costs of climate change would be equivalent to losing at least 5% of global gross domestic production each year due to impacts on water resources, food production, the environment, and health. The Review proposed investment on the order of one percent of global gross domestic product each year to divert disaster.[182]

At the release of his Review, the magnitude of investments being called for by Sir Nicholas Stern greatly exceeded anything envisioned by the authors of the Global Warming Solutions Act. According to California's share of national gross domestic product in 2007, the 1% figure being called for by Stern would have represented an annual investment of approximately $18 billion.

California would eventually collect roughly $1 billion during the first year of revenues derived from cap-and-trade. Occurring roughly five years after the measure's passage meant that they were already behind on compensation for damages alone. The sum, over that initial five years fell nearly $125 billion short of the amount Stern suggested as California's necessary investment to address global climate change. And, even this dramatic shortfall underestimated the larger sums required revision calculus when, in June 2008, Stern upgraded the estimate to

2% of GDP to address the growing effects of global warming.[183] By 2016, California had collected less than $5 billion from fossil fuel industries whose damaging costs to the public now soared skyward.

The Review's basic premise: Stern's analysis of global climate crisis as "the greatest market failure in history" should have raised anew serious questions about the role of AB 32's market mechanisms. The single act that precipitated Dr. Sawyer's dismissal as the state's highest scientific authority for implementing the Global Warming Solutions Act was his imposition of a regulation versus the demands voiced by a corporate gathering with a long and deep history of resisting public efforts to impose any restrictions on internal combustion engine or fossil fuels. Sawyers firing signaled what both Kip Lipper and public interest advocates had feared even before the first hearing of AB 32; 'regulatory flexibility' would become a device for undercutting the urgently needed actions.

The Stern Review might well have brought greater scrutiny to the "wisdom" of an emissions trading scheme but for an intervening event in what was now clearly a fateful and potentially extensively delayed journey. Ironically, even as Arnold Schwarzenegger's inner circle promoted market mechanisms and trading as the foundation for addressing a global climate threat, Mr. Market was on the verge of the greatest collapse since the crash of 1929.

CHAPTER 9

Hazardous Traits

> Every day, the U.S. produces or imports 42 billion pounds of chemicals, 90% of which are created using oil...These chemicals are put to use in innumerable processes and products, and at some point in their life cycle many of them come in contact with people – in the workplace, in homes, and through air, water, food, and waste streams. Eventually, in one form or another, nearly all of them enter the earth's finite ecosystems.[184]
>
> The California Policy Research Center
> The University of California 2006

Springtime for many years, has had a special meaning for Martha Dina Argüello, the executive director for the Los Angeles Chapter of Physicians for Social Responsibility (PSR-LA): preparing another annual presentation of the "Toxies:" a quintessential Los Angeles event, a gathering where one of California's more notable environmental health organizations displays its political and media savvy.[185] Originating during a retreat at a former nunnery, the idea started as a joke about California not needing any more "bad actor" chemicals on top of a bad actor Governor. Accompanying the laughter, a vision took shape.

A kind of Oscar ceremony is coordinated by a coalition of environmental health, policy, labor, environmental justice, interfaith, and other organizations to display the chemicals still at large in California. By the end of the retreat, the humorous exchange produced a plan: PSR LA would sponsor a gala with people serving in the role as one or another bad actor chemical. A slightly crazed actor would represent mercury contaminants, a not-so-hot actress would portray an infamous flame retardant, an aging and not too intelligent guy would be "Mr. Lead" and so on. PSR LA Staff readily agreed to name the award given to each as.... the Toxies!

Following a good humored-lunch, Martha returned to her usual multi-tasking. Over more than a decade, she and many advocates would be inspired by Richard J. Jackson, a pediatrician who would later become California's first Surgeon General. Indeed, Dr. Jackson would serve as a silent political partner with advocates and policy-makers across the state, including issues near and dear to Martha: lead removal, asthma and air quality, pesticides and integrated pest management to finding substitutes for hazardous dry cleaning chemicals and safer cosmetics. PSR LA came forward with the phase-out of reproductive-damaging baby bottles and created an extensive training program for health professionals - from physicians to lay "promotoras"[186] at work in neighborhood clinics, to sponsoring resolutions at statewide medical conferences.

Transition to a recognized force in political advocacy involved several hurdles. First, and foremost, was the need to attune physicians to community-level health issues. In addition to the discomfort that doctors typically felt with speaking in front of a camera, overall community exposures to one or more toxic substances meant that they had to shift the usual perspective from the individual patient. As a result, the organization worked to bring the needs of the community into focus. To effectively "treat" individuals suffering from the asthma of poor housing, or peeling lead paint, or contaminants from the nearby freeway, required something larger than prescribing treatment for just one patient. Such "seminars" yielded the reward of compelling professionals to expand their role as advocates.

Martha's recounting of her successes with advocacy on statewide policy always included stories about how physicians so equipped served crucial roles in conversations with legislators, especially in overturning corporate lobbyists' misrepresentation of the problems brought on by chemical contaminants. Among the earliest and most effective organizations to bridge the largely moot divide between various Latino legislators and dominant environmental organizations, where the face of environmental policy did not look like anyone in the neighborhoods many elected officials represented: This divide played perfectly into a stereotype fostered by industry that environmentalism, in California, was a preoccupation of people with little concern about jobs or about the difficulty of attracting businesses to neighborhoods characterized by abandoned industrial sites and dead storefronts.

Argüello, along with her colleagues in the environmental justice movement, worked strenuously to build a base of support shared by health workers and professionals at a neighborhood clinic, the recruitment of Latino physicians, and a circle of advocates located in Westside, Central, and Southside neighborhoods, places where many national environmental organizations were nowhere to be seen. Aside from marshalling neighborhood-based organizations, Martha Argüello and PSR-LA display a political savvy that distinguishes them from so many other nonprofit organizations: the ability to mobilize individuals for whom participating in the political process is new. And work with Korean owners and their Latino workers, to forge campaigns to replace dangerous dry cleaning chemicals with safer wet cleaning processes directly countered the hype that PSR was uncaring about jobs-consequences for employers and workers.

A crucial element assisting Martha and many activists across the state involved the push by Dr. Jackson and his political allies to frame issues as "healthy" instead of "environmental." In contrast to debates focused on fluid notions of 'environmentalism', public health professionals like Richard Jackson established a political baseline that corporate lobbyists found difficult to undermine: the health of individuals and their communities. Part of this may be rooted in a professional responsibility of "doing no harm" as a more natural fit with precaution (to avoid recognized hazards), than the alternative argument marshaled by corporate lobbyists: a reductionist study of the toxicology and calculations of "acceptable levels of exposure," classically meaning acceptable rates of harm.

Especially captivating for those working in the realm of environmental health, including *promotoras*, physicians, and nurses is a practical and daily commitment to translate Hippocratic obligations "to...keep the sick from harm and injustice," into concrete and creative political actions.[187] To the casual observer, Martha's easy, personable style may be confused for someone who appears lucky to land on her feet when life's trials throw others for a fall. This 'luck', like that of so many of her fellow advocates, is based on dedication to bridge community needs and political process: Which isn't to say that she always prevails in Sacramento. If asked about past frustrations, Argüello might readily mention one particular disaster: advancing green chemistry.

Action Delayed

By the late 1980s, various states and state-sponsored projects made headway: not to erect some state bureaucracy for monitoring end-of-pipe releases from tens of thousands of facilities, but to provide a framework for eliminating hazards in the production process, from the very start. Many states recognized that the national toxics law was deeply flawed. Given the corporate dominance that enveloped D.C.; trying to remedy flaws though a new Congressional bill was a fool's errand.

The state of Massachusetts Public Interest Research Group [MassPIRG] activists attracted nationwide attention and success establishing the Toxic Use Reduction Act. More than simply a chemical-by-chemical approach, the Mass PIRG combined regulatory and research projects analyzed whole groups of chemicals in the production process, identifying viable substitutes based on cooperative research programs with industry. Despite the collaborative approach, larger corporate interests beyond Massachusetts considered the program an unmitigated disaster due to the State's expanded regulatory powers to inspect, review, and regulate chemical uses inside industrial facilities.

The Mass PIRG success was instantly recognized as a model to replicate in other states. The corporate lobby countered with a campaign to insure that no such program be realized elsewhere. The California Public Interest Research Group (Cal PIRG) introduced a bill the next year to establish a sister program with many of the bells and whistles of the MassPIRG's toxics use reduction program.[188] While the Cal PIRG bill gained broad support and appeal among both environmental and labor groups, the corporate lobby advanced an alternate bill, SB14.[189] While Cal PIRG began with a strategic advantage by selecting a Senate Rules Committee member to author their bill, the corporate lobby trumped that -- by gaining the backing of the Senate leader and chair of the Rules Committee, David Roberti, to author industry's counter-measure. Industry lobbyists were wildly happy when the Pro Tem's bill displaced the CalPIRG bill with a program that gave the state essentially no regulatory purview over chemical plants and substituted a *voluntary* program targeting only one or two industries, every several years.

While the Massachusetts program advanced chemical substitution, applied research for reducing chemical workplace hazards, and an array of innovations adopted by industries across the state, SB14 effectively stripped California of a comprehensive agenda to promote alternatives to toxic substances. The classic explanation that the corporate lobby provided legislators who were considering more expansive statutes was that there *was* a law, this law passed to address such issues, and time was needed for its program to be implemented and evaluated. California activists were left to confront individual chemicals. Informal reviews among agency and legislative staff advised the state to eliminate the toothless program - and so remove the fiction that it did anything consequential to address chemical hazards. SB 14's enduring legacy was to effectively subvert a more comprehensive approach to re-engineer the state's toxics economy.

Flawed Federal Laws

In the search for models to promote community health, by the turn of the new century, mounting problems drew increasing attention to the toxic-bound economy across the nation. The federal Toxic Substances Control Act (TSCA) touted by industry people as all the law that was needed, was the subject of widespread disdain, based on substantive reviews. Ostensibly a federal screening process to evaluate hazards before chemicals were allowed to be used widely, the Act, in fact, provided no genuine review of chemical hazards, old or new. At the same time, the European Union was constructing a comprehensive program to rapidly evaluate and *restrict* chemicals that left many wondering why the U.S. remained unable to address parallel concerns.

As scientists investigated an array of previously unconsidered health and environmental consequences surrounding chemicals whose effects remained largely unexamined by federal law – workers, consumers, and communities angrily confronted authorities about the potential chemical contaminants in consumer products, workplaces, water, food, soils, and homes. The answer to questions regarding looming hazards was a haunting one: "We don't know."

Activists regularly approached legislative staff with proposals to impose new restrictions. While many of these individual chemical bills achieved success, it was clear that regulating even groups of chemicals one at a time would become a project extending well beyond the 21st century. Added to this mix were legislators who felt increasingly queasy about their role in arguments where conflicting views appeared to hinge on a scientific discourse and a formula for 'proofs' that they could only vaguely comprehend. Many activists had grown weary of simply knocking down bad legislation sponsored by industry. In this context, a group of professional legislative staff mobilized a campaign inside the capitol to advance a larger chemicals policy.

Discussions between environmental advocates and legislative staff initiated a variety of approaches to address the problem of toxics including litigation strategies, ballot initiatives, media campaigns, informational hearings, foundation programs, the redirection of agency budgets, and oversight hearings. Senior legislators urged the Attorney General to sue federal agencies for their failure to act. Added to these tactics, budgets and programs were supported to encourage collaboration between California's regulatory programs, academics, and activists from other nations to act on recognized hazards. Yet, even when successful, the outcome was too often an isolated program for preventing a single kind of toxic event, while most industry practices continued largely unaffected. Even with proper oversight and investigation, and documentation of failures in the principal federal law (TSCA), the public was left with an impression that the problem was located in government, rather than an understanding that such failures often originated with a design flaw purposefully engineered by corporate lobbyists.

Liberating Entrepreneurs

A variety of discussions in Los Angeles, San Francisco and between focused on the need to devise a fundamentally different tack for regulating chemicals. Among the most important contributors to these off-the-record meetings were researchers and faculty with the University of California, county directors of public health, and several professional organizations. A recurring problem surfaced as a simple question: 'How to design encouragements for industries to move beyond toxics?' And then I had one of my most instructive meetings, based on a meeting orchestrated by a representative from the private sector. The unscheduled meeting was initiated by an executive from a medium sized firm from another western state whose principal executive. Stepping into my office in the capitol, she began by asking that our conversation remain confidential then offered her reason for visiting California's state capitol.

"I'm here because we have found a non-toxic substitute for the formaldehyde commonly used in construction materials, including one of our major products. Our problem is that the other members of the industry are deeply opposed to our efforts to market our non-toxic product. And their opposition is quite simple: *they* don't possess a non-toxic substitute. To make things worse, many of our trade association competitors are anxious to expand their imports of even more contaminated products from their manufacturing plants outside the U.S."

I couldn't help but be curious: "So why come to California?"

The executive was perfectly blunt; "Unless we find a way to advance our product in the marketplace, we are concerned about being squeezed out of the market. Our competitors are more than simply 'unhappy' with our non-toxic product line; they want *us* to disappear." My enthusiasm peaked. While I was well acquainted with internal conflicts within industry groups, they did not typically come to my office to settle such disputes. The notion of designing a law *with me* to resolve a private sector dispute was verboten amongst the corporate lobby regulars.

The executive seated across from me, however, had already devised a plan: "We would really benefit from a tightening of Air Resource Board standards for indoor pollutants as essential to our marketing campaign. Everyone knows this state has been on the forefront. And, in fact, there is already a draft regulation in place that would give us a level playing field to sell our toxic-free product. Our major concern is that you consider helping the Air Board to ensure that their proposed regulation is not simply sandbagged. We believe our trade association is already engineering just such a plan."

My assistance, it turns out, involved nothing more than providing an open process for a parallel piece of legislation. While hearings for a legislative measure to further restrict the recognized toxicant fully afforded industry opponents the opportunity for debate, as we both suspected: no one from industry wanted to publicly call for the greater release of formaldehyde inside homes. The episode inspired the idea of a new approach for addressing California's toxic economy.

Green Chemistry and a New Science

Part of the impetus to integrate the larger problem of unregulated chemicals with a vision of what California should do to address this in a proactive manner was state recognition that, before long, efforts would be prepared in Washington, D.C. to "reform" the broken federal law. Given a seemingly permanent Congressional inability to forward a policy based on new science, California set the foundations for an alternative approach, eventually known as "green chemistry." The first step required a campaign to get past the old science and regulatory models that had contributed to frozen federal laws for nearly four decades.

The realization that chemical policy was fundamentally broken crystallized during a celebratory lunch for Dr. Richard Jackson, who had just been appointed to direct the National Center for Environmental Health at the U.S. CDC Centers for Disease Control and Prevention. A small group congratulated Dick on his good fortune in escaping the shifting sands of public health work in Sacramento. Dr. Jackson was already widely recognized for his finely tuned, cutting-edge scientific skills, combined with a knack to move things politically. Before departing, he shared one of the major achievements of his career: devising a nationwide program to investigate contaminants in the blood and tissues of Americans.

As always, Dick's focus was on a deep need. Not simply engaging a new scientific toy, his was a novel perspective on chemical contaminants in communities, workers, and children. Looking around the table at a group who collaborated with him during much of his earlier work on pesticides, Dick took a moment to fire imaginations once again. "So, I just returned from a visit with friends at U.C. Davis, conducting yet another series of studies with farm workers we've been monitoring in recent years in order to have them removed from field work when they have been over-exposed to specific kinds of pesticides. But, the most recent work at UCD is even more troubling! They are finding a much wider array of pesticides in study of the blood and urine of workers."

An adept public speaker, Jackson pauses to see that his audience is tracking. "Now the typical protocol that many scientists follow, is to evaluate what levels are appearing in workers and then move to research, to distinguish safe from unsafe…But this is absurd! Why are we taking a next step to parse the effect of contaminants inside people's bodies? Shouldn't we be taking another direction? These guys are spilling organophosphates in their urine: What is going on?

Shortly after his federal appointment, Dr. Richard Jackson released a study underscoring what he had spoken of earlier. In California, there had been a dramatic decline in the levels of lead in people's blood over two decades, following its essential elimination from gasoline and paints.[190] In subsequent years, the public health community would help advance further reductions of lead, finding no safe level for human exposure. With the memory of Dick Jackson's considerations in mind, I drafted a letter to the Legislature's environment committee chairs, calling on the University of California to author a study of chemical policy. Some of my friends referred to this late night entrepreneurial activity as "Bruce's letters from Hell."

In place of the usual critique of federal chemical policy, the California study would speak to the issue of alternatives to toxics. In place of a risk assessment approach (favored by the chemical industry, but increasingly discredited by an influential group of California scientists); and onerous bureaucratic avenues, the study would outline a precautionary reversal of the proof burdens classically imposed on government. This pathway would explore the potential to encourage private sector firms to move beyond replacing one toxic chemical with another.[191]

The impetus for the letter was a series of discussions with capitol colleagues who understood that even the legislative victories of past years frequently suffered the regulatory capture that industry lobbyists pursued as a long-term campaign. Foremost in this record of snatching defeat from the jaws of victory was pesticide manufacturers' release of a new generation of products that while less harmful than those now illegal, often posed other, less recognized hazards. That California's successes of the mid-1980s forced manufacturers to eliminate the most hazardous among a group of extremely toxic pesticides provided cold comfort to many tens of thousands of farmworkers who annually marched through and bedded down beside California's agricultural fields.

Another source of inspiration for jump-starting the debate on chemical policy in California arose from a group of scientists, both academic and regulatory, who acknowledged that most contemporary discussions of chemicals were pegged to older concepts, increasingly seen as a poor basis for understanding the broader array of hazards posed by chemicals. Most especially they offered "a shared rejection of risk assessment among California scientists" with decades of regulatory experience. Yet there remained a definite predisposition among political appointees and influential environmental groups in D.C. to maintain risk assessment as a cornerstone of federal chemical policy.[192]

During the early years of the new century such long-standing reliance on failed federal policies generated conversations on Main Street. Mothers would ask about foods, contaminants in breast milk, toxics in toys.... Neighbors openly questioned the wisdom of applying pesticides to lawns or flowers. Parents asked about classrooms where paints and other materials were touched by their kids. Entire communities confronted the release of gases by local industries. Protesters both collected samples and challenged permits allowing for discharges of air contaminants released by refineries. Families now expressed concern about effluents from unknown sources restricting fishing, or the content of what people were spreading on their faces each day. Questions about pesticides in food, plastics in children's products, particulates in workplace air, emissions from carpets, fire retardants in furniture, lead in toy jewelry, petroleum in shampoo, combustion byproducts in heating systems, volatile organics in small business applications, recycling of unsafe substances, disclosing transport of ultra-hazardous materials, drinking water standards, bio-monitoring for contaminants in human blood and tissues, and so many more topics reflected too many instances in which chemicals were largely unregulated.

In the fall of 2003, a report emerged reflecting the growing 'intersectionality' of groups working on the proliferation of toxic contaminants across California and their threat to women's health.[193] The effort, fostered by a partnership spanned Breast Cancer Action Commonwealth, *Lideres Campesinas*, and Physicians for Social Responsibility combined with the important work of community-based organizations including the Asian Pacific Environmental Network, Communities for a Better Environment, and the Center for Race, Poverty and the Environment. The publication, reflecting the work of those many engaged in a continuous and widespread effort to address an out-of control marketing, sales, use and disposal pointed to various actions that might be taken, including adoption of policies frequently referred to with a shorthand reference: 'first do no harm.'

Preventing Hazards

By the opening of the 2005/2006 session, numerous legislators noted the rapidly expanding concerns taking voice in every legislative district and nearly three dozen individual legislative measures were introduced to address a range of issues relating to toxics.[194] Despite the negative perceptions that typically accompanied such issues, numerous legislators recognized that, in their individual districts, addressing toxics was a winner among voters. What's more, even if legislators failed to have toxics bills signed into law, they at least demonstrated a willingness to take on an opponent the public viewed as endangering their workplaces and communities: the chemical industry.

Inside the capitol there was an entrenched opposition to even the most modest of changes. The soft underbelly of relying on the market to address such demands revealed industries with deep pockets – applying pressure behind the scenes to insure an impenetrable status quo surrounding chemicals. Moving from the prima facie case that evidence of contaminants in blood and other body fluids might provide a basis for quickly acting against toxic sources, instead, the bio-monitoring program would largely study, not act, on such contaminants.

There is also, within this simple story, a struggle that is common to many environmental issues. Is the purpose of addressing chemical hazards to perpetuate the use of toxic substances? Or, is the objective to set in motion a race to the top, to eliminate (wherever possible) recognized hazards and to adopt a precautionary approach to deal with chemicals?

An understanding of negative consequences means coming to terms with the social costs that result from chemicals appearing in commerce. Given our knowledge that a vast universe of products and industrial processes are integrally linked to petroleum (as noted in the U.C. Policy Research Center 2006 Green Chemistry Report), a key to various environmental statutes in California is assessing, and anticipating the regulatory costs that *should* be assigned to such industries. Yet fees often give polluters a "permit" to despoil the environment, thus making government complicit in wrongdoing. And, when pollution permits turn out, years hence to have been set too low– are even the most basic personal damages calculated and restored to affected communities, not to mention larger costs of destruction to human health and the environment?

The fact that many so-called "regulated industries" have a direct, often dominant role in setting standards, permits, and fees makes a mockery of the notion that "the people" are responsible for *avoiding* resulting contamination. Ergo, industry is too frequently able to sidestep even the highly inadequate compensation of fees for the release of a wide range of pollutants including plastics in oceans or fracking contaminants in ground waters or pesticide residues in waters, air basins and food or contaminants in breast milk and fetal tissues. At a practical level, regulatory fees are cheap corporate insurance to claim that their practices, however egregious, 'were in accordance with state and federal laws.'

It only follows that by the early 2000s, many in California held little enthusiasm for merely reforming a failed federal chemical law. In January 2006, Department of Toxic Substances Control's external advisory committee convened a meeting, seeking input for its newly appointed director. One recommendation for a new approach was a recent academic publication by Ken Geiser, one of the key intellectual forces behind the Massachusetts Toxics Use Reduction program.[195] The recommendation was a thinly disguised effort to reignite a wholly different approach that had been circumvented with the defeat of California's own Toxics Use Reduction Program. In place of a bloated federal regulatory agency tasked to evaluate tens of thousands of individual chemicals, an alternative would begin by quickly itemizing "high hazards".[196] Joel Tickner, a professor and colleague at the University of Massachusetts at Lowell, hosted an international summit to demonstrate the value of moving from older risk assessments to what many refer to as "new science," especially with respect to the precautionary principle.[197]

The battle between "old" and "new" science was not actually a conflict between scientists. As one of the participants at the Lowell summit would write, a central debate hinged on an essential *political* question: "whose science?" Concurrent with efforts to initiate a new chemicals policy in California, in 2006 a group of non-profit organizations in Washington D.C., active on the regulation of toxics for some years, began laying the groundwork for reform. Despite interest among a group of DC-centric nonprofit organizations, elsewhere in the country there were misgivings that pursuing a federal reform measure was a good idea.

A meeting scheduled for fall of 2006 generated a letter delivered via staff with the California State Legislature. A boldly headed title left little doubt about answers to D.C. groups - "Reasons for Not Introducing a Congressional TSCA Reform Bill in 2007" - challenged the notion of overhauling chemical policy, especially given likely emergence of a now widely criticized risk assessment approach. Specifics of the letter queried several major considerations: Timing, Federal location, Scope of Reform, Relation to existing law (Clean Air, Clean Water, CERCLA, RCRA), and whether Economic externalities of the chemical crisis (local costs for hazardous waste disposal - both public and private (for contamination of groundwater, the cleanup of brownfields, the treatment of wastes by sanitation districts, etc.) were adequately documented?

Recalling the episode of individual entrepreneurs finding ways to eliminate poisons (e.g., formaldehyde) that their industry associations tried to subvert as a new standard, the letter ended noting that certain private sector firms might already be advancing better alternatives than the typical D.C. approach based on the lowest common denominator of industry-wide performance measures, often forming the basis for cost/benefit and risk assessment calculations.[198] The response conveyed a characteristic exchange between D.C. based organizations and the rest of the world: "thanks, we got your memo." Beyond this, there was no further communication.

The long-standing disjuncture between the processes for making law in D.C. versus California reflected very different political process. However optimistic a case one could make for advancing a chemical reform bill in D.C., the process encompassed a concerted campaign lasting years and largely dominated by an overwhelming corporate lobby. Moving the political dial to affect the votes for hundreds of representatives meant a herculean effort. Smaller numbers in Sacramento roughly meant only having to move a handful of legislators in a few key districts. Not that legislative progress on chemical policy in Sacramento would be easy, but dominant Democrats forged different provisions than in federal laws (generally seen as setting minimally acceptable standards while California statutes often exceed any applicable federal requirement.) And so, to go to D. C. is what some called "forum shopping" - a practice classically used by industry to find the most friendly route to escape the rigors of harsh regulatory laws, especially in that bastion of citizen activism on the left coast, California.

The Impossible Task

A simple cookbook of how to undermine chemicals policy often incorporated one or more of the following: demanding ideal epidemiological *and* mechanistic evidence; and/or excluding individual kinds of scientifically relevant evidence because by themselves they are insufficient for a causal conclusion.[199] In the end, there is a circular game in which the corporate lobby crafts an extended and byzantine regulatory process, then blame government for failing to efficiently and affordably impose regulations. In the 2000s, many state activists began making alliances with local businesses to promote alternatives, while easing regulatory burdens or even providing incentives to further their dispersion to businesses unaware of how to change practices, or the availability of alternatives.

Even with a carefully orchestrated effort to lay groundwork for a comprehensive chemical policy, a coherent legislative package was missing. At the beginning of the 2007, a new legislator from Los Angeles expressed keen interest in carrying a bill, despite having little background or a conversant-staff. A larger problem stemmed from an environmental lobby lacking a fixed game plan, and leaving much of the drafting to capitol staff. When negotiation with the corporate lobby began in earnest, problems emerged, with shifting language. Basic questions surrounding key concepts in the bill remained unresolved. At the 11th hour, corporate lobbyists offered a classic "deal." A text already cooked, vetted, and approved was presented, and the young legislator had only a matter of hours to accept or reject the offer approved by Schwarzenegger's office.

Another in the series of legislative compromises that end in disasters and that were now emerging more frequently, set procedures for evaluating chemicals in a process that was arguably worse than having no existing law at all; it allowed numerous opportunities for indefinite delay, and challenges to any agency action. Its "crowning achievement" was limiting review to no more than a handful of chemicals. In an earlier time, negotiations with the corporate lobby often entailed first going through a series of defeats rather than accepting flawed amendments. Inside the capitol, some jokingly referred to this as "Getting to No," a substitute for the Win/Win strategy in which compromise allegedly benefitted both sides.

In the new era of term limits, many legislators found industry offers - backed by a governor - irresistible. Such was the case during the closing hours of the 2007 session. DC-oriented environmental organizations and their lobbyists joined their chemical industry counterparts: making rounds of capitol offices and announcing their joint support. How bad a deal? Corporate lobbyists could barely keep the grins of delight from bursting forth, on their faces. The level of success achieved by the chemical lobby cannot be overstated. "We now have a procedure for addressing chemical hazards," became a constant refrain inside hearing rooms. Years of groundwork for crafting an entirely new approach to chemical hazards in California were now fully upended. Industry lobbyists were more than happy for others to follow the latest innovation from California.

By the close of 2012 California, like many political subdivisions across the globe, possessed fewer resources to maintain pace with the expanding and increasingly complex world of uncharacterized chemicals. Even *if* green chemistry laws were fully implemented, regulatory agencies lacked the resources to address annual release of novel chemicals. The boom in nano-particles, for example, was largely outside the purview of state or federal law. The intrigue that awaited many voters turned not on who came into office, but on a world of private sector decisions largely beyond the purview of their elected representatives. In the midst of corporate structures achieving a status of too big to govern, government was being restricted to a status of too small to challenge private sector actors.

The upshot of a multi-year project challenging the proliferation of toxics had stalled by 2014. How did Dr. Jackson and Martha Argüello react? Martha was weaving a complex political tapestry, starting from a basis in community organizing, and she was painfully aware that DC-based environmental groups had once again thrown her people under the bus. Given the constantly moving political chessboard, others might have the luxury of bemoaning what went wrong, but Argüello moved forward with her group of foundation officers, environmental/civil rights advocates, union organizers, and so on. The disappointments with an aborted green chemistry program in some sense was only one in a multitude of struggles for an expanding group whose relied on a coalition of public interest advocates.

Legislative staff, agency directors, lawyers, scientists, community groups and activists who had vigorously joined the fight nearly a decade earlier had grown weary of a struggle that yielded so few controls surrounding tens of thousands of chemicals – following a financial debacle through which the state stumbled. Support was stinted by active legislative efforts to increase jobs, with one important exception. Many drawn to redirecting the state's toxic economy were now attracted to the latest battle: fracking.

CHAPTER 10

Cassandra Does Sacramento

The cast of luminaries began with Robert F. Kennedy, Jr., ushered around by one of the political groupies surrounding the recognizable environmental figure.[200] Kennedy's appearance meant press coverage, evident as numerous legislators eagerly filed into one of the capitol's largest hearing rooms. The jointly sponsored hearing began with a brief statement from the chairs.

Kennedy's presence befitted the hearings major theme: the assault on California's environmental laws. Though the attack arose from a variety of places, RFK's remarks focused on his favorite target: the Republican President, George W. Bush. By a later count, Bush II and federal agencies sought to undermine more than 300 federal environmental laws during eight years in office, included many of California's own.[201] Kennedy's uniquely unmistakable vocal character commanded instant attention in the typically noisy hearing room. Launching into a verbal assault on the Bush II administration, he cited case after case of legal and bureaucratic subversion.

The Kennedy presentation, "The Federal Role: Rollbacks and Preemption," largely summarized President George W. Bush's efforts to undermine environmental programs nationwide, but especially in California.[202] Before he was done, legislators had become inattentive. Kennedy's style, while persuasive and well-honed, was more of a lecture.

And legislators, like professors, were not an easy group to address. After his testimony and an early departure, much of the air seemed to leave the room with Kennedy.

Smart Money

Unbeknownst to most in attendance, however, a more controversial speaker quietly awaited his turn. For legislators scanning the hearing agenda, Thomas Van Dyck appeared at first glance to represent 'balance' in the hearing. In place of Kennedy's attack on the Bush administration, Mr. Van Dyck projected the image of a successful voice from the private sector.

Dressed for the role, Mr. Van Dyck introduced himself as an investment banker with a well-known financial group in San Francisco. Well spoken, neither loud nor theatrical, Van Dyck conveyed a distinct presence as one of the few people in the room who could speak about the intersection between the world of finance and the environment. Various legislators, especially the *corporados* from both parties sat-up, leaned-in, eyes focused and barely contained their enthusiasm to now receive a counter-argument to RFK's pro-environmental screed with the tantalizing subtitle for Van Dyck's presentation, "...A Private Sector Perspective."[203]

The Legislature's informational hearings operate with a kind of equal-time provision to present varied perspectives on a topic. His place in the agenda assured many in attendance that Mr. Van Dyck, the obvious Wall Street representative, would make short work of Kennedy and his entourage; revealing the costliness of California's excessive environmental programs, regulatory over-reach, and most vitally - the superiority of market-driven decisions by private sector entrepreneurs, bankers and others. Thomas, however, represented something other than the usual financial sector rhetoric.

The hearing room gradually quieted, attentive to the unlikely appearance of an investment banker at an environmental hearing. After introduction background, Van Dyck eased into his main discourse: environmental regulations were not simply good for California, but essential for the marketplace. Legislators were now dumbstruck. "What did he just say?" one legislator asked the committee staff sitting next to him. Van Dyck explained that without vigorous laws of the type that California pursued, many of the real dimensions of corporate accounting sheets remained invisible. It was vital for California to reveal the externalities and off-balance-sheet aspects of their operations. Many California environmental statutes provided at least certain kinds of transparency for investors to begin to differentiate companies from one another. Indeed, for Thomas's clients, he explained, the lack of transparency about corporate environmental costs often got them into trouble and angered investors.

Members were now on the edges of their chairs and the conversation was bubbling. It was clear that this lecture clearly went directly in the opposite direction from the routine objections that corporate lobbyists provided every week in one committee or another about the excesses of California's environmental regulations. If Democrats were silenced by the novelty of his statements, Republicans were flabbergasted! And one legislator who represented a rural county could no longer contain himself.

"Wait a minute. Just a moment ago you stated that among the preferred expenditures of your group are investments in organic agriculture. As a successful rice grower, I don't cultivate according to organic methods. But I can assure you that my enterprise and others who farm like I do are regarded as successful. Do you dismiss my achievements as a farmer, is that right?"[204]

If legislators had thought Mr. Van Dyck unprepared to deal with the rough and tumble of public political discussions, a surprise awaited them. "Sir, I in no way mean to disparage your achievements as a successful rice grower," Tom started in what some mistook as back-tracking. Instead, the dapper financier delivered a coup de grâce, "I am here to provide my expertise as a professional in the world of finance; and, *I am only telling you where smart money goes.*"

Hushed laughter immediately followed the unmistakable message: collecting short-term profits based on damaging environmental practices was not a wise *investment.* For those paying attention, Thomas Van Dyck's message moved to center stage: the orthodoxy that a sound financial order and aggressive environmental policies were at odds was a myth. One of Wall Street's rogue voices utterly demolished the corporate lobby's constant rant against regulations and replaced it with the sage advice from another realm of the finance world: the state's aggressive environmental laws not only benefitted Californians generally, these laws were essential for a flourishing economy.

Even though the day's news accounting focused almost entirely on Kennedy and his brief appearance, discussions inside the capitol returned to the new approach where Van Dyck artfully countered conventional thinking about economy, politics profit motives, and the environment. This rubric questioned a seemingly timeless practice of granting corporations a largely unrestricted go-ahead for a range of activities that went well beyond the corporate balance sheets to impact workers, consumers, communities, taxpayers and the conditions of their health and their environment. The hearing served as one more building block in the broader undertaking of promoting public involvement in private-sector decision-making.

The irony is that just as Tom Van Dyck was promoting a new thinking about finance and the public interest, America was verging on a scale of economic damage that had not been experienced since the Great Depression. A more enlightened financial strategy, led by "smart money" would be obliterated in a series of time-bombs unleashed by the predatory parts of Wall Street involving derivatives, credit default swaps, and other instruments of financial destruction.

Dangerous Money

I could barely find my phone amidst an overflowing desk. I did, however, recognize the voice of my trusted advisor on all matters financial: "It's time!"

I took the bait, "Pardon me, but what time would that be?"

"It's time to get out of this market: Completely. Things have gotten way too scary and you need to be entirely in cash. This is going to be very, very ugly."

It was the fall of 2007 and Casey had spoken increasingly in recent months, about his nervousness, regarding the world of finance.

Financiers, to my mind, were always a bit too pessimistic about such matters. On the other hand, since he was responsible for having built these structures for the great Satan (as he was fond of calling one of the largest corporate firms he worked for), he was in a position to know about such things. Truth be told, I had already invited Casey as a kind of seminar leader to various gatherings, my version of informal legislative briefings.

Governing involves the ability to predict coming trends that will occupy the most attention, and to forestall anticipated damages as much as possible: to maximize financial opportunities and rewards. It was quite the norm for constituents to consider it their political representatives' function to pave the way for 'more jobs,' as well as to pluck-up various negotiations for, if not worker health specifically, then public welfare. In the capitol, on a daily basis, my cohort of agencies, activists and consultants who dealt year-round with a specific issue (in this case, being Budget and Finance) as a way to reinforce governing ideas - to essentially make them whole.

If new regulations were to be put in place on any of a range of issues commonly engaged by committee staff, where would the funding come from? Whether fees up-front, or bonds, or borrowing from other new sources of revenue provided a partial answer, it was all part of the project of crafting effective legislation. The same was certainly true of Casey's professional, financial framework. And so, it seemed part revelation and part just extremely odd to me that legislators and legislative staff so rarely consulted with financial heads; and not the usual lobbyists for the banking and finance industries, but insiders who could speak to the cracks in the edifice of advanced capitalism.

I circulated a video clip to initiate these informal briefings.[205] The link contained a media project organized by a group of students at Yale University analyzing real estate prices with an animated video. Their presentation was both comical and terrifying. Their inspiration came from Robert Schiller, another figure from the world of finance. His simple conclusion, based on years of work: real estate prices verged on a frightening collapse. Schiller's cautionary work remained absent from any kind of public reporting and languished largely unknown -- except within the recesses of academia and among financial gearheads.

The Yale students artfully designed a roller coaster type of vehicle to illustrate how the prices of real estate in the US had grown over time. Starting somewhere circa the middle of the twentieth century, the video lasted for several minutes showing the trolley starting off at ground level, climbing, with occasional dips in a certain year or years, eventually passing a mountain, in its ever-upward climb. By the 1980s, the trolley was well off the ground; steeply higher as the decade progressed; and by the early 2000s the car now appeared to continuously, grindingly rise to such lofty heights that the houses that were once parallel with the coaster - were now visible only as tiny pinpoints through the clouds. While many talking heads invented reasons for how real estate prices would defy gravity, Schiller patiently explained that the more likely outcome would be a "reversion to the mean" – prices pulled inexorably back to earth.[206]

After receiving the dizzying roller coaster video, I called Casey to discuss the implications. "Okay, here we are again. Another piece of good news from the gloom and doom brothers. What are your recommendations for the state of California?" We kicked around several ideas and agreed on a plan for Casey's return visit to Sacramento to test a precautionary approach: anticipating a crash in real estate prices. In early spring of that same year, I invited a small group of professional staff representing finance, appropriations and budget committees. Casey was already known to several of those attending as "the guy who devised the plan for the state takeover of PG&E," but "Today I am here on another topic," he announced, "that Bruce and I have discussed over the past few weeks." Casey provided the usual handouts, summarizing the information assembled by Schiller and like-minded economists.

The first questions reflected a discussion that would repeat in a series of meetings over the next several days. A young legislative staffer demurred, "But I don't get it. You think we should do something just because some odd-ball economists think the sky is falling?" Others readily joined in, challenging Casey's premise that bad things might be on the horizon with a similar question: "Here, real estate seems to be the best bet that any of us could make right now. What are you proposing the state do, make bets against the real estate market?"

"Well, in a word, yes." replied Casey, "I want you to make that bet." The incipient laughter in the room stopped as soon as it had started as Casey elaborated.

"Yes, in fact, there is a tool used by finance companies that the public could use to protect itself against this type of asset bubble. One of these would be the creation of an inverse real estate bond. In the event real estate prices precipitously return to earth, Californians could have made side bets to protect themselves." One earnest young man, however, saw this as only a trick and expressed it so: "But why would we allocate scarce resources now?"

Casey paused, "Well, think of it as fire insurance. Of course, when you are paying the premiums, it seems like a silly thing to do....up until the moment your house burns to the ground. But, you cannot convince anyone, least of all financial markets, to provide you protection once your house has caught fire." The upshot of the meeting, however, was disappointingly predictable. While several of the consultants in attendance understood the potential impact, presenting a plan for how the state might respond posed a challenge. The notion that the Legislature might protect its constituents by anticipating bad things happening in the financial markets ran contrary to the popular mindset.

The political reckoning reflected a truth that everyone in the state recognized: if it was illegitimate for the state to intervene in financial markets, how was the state to make bets that markets might be on the verge of catastrophe? Even one of the Legislature's seasoned budget advisers could not make the connection: "I enjoy these theoretical conversations!" As she was about to learn, the state's lofty real estate journey was about to come plummeting to earth.

One or the Other

Casey expressed amazement at the byzantine nature of the California budgetary process. Digesting and translating the state's fiscal process appeared largely indecipherable to this Wall Street savvy analyst. He was fond of noting that at least the state's balance sheets did not seem to suffer from a trait so common among large financial firms – the manipulation, if not outright lying, about their financial condition. While

California's financial transactions might be archaic and inefficient with tracking revenues, the state did not reward those who distorted and disguised the state's accounts. In contrast, Casey regularly noted with incredulity rating firms, analysts and financial news reporters routinely boosting stocks regarded by insiders as largely insolvent.

During conversations regarding how the federal government continued to subsidize the private sector, Casey proposed turning this practice on its head. "How about if we have the State of California exploit the same tactics used by private sector firms to harvest tax benefits?" In a conversation punctuated with laughter, we agreed that such an approach was nothing short of inspired! Arranging another flight to California, I set up a new briefing, this time for committee staff whose work regularly involved the state's revenue and tax policies. Within a month, Casey arrived at my office with a new set of graphs and charts to share.

Briskly, Casey pitched the proposal that California should solve part of its budget problem by pursuing a tactic followed by a variety of the nation's largest firms: harvesting the federal tax code in order to gain revenues for the state. Taking this action, especially during the Bush Presidency, which attempted to withhold support of various kinds to that bastion of radicalism – California would be even sweeter. The presentation yielded an empty puzzlement in the cloistered offices on the fourth floor of the capitol. The staff director then repeated back to Casey the essence of the deal: "We would use the federal tax laws and game the feds to advantage California?" "Yep," Casey replied cheerily.

After a longer silence, the consultant responded with visible frustration, "But that would be dishonest!" Casey: "How so? If corporations are realizing such benefits in accordance with existing law, why is it dishonest for the people of California to benefit in equal measure?" The consultant's colleague from another committee could no longer hold back, "But this isn't the right thing to do. I mean, for God's sake, just because corporations are engaged in this activity is no reason that California should be engaged in the same kind of practice."

Having successfully pierced the belief in the sanctity of federal law, Casey responded smugly to the staff sitting across the table, "Fine. Don't take the money private sector firms feel they are entitled to for no better reason than the fact that their lobbyists created such beasts in the U.S.

tax code in the first place. But then at least make a public statement that you believe these practices, if not illegal, should not exist in the tax code." The consultants sat flummoxed by such a seamless pivot. Casey had not completed his argument.

"So, how about if you arrange a press release or better yet a public presentation, in the next fiscal year, announcing identified revenue sources amounting to several hundred million dollars that are available in the federal tax code, but that you think this is wrong and that the state of California will not stoop to such behavior? And oh, by the way, such holes in the tax code should probably be put to death and government provide for a more thorough-going investigation of corporate practices for separating taxpayers from their money." The committee staff remained steadfast in pursuing neither course of action. The unarticulated position was that the Legislature would bumble along, look to revenue streams and bond sales and keep a blind eye to private sector practices that would rapidly accelerate U.S. indebtedness, and erode the fiscal position of individual states.

As we left the meeting, Casey expressed impatience, "What don't they get that the world of corporate finance is propelling not just California, but the entire nation toward a more dangerous place? Taking no action is the same as encouraging more bad behaviors on Wall Street." To be fair, legislative staffers were largely overwhelmed by a world, the private sector, for which they had scant applicable knowledge and even less experience. Casey noted that even those legislators proclaiming business savvy from backgrounds of managing or owning a sizeable enterprise, did not have a clue about the world of global finance. The idea that the public possessed a group of professionals actively alert to financial hazards was belied by a history in which schemes such as Enron's gaming brought energy markets crashing down.

Casey's conversations produced a growingly familiar response among both capital staff and higher ups in the administration of various agencies with jurisdiction over California's finance: jaw-dropping incredulity. Casey's recap of current events in the private sector and what this meant for the public described a parallel universe for which the larger public, and certainly many professionals in the Legislature, had little basis for comprehension. For a generation of professionals trained in the legislative side of matters of budget and finance, government had no business in meddling with the world of private finance.

Among the few who did understand the import of such presentation, pragmatic political problems were manifest: How do I translate this into a plan for political action? What are the resources and allies I can draw on to make this case publicly? Who are my likely opponents and how do I navigate the fallout? And for those who would follow Casey this far, the idea of mounting a political campaign directly confronting Wall Street stopped everyone cold in their tracks! Everyone inside the capitol recognized the danger of confronting corporations and their lobbyists with a frontal assault on what many now regarded as their money.

Anticipating the Next Crisis

A more basic obstacle loomed large: the activities of a global finance complex vastly exceeded the abilities of the State Attorney General, State Treasurer, or the offices of the legislature to pursue a battle likely to last many years. With respect to plummeting financial catastrophes, both the public and elected representatives were captives of what Casey liked to refer to as "the same faith-based beliefs that held sway on Wall Street." Free markets required that government be removed from a fundamental "right" for corporations to manage everything from toxic consumer products to toxic financial products. With one important caveat: once a disaster emerged, the costs for privately orchestrated catastrophes would become a social responsibility, whereas profits were retained privately.

This was an active collusion, one we two had volleyed for several years. Not easily deterred, Casey adopted an approach that would become more broadly understood within a few short years.[207] Wondering aloud, "Why is it that the state cannot engage in profit-making? If we can't get the state to pursue catastrophe bonds (a kind of insurance policy when bad things would happen),[208] how about if we get the Treasurer to use state funds to 'short' the market with 'puts' for climate change, or bankruptcies, or....?" In meetings across Sacramento this presentation still bewildered decision-makers. The only groups prepared to take advantage of Casey's reputation as a savvy financial engineer involved private financiers who were completely uninterested in protecting the *public* interest.

As the crash of the financial markets surfaced in 2008 and viciously accelerated in 2009, the list of casualties exploded to include larger and larger numbers of homeowners. The number of foreclosures expanded to hundreds of thousands, in nearly every neighborhood across the state. By 2010 the reporting of home valuation by Zillow and others displayed in graphic detail of crashing real estate prices, Schiller;s long disregarded reversion to a mean value. Major media outlets around the state noted the real estate indices showing a continuing decline for most households. Reports of decreases in average price, in new housing starts, and increases in the number of households behind in mortgage payments, and in foreclosures were largely left to the financial section of the news. What to do, saw a blend of ongoing federal and state investigations and recommendations.

At the household level this often translated to a kind of purgatory where many families lived on the edge, waiting for notices directing them to vacate their homes. For so many who had leapt into home ownership or refinancing, this descent was a cruel part of their faith-based confidence in a free market over which they and the elected representatives exercised little control. Millions of Californians who were so devastated, for the most part, marched silently toward their fate. During this same period, news sources revealed that the financial bailout that banks and financial centers received during the early meltdown were made at an interest rate of 0.01%.

The fact that astronomical sums had been mobilized to save the banks 'too large to fail', while millions of households continued to evaporate was little connected or commented upon in the short-news cycle regarding the free money extended. Casey later reflected on his numerous meetings with government officials at various levels across California. Try as he might to simplify his explanation of financial transactions, few if any in the room could follow (and so too recognized that if the public did not have anyone on their side who understood finance, disastrous outcomes were hardly a surprise). For Casey it was all too clear that things were going to go from bad to worse if

Californians weren't simply to be eaten-alive most days of the year by finance capital types.

The plan began with a tiger team of financial analysts serving as a one stop shop for everyone from city managers to school districts. It would be a kind of 1-800 number service where questions about "free money" deals could be reviewed to discover potential scams. Casey's journeys to Sacramento: meetings with representatives from the Attorney General, the State Treasurer, the Legislature, State pension funds all resulted with the same interested postures, but little action. The regularity of these experiences only compounded his initial chagrin. Even as more cities teetered on the edge of bankruptcy the response was, at best, muted. Most cities lacked the expertise to answer detailed issues of finance. Many small governments depended on informal golfing partners gauging the safety of deals with bankers or private equity groups.

Professional guidance regarding risks was often lacking simple because even public employees with formal education in finance and economics had trouble dissecting and comprehending the terms for getting free money. In a memorable exchange, Casey visited a medium sized city. A group representing the county treasurer asked about a financial advisor's recommendation that the city to move its funds to a higher paying account. Amidst many local governments facing shrinking budgets, the offer seemed like an obvious good choice. After a careful reading of the terms for receiving these greater returns, Casey advised against the deal, pointing to provisions where the city was liable for substantial losses. Within a few years after dismissing his counsel, Casey read the 'deal' results – substantial losses.

The Next Trading Scheme

Another day, another call: Asking if I had seen the latest *Rolling Stone,* Casey laughed. "Well, we finally have a popular piece to distribute at your next finance briefing in the capitol." The article, by Matt Taibbi described the recent and ongoing financial disaster in terms familiar to anyone who had followed Casey's presentations at the capitol. Focusing on Goldman Sachs, the essay revealed a public reamed by the banking industry. The message appeared in various forms in the coming years as other authors dissected the aftermath of the latest global financial crisis. Turning to the final passages, I found a controversy that seemed to grow with each passing year:

> "...instead of credit derivatives or oil futures or mortgage-backed CDOs,[209] the new game in town, the next bubble, is in carbon credits — a booming trillion dollar market that barely even exists yet, but will if the Democratic Party that it gave $4,452,585 to, in the last election, manages to push into existence a groundbreaking new commodities bubble, disguised as an 'environmental plan,' called cap-and-trade.
>
> A new carbon credit market is a virtual repeat of the commodities-market casino that's been kind to Goldman, except it has one delicious new wrinkle: If the plan goes forward as expected, a rise in prices will be government-mandated. Goldman won't even have to rig the game. It will be rigged in advance."[210]

In the short term, the article would prove wrong, the Congressional effort to pass a cap-and-trade bill modeled after the California program failed. Indeed, many of the major environmental organizations bemoaned President Obama's not having moved more swiftly before the loss of Democratic majorities that might have ensured the enactment of a national cap-and-trade program. For many public interest advocates operating at the community level, the failure of a federal cap-and-trade would be quietly celebrated with sighs of relief that the nation had narrowly dodged a deeply flawed solution to global warming. Was an integral part of cap-and-trade architecture founded on a mechanism to enable banking and finance sectors to extract more profits? Even if Taibbi overstated the case that cap-and-trade represented the next bubble, his predictions of potential uses as a device for market manipulation were out on the horizon. In the coming years, the details surrounding California's cap-and-trade program (explained in the following chapters), would reveal tremendous economic value for the owners of refineries, confined animal feedlots and other major emission sources.

Thus, while astronomical sums had been mobilized to save the 'too large to fail' banks, professional guidance regarding risks was often lacking for the simple reason that even public employees with formal education in finance and economics had trouble dissecting and comprehending the terms for getting free money. In the meantime, public outrage over the world's latest financial crisis morphed into a discussion about public austerity. Without the kind of analysis presented by Matt Taibbi describing crimes by bankers and others against the public, leaders from Europe to the United States called for a tightening of household budgets and sacrifice in order to move forward from the financial wreckage. If convincing the public of their responsibility for the global financial meltdown appeared implausible, a greater irony awaited those who believed market-based programs held a solution for fossil-fueled crises.

CHAPTER 11

The Climate of Austerity

Walking into the Capitol during the first week of January, in 2011, one of the few reminders of Arnold's legacy was the giant metal bear, standing in front of the double doors to the Governor's Office like some discarded Hollywood prop. In place of the oversized couches and massive furniture previously dominating the entryway to a suite of offices, the reception area now contained only a single nondescript coffee table with half a dozen empty chairs. Walls previously filled with plaques and cabinets displaying Arnold's appearances from around the world, now stood bare.

Gone were numerous state police and guards. For the first time in years, the reception area was empty of people. No one was waiting and save, for the painters and movers, there was little in the way of the hustle and bustle that had surrounded Arnold's tenure. Missing, were the lines of kids and moms hovering anxiously outside the office for a glimpse of the actor governor. Inside the horseshoe semicircle of staff offices, the scene was no less stark. As I walked through, Governor Jerry Brown was just adjourning a meeting with a dozen people who occupied a space that now looked more-bare than any conference room for any of the various agencies surrounding the capitol.

Adjoining the Governor's suite an improvised conference room contained a collection of furniture that might best be described as early picnic set, wooden benches and tables that could have been used by the extras working on one of Arnold's movie sets. It could not be more perfect a setting for the newly elected Brown to make a statement about austerity and simplicity. The days surrounding Jerry's inauguration bespoke of the returning governor's emphasis that we were all entering a period of fiscal fasting.

It was a real-time elimination of California's days of excess. Beginning with an inaugural that featured hot dogs: Edmund Gerald Brown, Jr. started his third term off by closing several of his own field offices (e.g., Fresno, Bakersfield, or San Diego), eliminating the First Lady's Office, and downsizing of his office budget by 25%. In contrast to Governor Schwarzenegger's failed campaign to eliminate excessive regulatory controls, his deregulatory theme or so-called "blowing up the boxes," Governor Brown simply directed his Department of Finance to immediately reduce the budgets for virtually every agency across the state.

Brown arrived in Sacramento naming his budget director in advance of virtually all other appointments, even prior to assuming office. By early March, the Legislature had submitted its avalanche of roughly 2300 bills, and the Governor focused much of his time addressing structural deficits. Jerry met with legislators from both parties and successfully lobbied the Democratic leadership of both houses, unlike past governors, in order to meet a deadline for submitting a measure to appear on the ballot by June that asked voters to approve an increase in taxes while promising even deeper cuts in state programs. The Governor also announced a variety of additional cuts: closing foreign trade offices, terminating thousands of employee cell phones, downsizing the state's fleet of cars, and freezing the employment of new state workers.

Despite numerous reductions, Republicans championed additional cuts to public pension benefits as a major part of the problem of deficit spending and the portent crisis of unfunded obligations. As California rolled out its effort to address the budget crisis, many states - and especially those led by Republican governors - focused on the downsizing of public pensions, an expense the public could no longer afford. Further restricting public expenditures, however, glossed over a deeper structural problem: Nowhere in the Governor's budget did there appear a distinction between the burdens placed on the general public versus those placed on the owners of yachts, jets, sports stadiums, office towers, shopping malls, hedge funds, or the like. The lack of such distinctions fostered a prescription that 'we' needed to get 'our' financial affairs in order while obscuring any corresponding effort to tax corporate parachutes, bankers' bonuses, or any effort to curtail multiple corporate shelters to sidestep taxes.[211]

By the time Jerry Brown assumed office, journalists moved seamlessly from translating a fiscal crisis precipitated by reckless consumer excesses to the need for austerity in American households. Political reporting focused on the magnitude of necessary public sector cuts, yet avoided probing the role of ruinous private sector practices in precipitating the nation's worst economic depression in nearly a century. For both California and the United States, the government's lack of control over economic problems should have provided an historical foundation for governors to prevent problems stemming from private practices. Risky ventures generated in the private sector actors instead were converted, through a range of public bailouts, into a government responsibility.

Before moving to the minutia of financial instruments, the harvesting of tax codes, and so on, it is worthwhile to better understand the premise: the U.S. and California possess an ambiguous control over the private sector realm of the economy. The minimal kinds of control that the state might exercise, (e.g., transaction transparency, an explicit statement of what constitutes a violation of law concerning financial actions, a pattern and practice of enforcement against violators - relative to the potential gain) are not contained in the remediation of public law.[212]

In the aftermath of a great recession, many legal experts focused on a lingering question: what authorities did the federal or state government exercise over the private sector? If the destruction of the economy actually resulted from a private sector run amuck, the first order of business involved reviewing the public's legitimate right to exercise greater control over banks, finance corporations and Wall Street. Instead of this tack, attention turned to what many regarded as the more urgent task of getting the economy back on track. And the narrative of 'reviving the economy' appeared to call for greater corporate flexibility.

The notion that the financial disaster striking the US had a basis in too much regulation, however, ran entirely counter to the later studies of events. Even as 'austerity' became the watchword for responsible government actions, more sage observers of the time pointed to the need for a renewed regulation of private sector activities, including a Nobel laureate in economics, Joseph E. Stiglitz "...as we have seen, unfettered markets lead to economic and political crises. Markets work the way they should –only when they operate within a framework of appropriate government regulations; and that framework can be erected only in a democracy that reflects the general interest –not the interests of the 1%. The best government that money can buy is no longer good enough."[213]

As the esteemed professor in economics noted, his observations were rooted in a global uprising. "In May, I went to the site of the Tunisian protests; in July, I talked to Spain's *indignados*; from there, I went to meet the young Egyptian revolutionaries in Cairo's Tahrir Square; and, a few weeks ago, I talked with Occupy Wall Street protesters in New York. There is a common theme, expressed by the protestors in a simple phrase: 'We are the 99%.' That slogan echoes the title of an article that I recently published, 'Of the 1%, for the 1%, and by the 1%,' describing the enormous increase in inequality in the United States: 1% of the population controls more than 40% of the wealth and receives more than 20% of the income. And those in this rarefied stratum often are rewarded so richly not because they have contributed more to society – bonuses and bailouts neatly gutted that justification for inequality – but because they are, to put it bluntly, successful (and sometimes corrupt) rent-seekers."[214]

An Alternative Approach

The media covered the aftermath of the great recession with to-and-fro about where cuts in public programs should be targeted. In California the debate ranged from the closure of parks, to schools, to universities, and so on. Even on the left coast, no agenda including increased revenues could advance without being immediately challenged as a threat to the weakened economy. Jerry Brown's repeated and insistent call for a measure extending existing taxes to go before the public was successfully rebuffed by Republicans and the *corporados* across the aisle. So what might be an alternative approach?

Just as the political debate was reaching an impasse, and the public was fraught by renewed financial doom, an alternative appeared in the pages of the Wall Street Journal.[215] The article called for a program to recruit many of the unemployed in a massive public works program similar to New Deal policies aimed at reducing unemployment during the Great Depression. What is more, the plan called for financing the massive public works program with the sale of U.S. Treasuries; an act requiring Congress to raise the debt ceiling. The appearance of such a plan in the Wall Street Journal reflected the economy's precarious position - a shock only exceeded by the professional status of the author, Barton Biggs, as a former chief global strategist for Morgan Stanley.[216]

The 2012 Budget

On Thursday, January 5, 2012 Governor Brown unveiled the proposed state budget for 2012-2013. The $92.6 billion proposal promised to increase spending by 7 percent, even though the state faced a $9.2 billion deficit. The addition would be financed through economic growth, higher income taxes on those making at least $250,000 a year, and an expansion of sales taxes. [217] Key to the proposal was his ballot measure to increase taxes. Brown said the state would have to slash another $4.8 billion from education if voters failed to approve his tax plan at the polls in November. Brown dismissed the accusation that he was threatening to cut school funding to win support for his tax increase. As his finance director noted, public schools, kindergarten through 12th grade, account for 40 percent of state spending. Brown reasoned that the alternative facing voters of potentially serious cuts to education were so unlikely that he dared make a jocular reference to them. "That's where the money is," Brown told reporters at the news briefing.

The political calculus of "where the money is" always contains an intrinsic debate about whose money and their relationship to political power. To place Brown's proposed budget in perspective, an entirely different twist was being given that same day on the Nation's opposite coast. The speaker for the Harvard Law School Forum on Corporate

Governance and Financial Regulation, Robert Monks was the founder of a law firm providing such advice. His introductory remarks set the tone for the talk that would follow: "American corporations today are like the great European monarchies of yore: They have the power to control the rules under which they function and to direct the allocation of public resources. This is not a prediction of what's to come; this is a simple statement of the present state of affairs. Corporations have effectively captured the United States: its judiciary, its political system, and its national wealth, without assuming any of the responsibilities of dominion. Evidence is everywhere."[218]

Many states struggling with budget deficits and shortfalls identified various publicly-supported programs to cut, what their European colleagues referred to as "austerity measures". Mr. Monks placed the problem with public budgets in a wholly different context: "The social contract between Americans and their corporations was supposed to go roughly as follows: In exchange for limited liability and other privileges, corporations were to be held to a set of obligations that legitimized the powers they were given. But the modern corporations have assumed the right to relocate to different jurisdictions, almost at will, irrespective of where they really do business, and thus avoid the constraints of those obligations...." Per Monks, "Privileges have been preserved and enhanced, but the obligations have withered...the U.S. Treasury is estimated to be losing $100 billion annually from offshore tax abuses."

The Harvard lecture did not speak to whether cuts to one or more public programs might be necessary. Monks, however, sharply indicated that "deficits" must be placed in the larger context of the relationship between corporations and the state and of the history of who pays and who benefits nationally, and also in California's economy. While Jerry Brown could be lauded for taking on the rich with an increased levy on their wealth, he avoided a deeper and more profound debate about the role of corporate wealth and power in California.

The problem, for Jerry Brown as well as for others, is that while increasing taxes on a top 1% of income earners in California and across America could be applauded, in the absence of more systemic policies, such actions were only a superficial step. The rise of the financial industry has become all powerful. It affects and *infects* every American and thereby persuades the Treasury Secretary that the world will come to an end if such interests are harmed. *But, the average citizen does not have a lobbyist in D.C.*[219] The most severe critics of the US economy, included certain individuals the public might easily mistake as leading capitalists.

Jeremy Grantham, who directs one of the larger bond funds on the planet, in a newsletter to investors, directed blame at not simply a particular group (e.g., the 1%) or even a class of lobbyists who controlled various democratic institutions, but at the very basis of capitalism. "Damage to the 'commons,' known as externalities has been discussed for decades, although the most threatening one – loss of our collective ability to feed ourselves, through erosion and fertilizer depletion – has received little or no attention. There have been no useful tricks proposed, however, for how we will collectively impose sensible, survivable, long-term policies over problems of the "commons." To leave it to capitalism to get us out of this fix by maximizing its short-term profits is dangerously naïve and misses the point: capitalism and corporations have absolutely no mechanism for dealing with these problems, and seen through a corporate discount rate lens, our grandchildren really do have no value."

Grantham brought full circle the larger debate that subordinating regulations governing the "externalities" of production to the profit-maximizing drive by globally powerful corporations inverts what needs to be done – this from a man whose career has been built on managing money on a global scale. The message could not be more-clear nor more at odds with the 2012 election year messages, that resounded with a call to reduce regulations in order to provide more jobs, cheaper fuels, greater innovations, larger exports, and the like. For Grantham, and indeed many of his silent colleagues on Wall Street, the subordination of public control over production decisions by corporations portends that relaxing controls over greenhouse gas emissions, disposal of plastics to oceans, fracking of oil sands and shale, releases of genetically-modified organisms, nanotechnologies, or tens of thousands of chemicals with uncharacterized perturbations for public health or the environment will be cataclysmic at ever larger scales globally. What is more, when one closely examines the fact that these activities are largely unregulated in any meaningful sense but still does not act, one is choosing to be blind to historically bounded contradiction, stated by Grantham (but echoed by many, many others): "capitalism and corporations have absolutely no mechanism for dealing with these problems..."

From the perspective of a capitol insider, juxtaposing Governor Brown's budget to three proposals addressing the larger issues of finance and economy appears utterly unfair. A governor and his administration must deal with extremely constrained options and a very limited time frames and the immediacy of an impending financial train wreck that a lecturer at Harvard, the reflections of a past Republican budget guru, or the newsletter from a global money manager do not confront.

From another perspective, however, it is precisely such constraints and the need for Jerry Brown and other governors, as well as the President and Congress to act within them that creates the conditions for political disaster! As Monks, Grantham and certainly many others might declare, the fiscal crisis of the state cannot be legitimately resolved without addressing how this crisis emerged, who is responsible, and what can be done to ensure that future financial debacles are not simply a recurring feature of state or national political economy.

Conventional accounts treating the financial recession of the new century as surprise fail to take into account the early warnings that California was entering a dangerous period of financial instability. Leading up to the great recession, a series of private briefings in the capitol – point to the potentially catastrophic scenario that might be avoided if the state could pursue a much more aggressive agenda for controlling private sector excesses. Recognizing a problem embedded in Brown's spoken words captures perfectly the view of oil companies as the holders of a product that is simultaneously very valuable and very destructive: a quintessential lesson in the emergence of the market state.

Brown's thinking is a part of the American mythology that he spoke of years earlier. "In the sixties, there was a sense of reform in the air.... We would transcend mere profit. Subsequent years brought about a growing skepticism that's still with us. So there was a transition from a belief in government and public interest to this powerful doctrine that the market, buying and selling, is the principle that will make everything work at the end of the day. That's the dominant ideology that we live with in America today. That's our new religion."[220]

CHAPTER 12

Private Profits and a Punished Public

My "kids – like many kids – love Winnie-the-Pooh. Not the newfangled stuff, I'm talking about the original A. A. Milne stories with their wonderful illustrations ...we always loved how the stories in the first two books are named 'In which this' or 'In which that'..."

For a small circle of readers who eagerly followed one of the state's most talented environmental justice attorneys, Angela Johnson Meszaros' posting in the spring of 2011 yielded her typically humorous as well as insightful analysis of California's cap-and-trade program. "So, building on that excellent foundation - here's a chapter in the story of AB 32 - 'In Which the Air Resources Board Drives the Bus over the Cliff." Angela's literary style instantly grabbed her audience's attention to a seemingly sleep-inducing topic: the emissions trading of greenhouse gases.

In her inimitable style, Angela opposed the state's plan based on the history of exposures communities of color had suffered as a result of the South Coast Air Quality Management District's trading scheme. Angela outlined a broad-based and fundamental indictment of trading and offsets as already failing to provide a solution to climate change:[221]

13 Reasons Why Trading and Offset Use Are Not a Solution to Climate Change

1. Time is of the essence.
2. The European Union Emissions Trading Scheme (EU-ETS) has failed to deliver greenhouse gas (GHG) emission reductions.
3. EU-ETS has not reduced greenhouse gasses: windfall profits to polluters.
4. Trading stifles technological innovation needed to achieve long term goals for greenhouse gas emission reductions.
5. Global offsets, often unverifiable: lead to oppression, do not benefit our communities.
6. Trading is undemocratic, secretive, and excludes the public from decision-making about whether and how to address GHG emissions.
7. Trading intensifies financial incentives for fraud.
8. There is a broad-based rejection of trading.
9. Climate change disproportionately affects communities of color, fundamentally linking environmental justice to the need for real GHG emission reductions.
10. Failure to address the primary cause of GHG emissions will also fail to address the cause of negative health, safety, and quality of life impacts on communities of color.
11. Pollution trading can create and exacerbate existing "hot-spots."
12. Trading, investing, profiting, gambling on public health is just wrong.
13. There is a better way.

It is easy to see why Angela's blog discussions were troubling to defenders of emissions trading. Her posting pointed to a fundamental flaw in the Global Warming Solutions Act – market mechanisms threatened to drive California's strict air regulations over a cliff.

Nearly five years after the passage of the Global Warming Solutions Act, California had yet to initiate the law's most celebrated market-based feature: the emissions trading program. Among the various obstacles encountered was a not-so-small judicial matter. In a lawsuit by community activists, the entire trading program was challenged as having failed to fully consider more direct regulatory means for controlling associated toxic emissions – not simply greenhouse gases.

The matter of emissions trading was far from settled. On March 18, 2011 the Superior Court in San Francisco issued a ruling that the California Air Resources Board violated the California Environmental Quality Act by not properly considering alternatives to the cap and trade program in implementing the Global Warming Solutions Act. Judge Ernest Goldsmith's ruling rejected the state Air Board rationale for choosing a pollution trading program, stating that the law requires more than "a discourse on cap-and-trade justification." The decision requires CARB to fully analyze alternatives to the cap and trade program, and stops all implementation of the Scoping Plan - the cap and trade program as well as all other measures - until CARB complies with the law.[222] Angela Johnson Meszaros was among the several parties who were named as petitioners in the lawsuit filed against the CARB and challenging its cap-and-trade program.

For the next several months many in Sacramento anxiously watched, wondering if the environmental justice groups would derail the state's cap-and-trade program before it ever started. The suspense, however, was only temporary. A lifting of the stay ended on December 8th, when the judge gave a final order allowing CARB to move ahead with pollution trading.[223] Before achieving judicial victory over environmental justice organizations, CARB faced a new challenge to another facet of its trading: the use of "offsets" as an instrument to accommodate business interests. By 2011 Bill Magavern had served for nearly a decade as the Director of Sierra Club California. Bill had distinguished himself in numerous ways - as a thoughtful advocate when negotiating legislation, a fierce lobbyist when necessary, and, unlike many of his colleagues in the environmental movement, Bill was not disposed to sign onto a position simply because others were so inclined.

It was no wonder that Bill was widely respected around Sacramento and more than a little feared by those whose positions he opposed. Despite being a valued and vital part of the public interest lobby in Sacramento, Bill decided to take a leave from his position with the Sierra Club. Before removing himself from the myriad of issues that landed on his desk weekly, he completed his punch list: finding a replacement, tying up loose ends, providing briefings to his counterparts in D.C., and so on. Magavern's colleagues were no doubt sobered at the multitude of commitments that Bill juggled at the Sierra Club. Amidst all of these activities and with only about a month before his departure, Bill Magavern identified weighing-in on AB 32 as one of his final official communications to Governor Jerry Brown.

His May 9th letter cited the cap-and-trade rules adopted by the Air Resources Board during the closing days of the Schwarzenegger administration and called on Governor Brown to re-evaluate. "The rule has some serious flaws," Bill wrote, "that will limit its effectiveness in reducing emissions and generating green jobs, and call into question its compliance with the environmental justice requirements of AB 32." Of special concern was the use of offsets; "If polluters are allowed to outsource their emission reductions to other sectors and jurisdictions, the clean energy revolution will be delayed."

Additionally, the letter touched upon a host of issues; "Furthermore, we are especially concerned about weaknesses in the protocols for forestry offsets. Forest clear cutting and the conversion of native forests to tree plantations pose great risk to the climate, while simultaneously degrading forest ecosystems, water quality, and wildlife habitat, and impairing the forest's resilience to the impacts of climate change. Offset credits for even-aged management could become an incentive for the conversion of native forests to tree plantations."

Magavern echoed a caution articulated by a growing chorus of voices. A series of televised reports by Frontline, for example, provided graphic detail that paralleled an array of points mentioned in the Sierra Club letter. A growing number of environmental groups challenged the use of offsets, especially where these were given away to industry groups, including petroleum and energy corporations. The Sierra Club letter, however, went further than simply repeating some peripheral issues concerning the implementation of AB 32. Bill also raised a long-lingering problem dismissed by Schwarzenegger and company as well as the original authors of AB 32. "As experienced environmental prosecutors for the state have noted, "the cap-and-trade market poses significant enforcement challenges," and "offsets pose multiple additional enforcement problems, including jurisdiction, verification, and certainty."

The letter drove home the point that this perspective echoed that of one of the Governor's closest advisers, Ken Alex. And if its point might be confused as a narrowly focused technical/legal discussion, the final line emphasized that the newly elected governor might want to assume a broader perspective regarding this landmark act: "The time has come for a fresh look at how best to achieve the emission reductions required by AB 32." The letter re-opened an old wound - how would the state of California use market mechanisms to aggressively reduce greenhouse gases? The letter, in this sense, could not be more clear - it pointed to Ken Alex's testimony as a basis for the Governor to revisit the decision by one of his first, and closest, political appointees: Mary Nichols. It was also noteworthy in setting forth a challenge – from perhaps the only mainstream environmental group of national standing comparable to its sister organizations in D.C. The whole rush toward the particular cap-and-trade regime that had been voted-down by a Republican Congress should be seriously and profoundly reconsidered.

In this respect the Sierra Club letter reflected a gradual awakening among public interest advocates. Magavern's letter broke with many of the Sierra Club's traditional allies, especially the largest national allies with major offices in D.C. His message reflected a growing divide between the larger national environmental organizations and numerous community-based groups' daily experience of fossil fuel related crises: visited upon them in the form of industrial wastes: a legacy of exposures to toxic air contaminants, polluted waters, occupational hazards, unrestrained. The prevailing agenda among the larger, national environmental organizations supported a reform of private sector activities which included the use of market mechanisms.

Like other aspects of an America enthralled with the virtues of free markets, it was a difficult reverie to overcome. Divisions among public interest advocates might appear as subsidiary to the fact that a unified corporate lobby posed an overwhelming force, or underestimated the extent of erosion. What threatened the cleave was not simply a specific battle regarding poisoned atmospheres, but a broader public challenge to the extensive power corporations wielded - even over national allies.

The Legislative Analyst's Report

Roughly a month after Bill Magavern's letter, the Legislative Analyst's Office (LAO) submitted a report on cap-and-trade to Senator Pavley's Select Committee on the Environment, the Economy, and Climate Change. Representing an independent arm of the Legislature that regularly issued reviews of major public policies, LAO's report was a sobering reminder of a dangerous business terrain. The report described California's trading program as involving primary markets, spot markets, as well as derivatives markets. The LAO echoed what others had stated since the inception of the AB 32 Climate Solutions regarding potential for 'gaming" or distorting emissions trading markets; "Carbon markets are complex by their very nature in general; the more complex the markets are, the more challenging it will be to regulate them, and the more susceptible they become to manipulation and fraudulent activity."[224]

Noting the Air Board's proposal for responding to this regulatory gap, the LAO report cast further doubt: "...ARB has no experience in regulating such markets, and its lack of technical expertise and institutional knowledge of such matters increases the chances that market manipulation could go undetected, in spite of any monitoring efforts that it puts in place."[225] As if all of these questions were not enough, the LAO concluded that the Achilles heel of regulating the California market in ghg allowances was not even within the jurisdiction of state authority; "The [Air Resources Board] has concluded that it does not have authority to govern participation in the derivatives market because it is within the sole regulatory jurisdiction of the U.S. Commodities Futures Trading Commission."[226]

In January 2012, the Air Board postponed initiating the trading portion of its cap-and-trade program, apparently due to several factors. First, the organizational basis for trading by 2012 had largely fallen apart. The Western Climate Initiative, a nonprofit corporation based in Delaware, helped to create an initial market with four other western states: Oregon, Washington, Arizona, and New Mexico. The Western Climate Initiative was to create an auction for trading credits that would be used by the owners of sources of pollution. In 2012, all of California's western state partners had left the Initiative, with Quebec as California's only viable trading partner.[227]

The chairwoman of the CARB, Mary Nichols, disputed the Legislative Analyst Office report; "Cap-and-trade is very simple...I think we have a pretty good sense of what can go wrong."[228] One reporter assessing the differences in perspective best captured the sense of many capitol-insiders who believed they had seen this show before. Reviewing historic antecedent programs for industrial deregulation, the reporter summarized prospects for California's trading in the manner of a stand-up comic: "... let's recap: California has an alliance with Quebec to create a market in which emission credits will be bought and sold, overseen by a nonprofit headquartered in Delaware. Goldman Sachs will be involved. What could possibly go wrong?" [229]

Just as the Air Resources Board was putting its final touches on the start of its prized market mechanism for the trading of emission credits, a study funded by the National Academy of Sciences appeared in the pages of *Science* describing the latest in the ever devolving state of the Earth's atmosphere, this time with reference to the oceans. The findings detailed how the Earth's oceans might be acidifying at a faster current rate than at any time during the past 300 million years. Authors underscored study implications, noting that too much carbon dioxide in the atmosphere is making the oceans more acidic, threatening crucial parts of the marine food chain.[230] The *Science* article, like others to follow, should have provoked questions as to a largely unstated premise of emissions trading: 'Was there indeed time to initiate and orchestrate such a platform and so convenience corporations by selecting their most favored approaches towards release of inherently hazardous emissions?'

A Dubious Trade

As the California Air Resources Board tested its trading scheme in August of 2012, the global carbon market was becoming more precarious, with various observers predicting its impending collapse as greater numbers of participants moved to simply deploy their investments in alternative energy and related projects.[231]

By 2012, the problematic nature of using trading as a scheme to address market imperfections struck many observers as, at best, a very indirect and convoluted path toward addressing the dilemma of greenhouse gas emissions. For others, including many learned economists, the problem of emissions could be much more easily and directly dispatched by imposing an energy tax on sources; and by providing funds for low-income households to counter regressive consequences. Such duels among policy wonks, however, again missed the sleeping issue of why anyone entering the profoundly worsening consequences of fossil fuels would apply market mechanisms to a problem actually created by market forces?

By November of 2012, the California Air Resources Board claimed success with its test run for the trading of carbon emissions credits. The Air Board's trade timing coincided with the European emissions trading program. While California's press simply republished the Air Board's claim of success, Europe's press castigated the European trading scheme for failing to address the more fundamental and urgent measures needed to address an ever worsening climate. Integral to the critique of European emissions trading were criticisms that the transactions intended to promote investments to transform emissions sources provided little evidence of such change. Instead, observers noted that the tens of billions of dollars involved in emissions trading were largely mechanisms for delivering profits to traders.[232]

Indeed, in February, 2013 more than 130 environmental and economic justice groups called for abolishing the EU's Emission Trading System, declaring "The ETS has not reduced greenhouse gas emissions... the worst polluters have had little or no obligation to cut emissions at source."[233] California blended its trading system throughout with caps on emissions. The question remained: what was the value of pollution trading over straightforward policies directed at dismantling the use of fossil fuels? CARB's claim of success glossed over the fact that its trading price had barely budged from the minimal floor price of ten dollars a ton that it had set.

CARB issued no statement regarding how this floor price mostly matched the price of European carbon trades. The price they were celebrating was the same price that based European panning. More ominous still, the EU Commission was deeply troubled that falling prices for carbon emission trading appeared to provide insufficient incentives for businesses to transform their production practices. In what sense was carbon trading a success?

An Underwhelming Solution

Appearing in the same month as CARB's claims of success was an 84-page report issued by the World Bank argued that extreme steps were needed to address accelerating fossil-fueled crises. By late November, CARB's celebratory mood stood in stark contrast to a widely circulated essay authored by Chris Hedges that assessed where we stood collectively:

> "A planetary temperature rise of 4 degrees C – and the report notes that the tepidness of the emission pledges and commitments of the United Nations Framework Convention on Climate Change will make such an increase almost inevitable – will cause a precipitous drop in crop yields, along with the loss of many fish species, resulting in widespread hunger and starvation. Hundreds of millions of people will be forced to abandon their homes in coastal areas and on islands that will be submerged as the sea rises. There will be an explosion in diseases such as malaria, cholera or dengue fever. Devastating heat waves, droughts, and floods, especially in the tropics, will render parts of the Earth uninhabitable. The rain forest covering the Amazon basin will disappear.
>
> Coral reefs will vanish. Numerous animal and plant species, many of which are vital to sustaining human populations, will become extinct. Monstrous storms will eradicate biodiversity, along with whole cities and communities and as these extreme events begin to occur simultaneously in different regions of the world. The report finds there will be 'unprecedented stresses on human systems' as well. Institutions designed to maintain social cohesion and law and order, will crumble. The world's poor, at first, will suffer the most. But we will all succumb in the end to the folly and hubris of the Industrial Age. And yet, we do nothing."[234]

Did the state's celebrated global warming law undercut more serious and aggressive efforts to address increasingly damaging social, environmental, and public health consequences of this fossil-fueled storm? Indeed it was seductive to generate wealth by auctioning society's ownership of the air.[235] Such a tack both could now increase revenues for public projects *and* potentially distract attention from the precedent issue of whether a policy for trading revenues covered or curtailed the many damages resulting from the extended burning of fossil fuels.

In January, 2014, Jerry Brown submitted a budget to use the proceeds of AB 32 auctions to fund projects for sustainable communities, clean transportation, energy efficiency, natural resources, and waste diversion. Included in this budget was the use of $250 million to support a high-speed rail. The Legislature's budget staff warned that the Governor's budget was advancing projects having dubious links with the stated purposes of the law: to achieve greenhouse gas reduction.[236] Others suggested that the high-speed rail project would actually produce a net increase in greenhouse gas emissions. Budget review prompted a legislative hearing convened as an update on the Air Resources Board's progress with implementing AB 32.[237]

Publicity clips featured affirmations by minority activists of the the many important uses to which a new source of funding could be put in their communities. These notes of approval were steadfastly countered by Angela Johnson Meszaros. Angela, who always stood in solitude with compatriot groups she represented in ongoing legal action was quite distinctive on this occasion. Of course there was an enduring need for budget rewards to funnel in the direction of low-income populations. She heartily agreed. But, not only were credit auction profits being used for only remotely related purposes, but how could further pollution ever transform to a source to achieving ostensible gains?

In her introductory remarks as Chair of the Select Committee on Climate Change, Senator Pavley spoke optimistically of AB 32 and its positive influence in forming similar initiatives around the world. Sidestepping a detailed discussion of the law's achievements, the chair of the Air Resources Board, Mary Nichols testified that AB 32, while important, was but one part of a set of emissions reduction laws. Indeed, as massive as AB 32 was, the trading component of the "cap and trade" program accounted for only about 20% of emissions reductions. Other laws included California's standards for vehicle emissions, energy efficiency, buildings, appliances, rail and port operations, renewable energy, school buses and trucks, interstate transmission of clean energy, and so on. ARB chairwoman Nichols then underscored the importance of meshing the state's climate law with private sector interests; "...we must guide investments and look at pricing as a tool to incentivize [measures to control global warming]."

As a demonstration of Nichols' commitment to the private sector, she announced that the administration favored amending AB 32 to provide, among other things, free allowances for those companies facing no restrictions on their emissions of greenhouse gases outside of California. In yet another slap to the dirtiest of California communities (that balancing reductions could be achieved out-of-state and yet relieve culpable industries of some responsibility to lessen their outputs) Nichols concluded that AB 32 provided a framework "to do our share and build a sustainable future."[238] Bill Magavern was among a small group of speakers encouraging the Air Board to step up its work to address the state's most vulnerable communities. Mr. Magavern emphasized regulating not merely the small number of greenhouse gases, but the many additional or co-pollutants often released at major facilities in California.

Bill next turned, as was his characteristic fashion, to a topic otherwise disguised by Chairwoman Nichols as 'incentivizing change' in the private sector:' the Air Board's forthcoming proposal to allocate free allowances to oil refineries. In one of the clearest challenge to the Air Board during the joint hearing, Bill confronted whether the oil industry should also receive free allowances, in light of record profits. "Are they (oil refineries) *deserving* of offsets?" Bill's testimony clearly resonated with many watching the hearing, and left a lasting question: 'How could the Air Board defend a policy of providing free allocations to major corporations to pollute the air while those communities living downwind suffered the damaging effects?'

While the hearing displayed a chair and legislators happily celebrating California's progress in addressing climate change, more thoughtful observers didn't miss the fact that the hearing only further disguised the problematic nature of pollution trading. Among the issues ignored by the joint legislative committee was a question raised by the fiscal staff regarding the possible uses of revenues derived from pollution trading: what are the legal uses of these funds? The fiscal staff suggested, in the mildest terms possible, that this likely litigation might consume many years of judicial challenges.[239] Could California legally use revenues from pollution trading to fund alternatives to fossil fuels? The answer laid bare a fundamental paradox: scientists urged immediate dismantling of the fossil fuel economy, *yet* the revenues this pollution trading generated could not be legally used for such purposes?

Is Something Really Better Than Nothing?

While many younger legislators embrace a popular refrain that something is better than nothing, the Global Warming Solutions Act illustrates the fallacy of such a cliché. By opening the door on pollution trading, the state has arguably perpetuated the fossil fuel era. First, emissions-trading depends on a pricing structure susceptible to market manipulation by large energy corporations. Magavern's critique of free allowances distributed to petroleum refiners reflected the outsized political influence of political appointees. The history of Los Angeles' pollution trading scheme (RECLAIM) as well as the European Union's contemporary experiences with emissions trading reveals substantial uncertainties.

There also existed a parallel problem: when would prices reach a level where it made economic sense for fossil fuel industries to move toward alternative energy sources? When prices might rise to a level where industries would transition to clean energy sources, commonly cited as surpassing a threshold of $50 USD a ton, remained a mystery. 2025? 2035? 2045? The only certainty emerged from the unequivocal statement of scientists. The deadline for dismantling fossil fuels had already passed; postponing immediate and urgent actions meant that humanity would face a dramatically worsening situation.

Press accounts frequently portrayed opponents of emissions trading as a hegemonic fossil fuel industry unwilling to accept any intrusion on its extractive and polluting practices. This characterization misrepresented the actual political dynamic in two fundamental ways. First, while industry clearly preferred no form of direct regulation, emissions trading presented a potentially valuable mechanism for delaying direct regulations. Indeed, by 2016 the Global Warming Solutions Act had already delivered considerable value to *petroleros* by avoiding more onerous, direct regulatory restrictions.

Indeed, the value of cap-and-trade to the *petroleros* was overtly demonstrated what the South Coast Air Quality Management District decided to terminate RECLAIM in March, 2017. The *petroleros* had successfully gamed the Air District for many years; "By 2011, Southern California refineries had installed only four of the 51 catalytic reduction units needed to remove sufficient nitrogen oxides from emissions to meet clean-air goals... Pollution credits had become so plentiful and cheap in the RECLAIM market that refineries simply bought the credits instead of the equipment." Even as the Air District sought to remedy the situation, the *petroleros* resisted until the Air District's Board decided to terminate RECLAIM. At this juncture the lobbying group for California's refineries, the Western States Petroleum Association, pleaded for 'market-based solutions.' However, as Sheila Kuehl, a newly appointed member of the Air Board and an L.A. Supervisor noted, it was already too late; "Their greediness [indicating the regional refineries] made it easier to show that the program was not working".[240]

Second, various journalists entirely missed the distinction that, e ven as the Global Warming Solutions Act was being marketed globally as the Golden State's latest environmental innovation, many insiders extending from community groups to capitol staff had reached a very different conclusion: *the state emissions trading scheme was inherently flawed and far too weak to address the threat posed by petroleros.* For many advocates representing communities, public health, environment, workers, and even a select group of emerging solar, wind, distributed-generation infrastructure industries argued the Solutions Act undermined the obvious alternative: to immediately launch a massive public works project to finance and construct an economy based on alternatives to fossil fuels. Rather than being too bold, AB 32 was supplanting a more aggressive agenda to address widening and deepening crisis of global climate disruption.

Though it was but a part of a suite of laws, California's leaders marketed emissions trading as the centerpiece of a global warming solution around the world. Paradoxically, the direct regulatory laws that accounted for the largest part of California's decades-old effort to redirect its economy away from fossil fuels received only minor attention. The headline that it had achieved more than any of the other forty-nine states and the federal government only reflected a wealth of failures and inaction across the rest of the nation. Similarly favorable comparisons could be made between California and much of the rest of the world - except for some of its equally powerful and wealthy peers, including Norway, Germany, Sweden and Denmark, who pursued a more explicit and direct agenda for exiting the fossil fuel economy. In this sense, the international marketing of emissions trading both downplayed achievements (e.g., energy conservation, clean energy production) *and* concealed a dismal performance (e.g., a reliance on fossil fuels, the promotion of fracking, paucity of resources for clean energy production, the proliferation of toxic petrochemical products and byproducts).

From inside the Legislature, many felt that California's major achievements in addressing global warming were anchored in laws specifically designed to reconfigure the state's fossil fuel economy (e.g., appliance and engine emission standards, prohibitions on the interstate transmission of dirty energy, renewable portfolio standards, distributed-generation, net metering, community choice for sources of clean energy, community-based enforcement of clean air acts, replacement of dirty diesels, port emission controls, incentives for clean energy purchases). Emissions trading, by contrast, provided a tool with which to disrupt these other achievements by undercutting the rights of citizens. In place of a citizen-led program to redirect the economy, decisions about how to manage the crisis were left to a trading instrument entirely a creature of the private sector.

As Bill Magavern noted, various companies, including petroleum refineries, were now allocated free pollution credits without reference to their profits or to the impact of their facilities on surrounding communities. Emissions trading would soon become a pivotal point of conflict for communities long immersed in battles with some of the state's larger petroleum refineries.[241] Buried in the minutia of emissions trading, the fiscal analysis pointed to future auction revenues.[242] Noting that earlier auctions in 2012-13 had raised a mere $532 million in state revenue, the fiscal analysts postulated that between 2015 and 2020 California's cap-and- trade revenues were expected to draw $12 to $45 billion.

In early 2015 the rush to advance a range of proposals was a familiar scene, repeated over the years when new revenue sources created what staff referred to as a "feeding frenzy." Even if one accepted the high estimate of revenues (to reach some $9 billion a year over the five year period), would cap-and-trade revenues be sufficient to meaningfully transform California's fossil-fuel economy? For an increasing number of observers, even the high estimates for auction revenues were too low; "there should be trillions (not merely billions) of dollars of new investment going into clean energy technologies, new energy distribution systems, retrofitting all types of structures for energy efficiency, replacing all vehicles with new, high efficiency vehicles, and so on."[243]

Reminiscent of the stance of Governor Schwarzenegger's chief environmental adviser, Terry Tamminen, California was ignoring numerous other potential revenue sources, especially a range of fees and taxes to address the damages resulting from extracting, refining, processing, transporting, burning, and disposing of petroleum. Added to this list were the sums to be recovered by ending oil subsidies and other indirect forms of public support.[244] At the same moment as California's Governor and legislators celebrated the new-found wealth of pollution trades, the International Monetary Fund released a study analyzing the destructive subsidies provided to fossil fuels.[245]

The study noted that global subsidies for oil, gas, and coal would reach $5.3 trillion, and the US share represented 13 percent of this amount or nearly $700 billion.[246] In evaluating the external environmental and public health damages, Nicholas Stern unmasked the report's conservative calculus. "A more complete estimate of the costs due to climate change would show the implicit subsidies for fossil fuels are much bigger even than this report suggests.[247] Generating revenues through the trading of pollution credits produced an ironic effect of justifying greater fees placed on other hazards. Pesticides, for example, provided a pretext for removing a small set of "bad actor" chemicals, while the vast majority of other pesticides received approval for continued use. The result rationalized pesticides as an integral part of agriculture – shielding manufacturers from adopting alternative agro-ecology that might threaten to dismantle chemical-intensive agricultural practices.

A small fee on pesticides provided a kind of insurance, helping to perpetuate use by offering minor adjustments. The fee also underscored the role of human error – by field workers, pesticide applicators, mixers and loaders – thereby avoiding promoting alternatives. In a parallel arrangement, emissions trading could tinker with low carbon fuels, the conservation of forests, or the purchase of pollution credits while sidestepping more direct actions, including one suggested decades ago: outlaw the internal combustion engine.

CHAPTER 13

Adding Fuels to the Fire

The question came forth as a new political year in California began, with an inaugural address by the longest serving governor in California's history. Jerry Brown's return to the capitol encouraged many that California might once again resume its proper place as a leader in shaping national policy. Given the perennial paralysis enveloping Congress, the aspiration did not appear overly ambitious.

Beneath the enthusiasm for the newly elected governor, a perfect storm of contradictions encompassing energy, global warming, toxic substances, public health and the environment loomed on the horizon. On the evening of January 5th, 2010 the Governor attended a variety of inaugural celebrations around Sacramento, including a stop at the Railroad Museum. Seeing him across the room, a veteran lobbyist stole a rare moment when Brown wasn't being escorted by his closest political consultant and wife, Anne Gust. The Governor focused attention on the person introducing herself, a woman otherwise very recognizable among environmental advocates across the state, "Who are you?" Reintroducing herself the advocate, seized the moment to re-state opposition by one of the nation's foremost environmental organizations to what many regarded as the Governor's environmental Achilles heel – fracking.

Brown, however, brushed the matter aside. "Oh, that's all going to be resolved by the demand side:" Known for her tenacity, the advocate challenged the governor's optimism that consumer preferences would bring an end to a technology for extending the life of petroleum, "How is that going to work out, when fracked gas is simply exported to other countries?" Brown remained undeterred from his message. "It's still a problem best left to the demand side," as if repeating the economic rationale supporting a controversial method for obtaining natural gas resolved the issue, Brown ended the conversation, and turned away to another well-wisher.[248]

The Governor's formula of first resort to market mechanisms was becoming increasingly contentious. The history and tactics surrounding fracking suggested that Governor Brown was more and more on the wrong side of experts from the worlds of science, the environment and even finance. Embarking on what was likely the last chapter of his political career, Governor Jerry Brown was risking a legacy placing him on the wrong side of history. The political calculus for backing the burning of natural gas started as a sound idea.

First, the burning of natural gas had been identified by many as an easy method for reducing the comparative releases of greenhouse gases to the atmosphere - "as much as 50% less compared to coal, and 20% to 30% less compared with diesel fuel, gasoline, or home heating oil."[249] It was especially the logic of utilizing natural gas as a 'bridging fuel' that brought various groups, such as the Environmental Defense Fund, and President Obama and others to support the hydraulic fracturing or fracking of geologic formations to extract natural gas.[250] The storm impetus was a little recognized event whereby the incoming governor assigned his political appointees to carry out his vision for California.

Within a year of Elena Miller's assuming responsibilities, in 2009, at the Department of Conservation, "the number of permits granted for new drilling projects declined 73 percent. Indeed, their achievements were nothing less than a bold protection of water quality and the environment at a time when the approval of oil and gas projects was being fast-tracked with little, if any, review across the nation. At the same time there was a fourfold increase in applications, as energy companies sought to tap the vast potential of Monterey Shale, containing more than 15 billion barrels of oil."[251] In late 2011, Governor Brown fired both Elena Miller and the top conservation official Derek Chernow,[252] precipitated by a slowing of the permitting of new drilling projects.

As was later revealed in court documents, both Chernow and Miller confronted intense pressure from energy companies as well as the Governor's office to relax permitting standards for injection wells that oil companies use to pump production fluids and waste underground.[253] Even amidst such pressure, Chernow and Miller resisted the easy path of smoothing the way for expanded fossil fuel development, repeatedly warning Jerry Brown's senior aides that by overriding key environmental safeguards, permits granted to the oil industry would violate state and federal laws protecting groundwater from contamination.[254]

In October of 2011, Chernow learned that former governor, Gray Davis, working as an adviser for Occidental Petroleum (one of the nation's larger oil companies) called Governor Brown to complain about the slowing approval for oil field permits. Davis demanded that Miller, as the supervisor with the Division of Oil, Gas and Geothermal Resources, and Chernow, as a key advisor to State Conservation programs, be fired. When Chernow and Miller received a call from Brown's top energy adviser a few weeks later pushing them to immediately fast-track the approval of oilfield permits, Miller repeated that such actions violated the Safe Drinking Water Act and that the US EPA agreed with this conclusion. Chernow and Miller were fired the next day. Memos reportedly distributed during the next month to Department of Conservation staff explained how regulators could now bypass certain federally mandated environmental reviews and receive approval. Later documentation showed nearly fifty percent of permits granted during the Brown administration were flawed.[255]

If many in the public missed the news item, members of the corporate lobby quickly acknowledged the Governor's nod to their interests. "The Governor made the right decision," said Les Clark, executive vice president of the Independent Oil Producers. "If you continue to turn down permits that involve the oil industry, it's going to take its toll."[256] Within two months following Chernow and Miller's firings, Occidental Petroleum not only thanked Brown for advancing drilling approvals, but initiated the first of what would eventually amount to $500,000 in donations to Brown's campaign for a tax referendum.[257]

Undermining Alternatives

In early April of 2012 State Senator Fran Pavley described her notification bill as the necessary first step to begin collecting data on fracking in California. The bill called on oil companies to give their neighbors 30 days' notice before fracking, likening it to having your neighbor put up a sign if they were adding a second story to their house. "The purpose of this bill is not to stop fracking," Pavley said. "It's a good-government kind of approach."[258] Good government, it turns out, did not include taking decisive actions to prevent fracking from contaminating groundwaters or the considering the negative externalities of discouraging the development of wind, solar and other urgently needed alternatives.

Coinciding with Pavley's 'soft' approach toward fracking, a Massachusetts Institute of Technology study revealed the fiction behind using fracked gas as a 'bridge' to cleaner fuels; "[The MIT] study found that shale gas development could end up crowding out alternative energies. That's because as fracking spreads, it drives natural gas prices down, spurring greater consumer use, and so more fracking. In a country deficient in regulations and high in corporate pressures on government, this cascade effect creates enormous disincentives for investment in large alternative energy programs."[259] Within two years, MIT's slam of shale oil development expanded into a devastating critique of fracking generally. For the moment, however, California's governor and various *corporados* busily engaged in moving the deck chairs in the midst of an impending disaster.

Representatives from the oil industry opposed Pavley's measure, saying they supported separate legislation requiring public disclosure within 60 days *after* fracking occured. "We support disclosure. We support transparency. We believe in the technology," said Paul Deiro, a lobbyist for the Western States Petroleum Association. But, he added, "pre-notification is a step too far." Deiro claimed that advance notice would reveal proprietary information and undercut competitive advantages for oil companies, adding that energy firms were at the whims of the service contractors they hired to operate wells.[260]

A Bridge to Troubled Waters

On May 15, 2014 national news outlets carried the striking color image of a California now fully enveloped in a drought affecting 100% of the state.[261] Many in the blogosphere noted whoever still argued the impact of climate change -the debate was resolved for most residents of the state. California already experienced a worsening climate with consequences now including one of the state's most precious resources: water.

During the next week, Governor Brown appeared in venues ranging from Sunday morning talk shows with national audiences to gatherings of university academics; banging the drum that more concerted efforts for adapting to the coming climate had to be pursued, at all levels of government. Political messaging emphasizing 'demand side' of individual practices worked seamlessly with his priorities for a high-speed rail project, following in the footsteps of his father, a new statewide water project.[262] Brown became the talking head for extending the California model to a nation operating largely without a plan.[263]

Governor Jerry Brown's announcement about entering a state of emergency regarding prospective drought conditions was well past. An even earlier fire season was flaring in southern California. Numerous towns long dependent on private springs and wells, issued alerts for residents to begin cutting their water use by 20, 30, even 40 percent.[264] With the reminder that water forms a fundamental requisite for human survival, not simply for economic activities, many voices across the state decried that Sacramento was engaging in a grand schizophrenia of contradictory policies.

Even as individuals were being admonished to redouble water conservation efforts, the state was encouraging massive practices endangering both water resources and the state's climate. Earlier in the year at a meeting of environmentalists in Sacramento, John Laird, Governor Brown's Secretary for Resources, attacked prospective Congressional efforts to meddle in a state policy of unrestricted use of water by the state's agribusinesses. While many of those attending the summit were already fans of John Laird, the first question from the floor went to the heart of a simmering debate over fracking: "How does the Governor reconcile his recognition of a drought emergency while providing a green light to an industry that appears poised to contaminate the state's dwindling reserves of freshwater?"[265]

Laird, among the best spokespersons for the Governor, attempted to return the discussion to the Congressional crazies bent on making things even worse for both climate change and potential water conservation. Looking around the room many of Laird's admirers thanked their lucky stars for not having to publicly explain Governor Brown's perpetuating a 'better' fossil fuel with a familiar trait: to further contaminate the state's vanishing waters (i.e., the subterranean injection of numerous and often uncharacterized chemicals and the inherent hazards of contaminating groundwaters).

Even with mounting and damning findings against fracking, environmentalists confronted a distinctly challenging conflict. National environmental groups presented expanded drilling as a smooth glidepath for transition to less damaging energy forms, ostensibly providing for local jobs and a lessened reliance on foreign imports. Echoing the earlier messaging of emissions trading, fracking was framed as a market solution involving minimal regulatory intrusions, while overlooking its potential for ruining groundwaters from increased contamination. The corporate lobby justified the complexities of fracking to distracted legislators with a favorite refrain: it was based on sound science. Their explanation encountered one small problem: the scientific support for fracking was unraveling.

In the summer of 2014, an historian of science at Harvard University, Naomi Oreskes, concisely pinpointed the problematic nature of fracking via her not-so subtle subtitle: "why fossil fuels can't solve the problems created by fossil fuels."[266] Professor Oreskes began with two basic questions: Doesn't natural gas have a smaller carbon footprint than other fossil fuels (e.g., coal, petroleum)? Isn't replacing coal with natural gas for electricity: better for the environment, at least in the short term? "No:" answered Oreskes, further explaining a troubling component of natural gas production: methane.

Methane, while lasting for a shorter time in the atmosphere, represented a substantially more potent global warming gas. "While CO_2 persists in the atmosphere for centuries or even millennia, methane warms the planet on steroids for a decade or two before decaying to CO_2."[267] In light of evidence of leaking methane from hydraulically fracked wells, coupled with a massive projected increase in the number of wells, fracking provides a dubious benefit over other fossil fuels. Having demolished the empirical argument supporting natural gas and fracking, Oreskes turned to a less noted impact: fracking served as an effective vehicle to delay or defeat alternatives such as solar and wind.

Following extensive reviews of the scientific evidence, Oreskes concluded that unless we immediately and decisively exited fossil fuels, we risked societal collapse.[268] It was the same conclusion that other observers, including prominent climate scientists, would later conclude.[269] The statements by Oreskes and many of her academic colleagues provided a clear challenge to Governor Brown's faith in the demand-side of free markets as a tool for resolving the worsening climate crisis. A common theme raised by many in the world of political work notes that once a legal, physical, and commercial infrastructure has been cast in one direction, flow along another path becomes increasingly difficult. If Brown's vision was clouded by a misplaced faith in markets he was hardly alone.

"More Complicated than I thought…"

It was February 11, 2015 with Senator Pavley chairing yet another committee hearing on well-stimulation technologies, including the most notorious one: fracking.[270] Beginning with a preemptive caveat, she asserted that the hearing would not discuss whether or not fracking should be taking place in California. The day's witnesses were instructed to focus on the *implementation* of her bill. Emphasizing that her bill was the most far-reaching of any state in the nation overlooked the fact that fracking remained largely unregulated. Even more striking were those congratulating Pavley for her work on fracking. Testimony from the Republican vice chair of the committee constituted a curious study in contrast of images: the touted environmental legislators received encouragement from fossil fuel supporters while environmentalists prepared to deliver their critical assessments.

During testimony summarizing the first volume of scientific studies, Senator Pavley asked about the implication of a "data gap" regarding chemicals used during well injection. The response recounted what was already widely known. Of the at least 400 chemicals commonly used in California well stimulation, scientists found it "overwhelming to understand the entire chemistry of this process." The absence of complete health and environmental data on these chemicals, coupled with concurrence that there was "no point at which you get it [injected chemicals] all back" combined with inadequate understanding of where fresh water was located throughout the state - made outcomes uncertain relative to fracking and associated approaches.[271] In place of what many might conclude was compelling evidence to impose a moratorium on fracking, Senate Pavley offered the understatement of the hearing, "....well, [it is] more complicated than I thought..."[272]

Standing apart from a three-hour hearing filled with scientific minutia, were another few precious moments of testimony at its conclusion. The representative of Clean Water Action, an environmental advocacy organization, reflected a much wider sentiment of the environmental community. Here, it was argued that the Legislature should consider fracking from a 30 year perspective - the same interval during which petroleum and gas development had been systematically mismanaged. The revelation of more than 900 open pits with petroleum wastes spread across California's Central Valley pointed to incalculable impacts on air, water, and public health. This larger perspective cast doubt not simply on fracking, but on whether the petroleum industry could be effectively regulated at all.[273]

By the close of 2016, a small group of termed-out legislators would gain more unmerited praise for achievements in environmental law and policy. Amidst the accolades, deeper examination of fracking illuminated a dark side to political decision-making across the nation. The proximate cause for compromised atmosphere, of course, resulted from a monolithic petroleum industry assisted by a larger corporate lobby. This aspect of money in politics, however, only revealed the most obvious dimension. The more subtle aspect reflected what many political workers called 'neoliberalism.' The essence of neoliberalism conveyed a popular sense that the proper role of government vis-a-vis the private sector was largely limited to keeping markets free. Neoliberalism reflected an attitude long ago captured by Governor Brown and many modern legislators: a mythology that our greatness arose from enrapture with markets. Growing and profoundly detrimental crises of the 21st century were predicated on a deeply flawed myth.

Damaging one of the world's largest and most vibrant economies, markets freedoms now generated corporate-sponsored crises. It would be a mistake, however, to characterize Governor Brown as a zealot for unrestrained markets. In the context of what appeared to be a fossil-fuel free fall, Brown voiced a moral outrage against those who burn the planet for profit. "Opposition to climate change borders on the immoral... You can't just sit around and engage in rhetoric because some of your donors and your constituents are saying, 'Well, we want to make a profit.' The coal companies are not as important as the people of America and the people of the world, and I think this has to be almost at the level of a crusade to wake people up and take the steps intelligently, carefully, but nevertheless forcefully from this point going forward." [274]

The justified attack on coal yielded a perplexing result. Why did the Governor and so many legislators fall short by embracing the supposed virtues of yet another fossil fuel? Instead of emboldening public action against fracking with aggressive regulations, the governor opted for one of the largest economies on the planet to leave fracking to an arena marked by manipulated prices, uncharacterized and unregulated chemicals, tens of thousands of oil-contaminated properties, communities exposed to refinery emissions, and polluted urban streams and estuaries.

CHAPTER 14

Race, Poverty and Trading

Well, "it looks like you are the winner!" Jesse Marquez, known for standing out in public meetings, would remember coming in first as something not to celebrate at one of the early gatherings of environmental justice activists. There, the organizer asked the many gathered to stand shoulder to shoulder, against the back wall, in a row facing the front of the room.

When the organizer asked everyone who had an industrial smokestack in sight of their home to take a step: Jesse, along with most of the rest of the room moved forward. Next, he asked those with a relative suffering asthma to take another step. More steps forward awaited those with contaminants in their drinking water, a contaminated and abandoned industrial site near their homes, a suspected cancer cluster within their community, a neighborhood rail yard with diesel pollutants, idling trucks at proximate ports, and so on. Jesse was somewhat surprised to be standing alone at the front of the room at the end of the exercise. As he later mentioned, "It was not a race I wanted eagerly to win." Not that those a few steps behind him were any better off for not "winning" the race for living in the worst neighborhood.

After the shared dark jokes among the participants, Jesse Marquez reflected that his trajectory had been set some forty years earlier. At the age of sixteen, he lived with a refinery across the street, where "with the first explosion, the house vibrated. Two more blasts generated enough heat to force my family to flee over the backyard fence. Two workers were killed and 150 people – workers, as well as neighbors – were burned."[275]

Jesse described it as a crystallizing moment, propelling him into the ranks of environmental justice activists. As the longtime director of the Coalition for a Safe Environment, Jesse Marquez challenged operations sponsored by British Petroleum, ConocoPhillips and others, including fourteen projects at the Ports of Los Angeles and Long Beach. In his view these sites were thinly disguised efforts to turn his predominantly Latino community into a dumping ground for industrial pollution.

Jesse's work as an activist most typically involved "brownfields" or various contaminated properties. The typical brownfield site is a former gas station or similar facility now with warning signs posted about hazards posed by lead, petroleum, or other such wastes. Jesse's environmental justice brethren labored for many years to address the legacy of hazard sites in communities recognized by some of the larger and more notorious: Stringfellow, Casmalia, Buttonwillow, Kettleman Hills, Rosemead, Hunters Point, Barrio Logan and Vernon. Well publicized toxic struggles occurring in the 1990s, fostered a popular misconception that new regulations protected citizens, and communities no longer suffered the damaging health effects by the early 21st century.[276] A more careful accounting of brownfields revealed tens of thousands of contaminated sites remained largely untouched.

Even for those areas having been approved as fully remediated public health controversies remain regarding the adequacy of standards and practices for removing contaminants. Many having vigorously pursued environmental cases were still only beginning to establish a statewide network to address larger scale violations. The less reported situation, as Martha Valdez pointed out many years before, "...the brutal fact is that many environmental laws simply pushed toxics problems into someone else's neighborhood." Over the years, many agreed that the state's most endangered environments extended not simply to those areas surrounded by trees, meadows and wildlife, but included communities of millions bounded by freeways, concrete and steel. Bringing attention to the human dimension of threatened environments, in the early 2000s Jesse joined other community activists challenging city leaders, legislators, and agency directors about the continuing problems posed by industrial release of toxic substances by conducting "toxic tours" around various parts of Los Angeles.

Toxic Tours

In the early years of the Schwarzenegger administration, Jesse Marquez and other community activists invited the then Secretary for California Environmental Protection Agency [Cal EPA] and staff to join a bus tour passing through various neighborhoods in Los Angeles where communities struggled with the common variety of problems that placed Jesse first in the stepping game: releases of toxicants from refineries, contaminated and abandoned properties, diesel particulate emissions from idling trucks, ships and locomotives at ports, discharged wastes from chrome plating shops, pesticide applications at schools and parks, the illegal disposal of wastes into streams and estuaries, tanker truck discharges of wastes to sewers, and so on.

As the "toxics tour" progressed that day, many leaders realized how little they knew about the constant barrage of environmental assaults that typically marked life in LA's various neighborhoods. One of the state's chief enforcement officers, Gale Filter, deputy director Enforcement and Emergency Response at California's Department of Toxic Substances Control, had created the Environmental Justice Enforcement Initiative, a community-based policing task force prized for focus on "spotting and squishing" environmental harms. In this professional history, Gale steadily honed a creative approach to enforcement. Inside the state capitol, Gale Filter's supporters advanced his activities in budget hearings with an approving nod in his direction: 'Is this not what we expect from our district attorneys?'

Gale's professional career, it seems, had always been steeped in controversy. Beginning with his first job in the district attorney's office in Imperial County, his boss explicitly defined the realm of Gale's work; "Your job here is to go after robbers, rapists, and murderers." Yet, it was not long before he uncovered a major violation involving the operator of a hazardous waste facility covertly and illegally returning hazardous materials to the United States for disposal. The practice reflected the kinds of illegal practices Martha Valdez and others had warned about years earlier – the maquiladora zone – representing an expansive complex of manufacturers based along Mexico's northern border, many owned by U.S.-based corporations.

After filing charges for violations of hazardous waste laws, Gale received a call from the firm's Boston attorneys informing him that their legal team would be flying to rural Imperial County to review and argue the case. Only later did Gale learn his opponents represented a law group possessing a notorious national reputation for aggressively defending its private sector clients.[277] Toward the close of the phone call, the Firm's legal assistant asked Gale if a more relaxed dress code wasn't acceptable for their forthcoming visit to Imperial. Gale immediately expressed an unrestrained outrage, "I'm offended! What makes you think our treatment of the law is somehow different? I expect no lesser regard than if the meeting were taking place in Boston, including the proper business attire."

When the team finally arrived, after a long car ride, Imperial's climate had already reached its normal excess of 100 degrees. Fully attired in wool suits, the Boston legal team was formally introduced to Dr. Filter – wearing khaki pants and Hawaiian shirt. The team glanced at the open window with the county's nearby animal feedlots. In place of the usual extensive deposition, after a brief pause, the Boston legal team asked if Gale had a settlement figure in mind. Within forty-eight hours, Foley's client agreed to $400,000 - the second largest environmental settlement to that point in the history of Imperial.[278]

In the coming years, Gale became an increasingly recognized figure in the enforcement of environmental laws. He later recalled, "Hell, it was not exactly hard finding environmental cases; it mainly involved opening the door and walking outside." His humor and modesty, however, hid a willingness to readily dive into cases that were politically sensitive. By the late 1990s, Gale was assigned to the Circuit Prosecutor Project, initiated by a group of activist attorneys with the backing of legislative staff. Prosecutors assisted DAs with how to build a successful case for those who polluted state waters, air and land.[279] By the mid-2000s, more than 2000 cases spawned a calculus of whether such violations were worth the distinct possibility of stringent penalties including the possibility of prison time for what had too often been considered a victimless crime.[280]

Via personal testimony in legislative hearings, Gale provided a striking challenge to a business-as-usual mentality, particularly with respect to enforcing violations of air standards. Did this relationship between the local air board and industry perpetuate community exposures to dangerous air contaminants? How to address consequences for politically powerless communities around the state? Preparing his testimony, he listened to a law-and-order legislator express his dismay that so many resources were being directed at environmental issues instead of the real crime affecting communities, pedophiles who threatened our children: should district attorneys not more exclusively pursue burglars, murderers, or sexual predators? Gale responded with a full voice.

"With all due respect, I think that I can speak with authority, having prosecuted all manner of cases - from burglary, to molestation to murder... the conclusion is inescapable: every day around this state thousands of children are done much greater harm by violations of air standards than by a diminishing number of sexual predators." A stunned silence in the hearing room broke by whispers, "Did you hear what he just said?" Legislators were now challenged with a very different interpretation of what posed the greatest threat to the state's children.

Gale Filter's observations remain haunting for many whose tendency is to evaluate safety by looking to the police blotter. For many Californians, there was a growing sense that there were no cops on the beat when it came to an array of environmental hazards. The litany of environmental crimes incorporated by local attorneys spanned a diversity of issues: abandoned chemicals, industrial releases of air contaminants, discharges of effluents to creeks and waterways, illegal disposal of hazardous wastes and more across L.A. where communities struggle with many problems affecting their neighborhoods. As the "toxics tour" progressed that day, Gale realized how little he knew about the constant barrage of environmental assaults that typically marked life in L.A.'s various neighborhoods.

Gale reflected later that the toxics tour transformed the abstract phrase "environmental justice" into an awareness of the daily struggles faced by many of the state's urban poor. Midway into the itinerary, Gale took a detour from the toxic tour, to join a local council member from Maywood, a small city with more than its share of endemic exposures. The counselor's destination was a small manufacturer of plastic parts, but the problem was the business across the street at a facility that would become among the more notorious in the state, the Exide plant. The plant's activities included the recycling of lead acid batteries, a product as integrally linked to the state's fossil fuel complex as the internal combustion engine. As with so many other dimensions of fossil-fueled economies, among the damaging effects of lead acid batteries were so-called 'externalities', in which taxpayers bore a financial burden to remedy damages to public health resulting from the contaminants affecting the many neighborhoods surrounding the Plant.

Workers from the night shift explained to Gale that they typically retreated to the lunch room around midnight, sealing windows and doors with wet towels in order to staunch the profusion of lead particles coming from the Exide plant. Even with such precautions, several of the plastics workers were informed by their doctors that their blood showed elevated levels of lead.[281] In the days that followed, the local air district convinced leadership at Cal EPA that it would correct the problems at the Exide plant. But, for locals, the legacy of problems at Exide would continue for years to come. Gale grew more frustrated listening to environmental justice advocates explain, in episode after episode, events replicating a dizzying array of toxic harms.

At the end of his visit to Maywood, Filter rejoined the group of local activists. Gale, rarely comfortable simply sitting, had heard enough. "Okay, so let's talk about how you collect evidence that can be used to prosecute these bastards." Having grown up on the Southside of Chicago, Gale deeply respected enforcement grounded in teamwork with policing. He gave an impromptu training course instructing how neighbors could collect facts and evidence necessary for pursuing violations involving the nearby refinery. At the end, Gale provided his contact information saying that they now were part of his team to bring action against the refinery and anyone else who thought they could simply get away with poisoning their communities.

While the chief enforcement officer would later be shunted aside, the support renewed Jesse and fellow activists to pursue a broadening number of violators in their communities, including major emission source facilities involved in transporting, processing, and burning fossil fuels. Among the various successes achieved by many community activists, one important foundation arose from provisions of both the state and federal Clean Air Acts authorizing citizens to sue for violations of clean air laws. Being empowered as a policing force, citizen complaints provided a crucial tool against polluters employing assorted legal tactics to resist changing business-as-usual practices. Even as Jessie Marquez utilized these legal tools, cap-and-trade motored its way toward undermining community enforcement in both California and across the nation.

Trading Protections

As the trading provisions of the Solution Act deployed in California, the export model of cap-and-trade took root in federal programs. And by early 2014, Jesse and his fellow activists gained greater appreciation of just how bad things might get for communities living in the shadow of refineries and of other facilities emitting greenhouse gases and additional co-pollutants. In 2013, U.S. EPA released a set of proposed guidelines to address the emissions; specifically pertaining to electric utility generating units.[282] On the positive side, the federal government now joined California in devising more specific regulations to address another fossil-fuel problem. On the negative side, the feds now joined a dubious solution – California's emissions trading scheme.

After much discussion, numerous public interest advocates challenged the proposed federal guidelines for electric utilities emissions. The extensive legal work, written by Brent Newell, a noted attorney with the Center on Race, Poverty & the Environment (CRPE), presented a multi-faceted argument noting deficiencies in U.S. EPA proposed guidelines.[283] The letter began by noting that regulations were bound by both Civil Rights laws and U.S. EPA's own environmental justice guidelines. More than simply an empty phrase, this U.S. organization had a particular duty: "EPA should not promulgate regulations which themselves inflict an injustice on poor people and people of color." Yet, as Brent Newell wrote in the next sentence, U.S. EPA was failing to meet this duty.

"Climate Justice Advocates do not want EPA to allow states to use cap-and-trade and deny environmental justice communities the benefits of carbon reduction policy."[284] Under the proposed EPA rule to allow trading, electric utilities could sidestep existing performance standards; instead, measuring a source's emission would then be done by purchasing reductions from another, even distant source. The Clean Air Act clearly never specifically authorized trading as a standard of performance. As Jesse attested, trading instantly inverted the notion that individuals could enforce violations of clean air protections for their communities. By allowing electric utilities to engage in emissions trading, CRPE underscored that hazards would continue unabated at particular facilities and additionally the victims would remain those same groups who typically lived next to refineries and other such sources: poor people and people of color.

The CRPE letter alerted EPA that use of cap and trade would undermine precisely the right to eliminate hazards in their neighborhoods that advocates had worked for years to achieve:. As Jesse's own experience attested, and the CRPE letter noted, there was nothing neutral about the boundaries of cap and trade for surrounding communities; "In California, for example, the residents living near facilities subject to California's cap-and-trade program are overwhelmingly people of color."[285] The final argument also reflected a topic near and dear to Jesse and his colleagues: enforcement. CRPE noted that the Clean Air Act required each emission source to achieve continuous emission reduction(s) based on specific performance standards.

All of these arguments combined with one additional flaw: the EPA-proposed guidelines actively undercut a long-standing obligation to ensure that states comply with the Civil Rights Act, which explicitly required that agency to analyze, consider, and *prevent* the "disproportionately high and adverse human health and environmental effects of [EPA] programs, policies, and activities on minority and low-income populations."[286] In terms of cap-and-trade, while acknowledging its guidelines might result in increased pollution, "EPA has concluded that it is not practicable to determine whether there could be disproportionately high and adverse environmental or human health effects on minority, low income, or indigenous populations from this proposed rule."[287]

Mischaracterizing Opponents

Press accounts frequently portrayed opponents of emission trading as a hegemonic fossil fuel industry unwilling to accept any intrusion on its extractive and polluting practices. This characterization misrepresented the actual political dynamics. First, while industry clearly preferred no form of direct regulation, emissions trading presented a potentially valuable mechanism for postponing compliance with direct regulatory requirements. The Global Warming Solutions Act had already delivered considerable value to petroleum interests by avoiding more costly direct regulatory restrictions for nearly a decade. Second, as CRPE's Climate Advocates argued, cap-and-trade opened the door for dismantling citizen suits against refineries and other major emission sources.

Many of the most important state environmental laws were grounded in the legal rights of citizens to control their economy. But, emissions trading contained in California's Global Warming Solutions Act facilitated using markets as a legal device beyond the reach of citizens or their exercise of democratic rights. While industry bemoaned cap and trade as yet another example of over-regulation, this simple presentation by too many journalists utterly failed to denote that public interest opponents of cap-and-trade represented a dramatically different argument from that of industry opponents. For many representing communities, public health, environment, workers, and even a select group of emerging solar, wind, and similar alternatives, the Solutions Act distracted attention from the obvious and immediate launch of a massive public works project to finance and construct an economy based on alternatives to fossil fuels.

Integral to the petition submitted was a central issue ignored by so many older mainstream environmental organizations: racism and discrimination. Jesse Marquez, Angela Johnson Meszaros, Gale Filter, Brent Newell, Rossmery Zayas, Martha Argüello, and many others at the community level readily identified with themes raised by their legal team: advocacy relating to race, poverty and the environment involved more than simply distributing trading revenues. The fact that California's major hazardous emission sources occurred in neighborhoods dominated by poor people and people of color was hardly news at the signing of the Global Warming Solutions Act. Many fellow activists achieved some measure of protection by pursuing subsequent legislation and regulatory language for communities lacking the resources, legal talent, and experience to track and organize politically, to intervene.

One obvious question emerged from this episode: What was the likely outcome of emissions trading as an export model to other states, regions, and nations for poor communities everywhere? Under the EPA's proposed rule to allow trading, electric utilities could avoid meeting existing performance standards. Instead, measuring a source's emission would now be done by purchasing reductions from another, even distant source. Yet, the Clean Air Act clearly and specifically never authorized trading as a standard of performance. As petroleum refineries were allocated free pollution credits without reference to their profits or the impact of major emitters on surrounding communities, solutions predicated on emissions trading, as crafted by U.S. EPA and others would increasingly become a pivotal point of conflict for communities long immersed in battles with major fossil fuel facilities.[288]

Nearly a decade after the enactment of AB 32, Martha Argüello would reflect on the short history that "...Mostly I am reminded of 2006 and all the work, negotiations, and fights we had over one little word: 'may'. Specifically "the state board may adopt a regulation that establishes a system of market-based declining annual aggregate emission limits," a system that became cap-and-trade. That 'may' was a nod to the voices of environmental justice advocates who recognized the inherent flaws of cap-and-trade and the negative toll it would take on impacted communities. At the time, that one word meant that we would develop real solutions that would both meet our climate targets and address the immediate health impacts associated with pollution. Instead the state decided to put all its eggs in the cap-and-trade basket."[289]

"...[T]en years later, we do not know what would have happened if the needs of environmental justice were addressed by decision makers. Who knows how many children would not need inhalers in Fresno or how many babies would come into this world at a healthy birth weight in South LA? One thing I do know is that ten years ago we had an opportunity to take bold action to address existing health disparities in fence line communities and we did not take it."[290]

CHAPTER 15

Climate of Compromise

On the last night of California's 2015 Legislative session the leader of the State Senate, President Pro Tempore Kevin de León, passed one of the more important laws of his legislative career: the Clean Energy and Pollution Reduction Act, Senate Bill 350. Advancing an essential element in California's suite of climate change laws, his success yielded only a muted celebratory mood.

Bill Magavern reported days later, a deeply disturbing transaction accompanied the victory. A large bloc of moderate Democrats joined virtually every Republican to strip a central provision of SB 350 – a phenomenon reaffirming the emergence of a new kind of legislator who, in such instances represented the oil industry rather than their own constituents.[291] Among the differing accounts of what happened, the most striking came from an interview with the Senate leader. "Sitting in his office the morning after he broke off negotiations, de León went down the list of people who had spoken favorably about SB 350 or endorsed it: Pope Francis, President Barack Obama, U.S. Sen. Dianne Feinstein, U.S. Sen. Barbara Boxer, Rep. Nancy Pelosi, Gov. Jerry Brown, past Assembly speakers and leaders of the state Senate, California Democratic Party Chairman John Burton. They didn't matter, not compared to the power of oil."[292]

SB 350's beginnings had been especially auspicious. Reflecting Governor Jerry Brown's State of the State speech in January of that same year, SB 350 set forth a particularly aggressive agenda challenging the state‘s reliance on petroleum. It encompassed three objectives drawn from Brown‘s speech: requiring utilities to acquire 50 percent of their energy from renewable sources by 2030; increasing energy conservation in buildings by 50 percent by 2030; and, in a novel approach, mandating decreased petroleum in transportation fuels some 50 percent by 2050. On the concluding evening of the Legislative session on September 11, SB 350 received the necessary votes in both houses, passing to the Governor for his signature – with one fundamental change: a last minute amendment eliminated the mandate requiring a fifty percent reduction in transportation fuels.

Even absent this major provision, the legislation represented another advance in California's decades-old trajectory of dismantling the fossil-fueled economy. The long trek of gradually decoupling society from fossil fuels would likely be embraced by others around the world. The understory, however, spoke volumes as to the political conflict surrounding the fossil-fueled crises. Early signs in 2015 suggested the political forces supporting SB 350 were unstoppable. For many legislative measures, authorship by either legislative leader typically assured its passage. Combined with governor's support, such bills only rarely confronted any significant amendments. In this instance, however, both the Governor and de León were forced to jettison a central provision of their legislation in order to salvage the other provisions of the bill.

For many pundits writing after-the-fact reviews, the blame extended in all directions. Some opined that the Governor and his staff had waited until too late to negotiate with a growing number of ambivalent legislators. Others felt that the responsibility rested with poorly managed negotiations, the absence of a more sophisticated grassroots campaign, or ill-timed votes. A few political veterans viewed the defeat as symptomatic of a changing national political landscape.

The reasons for an unstoppable legislative measure stalling to near failure began and ended with the power of an entrenched corporate lobby having the wherewithal to influence, what others might call intimidate, a large number of legislators.

Throughout the year oil interests opposed SB 350. Corporate lobbyists, however, recognized that defeating a Senate bill carried by the Senate leader as largely futile. The usual game plan in such situations meant waging war in the other legislative chamber. Intimidating members of the Assembly held a tangible advantage for the corporate lobby. First, newer, less seasoned-legislators who were on a near-constant cycle of re-election every two, rather than every four years, felt the threat of opposition from a major financial interest viscerally. They imagined large sums flowing to their opponents. Second, many Assembly members were uncertain of their constituent response to the framing of messages by oil companies and their allies.

The political might exerted by California's petroleum interests, the *petroleros*, was legend since the early part of the 20th century. As described by Steve Early, the State's *petroleros* wielded a power long recognized by citizens and their representatives everywhere, including one of the largest refineries located in Richmond: We "should have expected that companies with robber baron roots might have tangled with its downwind neighbors a few times before. Upon closer inspection, for much of the twentieth century and onward, refinery bosses and lobbyists were skillful at winning local hearts and minds. To achieve business goals, Standard Oil of California had employed more than a century's worth of corporate paternalism, targeted philanthropy, slick publicity, and political patronage… [When] public revulsion turned John D. into a much-detested national figure: so the Rockefeller's launched a 'massive philanthropic campaign, donating large sums to various causes, to refurbish the family image.'"[293]

The purpose of early political campaigns, moreover, was not limited to a short-term tactic aimed solely at voters. Behind various campaigns, the *petroleros* endeavored to weaken their political opponents, particularly labor. "To this day, when union leaders take independent and sometimes controversial positions on health and safety enforcement or environmental protections, refinery supervisors are able to quietly agitate among employees about getting out of a union that is 'working against their interests'... In Richmond, the results were disastrous. Standard Oil mobilized anti-union workers and a hostile local press." [294]

The *petroleros*' capability to conduct ground wars inside political districts grew enormously in subsequent decades. During the summer of 2015, the oil companies began to unleash very targeted media campaigns calling on voters to reject the "extreme" legislation taking shape in Sacramento. Their messaging portrayed a future of gas rationing, high energy bills, and long lines at petrol stations as the probable result of SB 350. For Assembly members who lacked the might and imagination to stand in opposition, corporate campaign also provided a stark preview of what the next primary race might hold for legislators tempted to face their wrath. For many outside of California, the expenditures of multiple millions of dollars month after month always appear otherworldly. In several states where only fractions of these amounts are in play, the expenditures appear wasteful. Yet, from the perspective of fossil fuel corporations – supplying vast sums to stymie actions in places such as California makes good business sense.

The victory of the petroleum interests, however, was perhaps a mixed one. While their core provision which eliminated the timetable for reducing petroleum by 50% over the next fifteen years was achieved, another set of provisions added to the bill during its final amendments significantly advanced precisely the same objectives. The amended bill now effectively allowed the state's utilities to electrify the transportation grid. What the *petroleros* had gained by stripping away the more general provision of law, requiring a 50% reduction in transportation fuels was now compromised by the additional requirements to electrify transportation coupled with the bill's other provision that 50% of electrical generation would come from renewable (i.e., non-petroleum) sources. The support from the public utilities appeared to stem from the fact that, with the declining fortunes of added renewable energy sources, their compensation in electrifying the transportation grid might provide a brighter future.

Beyond any specific bill, many insiders overlooked a not-so-subtle political transition: the corporate lobby and their clients had already been preparing to capture various newly elected legislators. During

2012 and 2014 elections, the Coalition to Restore California's Middle Class, a campaign committee funded exclusively by Chevron and several out-of-state oil companies in conjunction with the California Chamber of Commerce, supported election of ten business-friendly, moderate Democrats, the group here referred to as '*corporados*' who then played a pivotal role in forcing de León to abandon core provisions of SB 350.[295]

The rise of moderates in California's Legislature resulted in part from voter approval of ballot measures that revised primaries to allow the top two vote getters to compete in general elections (in contrast to traditional party-based affiliation runoffs of the top winners).[296] In a state long dominated by Democrats, the top two approaches provided a critical entry point for corporate expenditures unleashed by Citizens United and parallel rulings to alter election outcomes by pitting progressives against moderate Democrats with an immediate and unmistakable effect. "Under the old system, these moderates would never have made it to the November ballot..."[297] By 2012 and 2014 staff inside the capitol witnessed a shift in floor votes based on the emergence of the *corporados*. The ascendance of corporate money over party leadership signaled the decline of traditional allies – environmentalists, teachers, nurses, trial lawyers and others often defined by social interests, especially the middle, poor and working classes.

Devising a strategy whereby enough votes can be patched together to move legislation through committees to the floor and the Governor's desk, however, has often been a much different task for many corporations in the place called California – directed at creating votes they can count on. Additional dividends on the investment by petroleum and allied interests yielded modified term limits that allowed for Assembly members to serve for a maximum of 12 years, in contrast to older provisions limiting them to 6 years. As the primary objective for many corporate lobbyists involved keeping progressive laws from descending on their clients, in the summer of 2010 this objective was facilitated by passage of the Top Two Primaries Act.

In California Republicans who set out to destroy their own party by waging wars on Latinos, gays, women, and unions, made the corporate lobbyists job increasingly difficult. With the creation of a new electoral model based on selecting the top two candidates receiving the most primary votes as competitors for the general election, the corporate lobby task eased greatly, now to only favor the moderate, more business friendly candidate's corporate campaign expenditures fostered for many electoral races, in the general election. As one professor of law noted, "Sophisticated, well-funded special interests are playing a long game. It makes a lot of sense to invest early in people who are attuned to your needs and are in position to vote your way when the time comes."[298]

Even more attractive, corporations do not have to win a majority in either the Assembly or the Senate. An electoral calculus based on "assisting" a small number of *corporados* would constitute sufficient votes to block progressive climate; and other legislation threatening the corporate lobby's business-as-usual agenda. As SB 350 illustrated, corporations could engage in less adversarial conflicts over climate change by stripping away specific provisions rather than having to defeat an entire measure outright. By 2015, the corporate lobby's success with assuring the victory of ten *corporados* in the Assembly was nothing short of a coup d'état.

Financing also yielded yet another payoff: shaping a more sweeping means by which to defeat further intrusions of law on the *petroleros*. Part of the messaging used by the oil companies during the summer campaign against SB 350 involved a familiar theme: jobs versus the environment. Various legislators incorporated the industry line into their own line pressing the need to balance both issues. One recently elected legislator framed the anomaly as a classic example of political compromise, "I'm trying to make sure the well-being of our poorest communities is not sacrificed for the sake of clean air. I should not have to choose between good jobs and clean air for my constituents. We deserve both."[299]

For *petroleros*, stripping away a central provision of the proposed climate law served as a classic example of political compromise. Simply slowing down or making otherwise decisive efforts to dismantle fossil fuels more-vague served as at least a temporary win, perhaps until the opportunities of a new election. From the perspective of scientists tracking the advance of fossil-fuel-induced disasters, the time for delays and incremental changes had lapsed.

Winners & Losers

Of course, the messaging by the *petroleros* that jobs – especially among the poorest workers – would be lost if one moved too quickly toward renewables was based on specious arguments. During the prior year, a group of researchers at Stanford University devised a plan by which California could fully eliminate its use of fossil fuels in transportation, electric power, industry, heating and cooling energy needs by 2050. Furthermore, the plan "would create a net gain, after fossil-fuel and nuclear energy job losses are accounted for, of about 220,000 manufacturing, installation and technology construction and operations jobs. On top of that, the state would reap net earnings from those jobs of about $12 billion annually."[300] The Stanford study was but one of various technical discussions focusing on moving to a post-petroleum world.[301]

What the *petroleros did* have correctly in their political campaign was tapping into the public's uneasy sense of a plan fomented by *los politicos* in Sacramento. As a sage labor organizer observed, the architects of SB 350 unnecessarily sowed the seeds of discontent by ignoring an obvious pitfall: what would happen to those workers tied to fossil fuels and associated industries?[302] Adding legal provisions to address the fate of workers in refineries, automobile sales and maintenance shops, chemical plants, and elsewhere certainly required a more complex plan; the governor, however, possessed a stable of skilled consultants. In certain legislative districts such as Martinez and Benicia, having a disposition supportive of large corporations and ignoring the economic consequences for local communities created potential for turning a constituency otherwise sensitive to the issues of fossil-fueled hazards towards corporate-sponsored candidates. Worse still, for other refinery locations, such as Richmond, ignoring the needs of labor eroded support in a stronghold for progressive Democrats.

As would be demonstrated in the coming months, political miscalculations of this character had been repeated across America with devastating consequences. The corporate-financed narrative to combat measures such as SB 350 was not without its own set of problems. Extensive polling found that two-thirds of California's likely voters consistently and strongly supported regulations to reduce greenhouse gas emissions. Moreover, the same polling data found a plurality of supporters stated that actions to reduce global warming would lead to more jobs (44%), less than a third saying the actions would have no effect on job numbers (30%), and just 14% replying that the result would be fewer jobs.[303] Polling data frequently disguises unexamined premises and the same held true for the issue of jobs versus the environment.

If one of the premises embedded in images and messaging by *petroleros* was that job creation and the economy should be left to private sector forces, its corollary was doubly emphatic: In no instance should economic decisions be left to the public to decide. The state's history over the last century suggests that the public's promotion of economic winners has played an often pivotal role for the disparate major state economic sectors (e.g., biomedical/biotechnology, agriculture, computers/ software, alternative energy). Taxpayers frequently fronted essential educational research support, physical and virtual infrastructure, tax breaks, and subsidies for industry. The very strong evidence points to the fact that the public has been at the forefront in providing the foundations for later economic winners.

The elimination of losers, while more controversial, suggests a different narrative than one where some industries simply fail as a result of market forces. Especially in recent decades, many products first identified by public-interest advocates as posing hazards were subsequently eliminated by active campaigns. In addition to infamous 'goods' such as tobacco, lead and pesticides, citizens actively supported limiting toxic substances detected in furnishings, flooring, construction materials, automobile components, jewelry, packaging materials, art supplies, electronic equipment, cosmetics, clothing, processed foods, and numerous consumer products. While virtually each of these decisions confronted private sector push-back, the state has been led increasingly by a public exerting substantial control over the shape and direction of the economy. Interestingly, the elimination of these bad actors, in many instances originated with public support for regulatory agencies clearing the way for cleaner innovations and alternatives by imposing costs and more stringent regulations on older, dirtier industries.

The push-back by the corporate lobby has also characterized most every attempt to eliminate the losers supported by dominant economic interests. The hyperbole that any restrictions imposed by the public via the exercise of their democratic rights will result in a loss of jobs, worsen the business climate, drive innovations to other states, or permanently damage the state economy has been a constant refrain of the corporate lobby. In many instances voters have rejected the notion of a falling sky when their government acts to force products out of the economy - especially where the dangers have been well-documented. While everyone once appeared to have a cigarette dangling from their lips, we no longer think about tobacco as providing a positive contribution to society, even if there is a corporate lobbyist prepared to extol its virtues.

The promise posed by a citizenry actively exercising its democratic rights over their economy is the threat that *petroleros* may suddenly awaken to find themselves among the walking dead. Within the context of changed election laws (e.g., "top two" method for electing candidates[304]), enhanced corporate expenditures disguised as free speech (e.g., Citizens United),[305] and an expanded reach of the corporate lobby to elect *corporados* as representatives, the picture might appear bleak for the public interest lobby. Yet, this sketch too easily dismisses a more subtle political shift: popular discontent over a world divided between haves and have-nots, a broadening coalition of public interest groups.

Broadening Alliances

The dynamics of politics meant that possibilities also existed to reverse whatever advances were achieved by public advocates and their public interest allies. After every public interest success, corporate lobbyists would pose challenges to agency regulatory hearings, introduce legislation to reverse enacted measures, file judicial appeals, sponsor federal law to preempt California's statutes, and/or set in motion so-called international trade "agreements," to erode democratic rights over a privatized economy. On the political front, the *petroleros* could be expected to more firmly cement their relationship and control over local, statewide, and congressional offices.

The considerable attention drawn by measures such as SB 350 distracted the media from other proposed statutes of substantial importance, not the least of which was a little noticed one supported by a lesser known environmental organization - the California Environmental Justice Alliance. The Alliance organized in the early 2000s, held a large meeting - its *Congreso* - during August, 2015.[306] It included dozens of organizations from across the state, many of these smaller community groups, focused on what was perhaps the leading edge of environmental organizing across the nation - the role of environmental justice.

A bill supported by the Alliance relating to greenhouse gases was among the measures enacted at the close of the legislative session.[307] Over the last decade the environmental justice movement had succeeded in bringing more agents of communities of color into state governmental bodies, including the state's environmental programs. Enlarging representation on local boards and state agencies, these groups have gradually accumulated a power rivaling much larger environmental organizations generally lacking an essential feature of the Alliance and its partners: the ability to mobilize and sustain political action by large numbers, especially among the poor and communities of color.

After attending the Alliance's Congreso, Bill Magavern commented on its impressive display, particularly for such a young organization, bringing together so many groups from across California. Unlike staid gatherings of older environmentalists from years past, the Congreso was visually striking. In place of sessions dominated by Anglos reflecting issues from an earlier era, the Congreso included many younger participants. The new face of diverse communities heralded a new energy dedicated to combining a commitment to both social justice and environmental issues too long neglected by wilderness/conservation preservation organizations. The Alliance, in gaining greater representation inside California's bureaucracy, moved far beyond a narrow achievement for constricted self-interest to spawn a broad-based victory for a network of community-based groups.

More than simply stewarding another bill into law, the multi-faceted organization with a reach into regional neighborhoods now provided push back against precisely the corporate machinery that so frequently defeated communities exposed to toxic wastes, refinery emissions, polluted waters, contaminated air, elevated illness rates, occupational injuries, and other damages to public and community health. The Alliance and its partners now possessed the wherewithal to challenge the position of *corporados* who regularly characterized efforts to dismantle fossil-fuels as a threat to jobs, the economy and their allies in corporate lobby.

Alternatives to Market Solutions

During the summer of 2015 some seventy-nine organizations representing many dozens of communities across the state gathered in Sacramento to discuss new approaches addressing a broad range of social, political and environmental issues. Many attending had long been at the forefront of community-level actions. Their purpose was to address "Climate change as one of the biggest issues facing low-income communities and communities of color in California and across the globe. Despite being an international leader on climate, many of our policies fail to address the needs of communities who are already bearing the burden of dirty fossil fuels and who will be hit first and worst by climate change."[308]

The Alliance's Sacramento meeting was far more than a statement of intent. Acknowledging the inspiration by many others, working locally against dirty power plants and fracking, their purpose involved bridging the many isolated struggles of individual activists into a larger, more enduring organization. Panelists Antonio Diaz (People Organizing to Demand Environmental and Economic Rights); Juan Flores with the Center on Race, Poverty and the Environment (CRPE); Christine Cordero with the Center for Story-Based Strategy (on Climate); Penny Newman with the Center for Community Action; Diane Takvorian along with Carolina Martinez, Jorgé Gonzalez and Tuan Luu representing the Environmental Health Coalition; Mari Rose Taruc of the Asian Pacific Environmental Network (APEN) and Elma del Aguila of Central Coast Alliance United for a Sustainable Economy (CAUSE) said, in a combined statement of mission: "Our heartaches drive our passions that drive our innovations... [so the] tragedies we experience in our valley communities, to our coasts, to our homelands, are not repeated."[309]

Their shared agenda recognized that a key to successfully achieving major changes to climate policy involved building on the "leadership of communities directly impacted by the causes and consequences of climate change." Among the items contained in the vision statement on the Alliance's website were those placing equity at the center of the climate debate, as a means for ensuring that environmental justice would be a priority in the formulation of climate laws. Moreover, the Alliance noted its approach was not merely to provide principles, but rested on a tradition of democratic representation and action.

Distinguishing this gathering from many of the established, wealthy environmental organizations holding sway in D.C. was a tacit, if not explicit, rejection of remaining confined to existing political relationships. The Alliance's many partners challenged the silent premise that the public would receive good things from a political structure dominated by corporate lobbyists. The Alliance's approach involved many issues, but perhaps most strikingly was its take on the state's premier climate change law. "We believe that cap and trade is destructive to environmental justice communities and we want to fight for alternatives to market systems that continue to oppress our communities."[310]

As Congreso speakers assembled on the steps of the state capitol to encourage public interest allies to fight against fossil-fueled disasters across the state, like-minded legislative staff inside the capitol were engaged in a parallel endeavor. The political quest was not solely a critique of the pollution trading scheme. The Alliance pursued a blend of positive approaches, including support for both expanded regulatory laws and devising support for advancing clean energy projects and a just transition for the many workers tied to an expiring industry.

Even as the Alliance and its partners conversed about tactics and strategies for the next legislative session, California's political terrain was shifting. Within the next year, the context surrounding everything public interest advocates had worked to achieve over the past five decades would confront a dramatically altered political context. The war that *petroleros* and their corporate allies had waged on California was entering a new phase.

CHAPTER 16

The Pontiff, Politicians, and Paris

It was vintage Arnold Schwarzenegger. "I don't give a damn if you believe in climate change." The message was delivered via Twitter, yet everyone could imagine hearing the unmistakable voice of California's former governor. Even though Arnold was only an observer at the Paris meetings discussing a global climate treaty his words captured an essential political shift occurring across the world. Arguing that fossil fuels accounted for tremendous damages especially in terms of public health, the edict called on followers to join him in advancing "a smarter, cleaner, healthier, more profitable energy future."[311]

Schwartzenegger's December demand that the public recognize the end of fossil fuels marked a year where his successor, Governor Jerry Brown, presented a detailed plan in January to dramatically reduce the state's uses of fossil fuels. By September, much attention focused on battles surrounding legislation that would make permanent provisions of law to both reduce fossil fuel use and promote energy conservation. California conflicts over fossil fuels during 2015, however, were more than simply an argument over technical details. Embedded in the battles extending from California to France was a more profound conflict centering on citizen rights versus the rights of corporations.

Technology & Markets

As Governor Schwarzenegger was making the case for faith in market solutions combined with California's environmental laws, his successor, Governor Jerry Brown was voicing a similar missive at another meeting across Paris. His message to a multitude of attendees representing cities and states was equally to the point: California possessed many solutions to a worsening climate crisis. The evening celebration of California's policy innovations at the posh hotel, however, was punctuated with the unscripted protest by community-based organizers from the Golden State, including a youth organizer, Rossmery Zayas, from Los Angeles. Brown was confronted by a group of citizens whose trip focused on delivering a clear message of dissent:

"We're from California: Let us tell you the truth about what's happening in our communities."[312] In representing a decades-old California public interest group, Communities for a Better Environment, Rossmery Zayas was part of a coalition of globally-linked community activists at the Paris climate meetings. Among the central issues at the heart of the critique of those talks was the approach that both Governors Brown and Schwarzenegger advanced as an export model law for solving climate change: a program called cap-and-trade.[313]Joining Zayas' protestations were others, including representatives from Idle No More-Solidarity East Bay, whose members stood directly in front of the governor shouting, "Richmond, California says 'No' to REDD! No' to evicting indigenous people from their forests: 'No' to poisoning my community!"[314] The chant, joined by others in the room, illuminated what protesters regarded as a deeply flawed piece of pollution trading. REDD (Reducing Emissions from Deforestation and Forest Degradation) was a collaboration of 29 states, that many supporters of cap-and-trade hoped would serve as a pivotal piece in the trading of pollution credits for "preservation" of forests elsewhere. For Rossmery Zayas and others from California, allowing refineries and others to engage in pollution trades meant that communities in Richmond, Wilmington, Carson and elsewhere around the state would continue to be subjected to hazardous emissions.[315] A clearly flustered Governor Brown was quickly escorted to an exit by organizers of the conference.

While the media virtually ignored the notable fact that an organized group of climate activists had traveled a great distance to confront California's Governor in what was essentially his only public speaking engagement, Brown was clearly ruffled by the confrontation.[316] California pollution trading program, especially features allowing those owning polluting refineries to make an exchange based on a commitment to preserve distant forests, struck many as an environmental injustice. The legal details of this exchange cast doubt on basic premises: including whether forests were actually being preserved, as well as the health impacts affecting those living near polluting industries. Public challenge to the Governor's support of cap-and-trade was hardly new.

Indeed, months before arriving in Paris, Governor Brown had tried to field an even more fundamental interrogation of the Global Warming Solutions Act authors. This citizen to corporate conflict emerged most visibly with a statement issued by a person who had never before played a role in California politics. Just as the capital was reaching that point in the year when it would break for its usual summer recess, one of the world's foremost religious leaders, Pope Francis, issued a 170-page statement that news sources immediately reported as focused on climate change. In fact, the Pope framed his discussion in terms of an unequal social order fostering a climate crisis threatening the survival of humanity.[317]

The Pope's message was wide-ranging as well as specific, identifying both negative and positive issues relating to climate change. Especially striking was the pontiff's critique of one particular item. Pope Francis' message could not have been more explicit: cap-and-trade was a bad policy, a diversionary tactic to benefit the wealthy while avoiding the imperative of fundamental changes necessary to save the earth and humanity.[318]

> "The strategy of buying and selling 'carbon credits' can lead to a new form of speculation which would not help reduce the emission of polluting gases worldwide," the Pope wrote. "This system seems to provide a quick and easy solution under the guise of a certain commitment to the environment. But in no way does it allow for the radical change which present circumstances require.

> Rather, it may simply become a ploy which permits maintaining the excessive consumption of some countries and sectors."

If the Pope's message was lost on most legislators and staff, the statement had clearly gained the attention of the capitol's most prominent Jesuit, Governor Jerry Brown. Within weeks Governor Brown flew to Rome to attend a meeting with the Pope along with dozens of officials from around the world. Governor Brown was clearly a leader among those confronting the global climate crisis. It was also evident that Brown sensed he was holding onto contradictory positions.

In discussions with the press, the Governor insisted that "cap and trade can be part of a very imaginative and aggressive program".[319] The next day the press carried a further explanation from Brown; "California has a uniquely constructed cap and trade. It is very tightly regulated and it is not the only thing. I get the impression that [Pope Francis] thinks a market solution is not enough. We have a renewable energy standard; building standards; we have research and development, subsidized electric cars."[320]

Governor Brown's American Mythology

While dismissing the not-so-small matter of allowing corporations to purchase rights to pollute, the Governor acknowledged the "fierce opposition and blind inertia" of "well financed climate change skeptics" undermining more decisive efforts to address the climate crisis.[321] Indeed, the Governor seemingly joined the Pope in linking the climate crisis with a dysfunctional capitalism. "We have very powerful opposition that, in at least my country," Brown stated, "spends billions on trying to keep from office people such as yourselves and elect troglodytes and other deniers of the obvious science."[322]

"California is now deriving 25% of its energy from renewable sources and has the "most efficient" buildings in the U.S., as well as 40% of the country's electric cars," he stated. "But we are not stopping there," adding that he wanted renewable energy to reach 50% and gasoline use in cars and trucks to drop by 50% in 15 years."[323] Even in defending his legislative proposal, supported by nine of the Legislature's most recent leaders, Brown spoke with an ambivalence that echoed many across the state, "[Oil companies] have a product that is highly destructive, while highly valuable at the same time: And we are trying to work out the right policies ...We're going to intensify our efforts to lower carbon fuels and lower carbon pollution, now and into the future." [324] The problem embedded in Brown's spoken words is captured by recognizing oil companies as holders of a product that is simultaneously very valuable and very destructive. His thinking is a part of the American mythology that he spoke of years earlier.

"In the 60s, there was a sense of reform in the air....We would transcend mere profit. Subsequent years brought about a growing skepticism that's still with us. So there was a transition from a belief in government and public interest to this powerful doctrine that the market, buying and selling, is the principle that will make everything work at the end of the day. That's the dominant ideology that we live with in America today. That's our new religion. That's our mythology." [325]

Statement to the Vatican conference went even further, noting that the global goal would require a "revolution" in the use of fossil fuels. "We are going to have to set a clear goal," Brown told a crowd of mayors and public officials from around the world. "And that goal is almost unimaginable. One-third of the oil that we know exists as reserves can never be taken out of the ground. Fifty percent of the gas can never be used, over 90 percent of the coal. Now, that is a revolution."[326] Skeptics among the press noted that if indeed the Governor intended to alter the course of America's third-largest oil producing state, Brown would have to radically rewrite a posture of general support for its oil production.[327]

Added to such skepticism were many environmental/community organizations: struggling to reverse the Governor's *laissez-faire* attitude toward fracking. The skepticism regarding the California Governor's contradictory stances towards fossil fuels was echoed by others in his administration. Mary Nichols, for example, stated, "California is showing the world how to throw off the shackles of fossil fuel dependency. No longer must economic growth result in smokestacks and pollution."[328] Secretary Nichols' statements revealed one of the recurring problems with approaching the climate crisis as a largely technological project. The Pope, by contrast, presented a critical perspective on "models of production and consumption," and the larger context guiding technology. Found in Naomi Oreskes' introduction, "The pope addresses head-on our prevailing economic practices and the modes of thought that insist – despite considerable evidence to the contrary – that we just need to let markets do their "magic."[329]

By the summer of 2015, discussions of global climate change were beginning to take on a different character. The public, for one, appeared to be losing interest in energy company-sponsored denials. Perhaps it was a growing realization that the crisis was already upon us? While news reports cautioned that the latest storm, drought, fire, flood, record temperature or other calamitous weather event was not necessarily a result of climate change, everyday conversations made the connection. The initial steady flow was now becoming a raging flood of literature, scientific findings and reports. Seemingly no day passed without an update on a vanishing species, coral destruction, or habitat loss. The recorded march of disappearance of lakes, streams, and aquifers was joined with notices describing the loss of mountain snowpacks, glaciers, and ice shelves.

A Misplaced Faith in Markets

The conversation was not simply passive. If the public had not fully awakened to the broader destruction wrought by fossil fuels, there was incipient recognition that something actually had to be done about the prime culprit. Conservative institutions of international finance acknowledged that the fossil fuel era was drawing to a close.

A 2015 report by the International Monetary Fund joined increasing evidence underscoring the imperative to dismantle the fossil fuels complex. The report noted that immediate end of government subsidies would yield positive benefits for people around the planet. Were subsidies eliminated that year, it would raise government global revenues by $2.9 trillion, cut global CO_2 emissions by more than 20 percent and reduce the estimated one million premature deaths from air pollution by more than half. They would also raise "global economic welfare" by $1.8 trillion, or 2.2 percent of gross domestic product.[330]

British economist, Nicholas Stern, author of the U.K. government's influential 2006 review on the economics of climate change, called the 2015 IMF analysis "very important," noting it "shatters the myth that fossil fuels are cheap by showing just how huge their real costs are." Stern described calculations as a "conservative" accounting of actual environmental costs: "A more complete estimate of the costs due to climate change would show the implicit subsidies for fossil fuels are much bigger even than this report suggests." Even the IMF critique of fossil fuel subsidies did not capture the growing evidence of negative consequences surrounding their burning. Within California, the blossoming of alternatives had virtually none of the subsidies extended to fossil fuels.

Several major related facets of fossil fuels represented a larger, toxics-based- economy. One of these aspects includes an extensive agricultural complex built on petrochemicals and energy-intensive inputs. Energy companies are frequently characterized as resisting conversion of retail or wholesale energy to safer alternatives. Added to the toxic economy is a vast array of consumer products derived from fossil fuels. Transcending each of these facets is a global financial sector perpetuating fossil- fueled economics. The manufacture, transport, and disposal of fuels constituted yet another crisis, such as the damages resulting from the massive pollution of oceans by plastics debris.

The Politics of Problems, Framing Solutions

In 2015 one of the world's most influential religious leaders urged more than a billion faithful to care for a too long neglected Earth. More than constant nurture, Pope Francis called for action against the principal threat identified by a single word: capitalism. In preparing his encyclical, the Pope gathered scientists from around the world to summarize their analysis of climate change and the disaster confronting the world's populations. As a consequence, the 170 page treatise reflected Pope Francis' early training in chemistry, which added an interesting depth to what might otherwise have been an ethereal collection of moral edicts.

Paradoxically it was this global figure, operating outside the world of California politics, who lead with an ethical, moral phrasing that is so often incompatible with how politics is engaged at the capitol. The papal message was both simple and devastating to those at work designing the technocratic program for trading pollution credits; capitalism represented a tyranny threatening both democracy and the survival of life on this planet. In the secular political world, the Vatican dicta would normally go unnoticed. In 2015, however, California's Governor, a former Jesuit priest-in-training, was struggling with roles that clashed throughout his political career. Growing up in the household of another governor, Edmund G. Brown, Jr. became a consummate politician. Crafting pragmatic deals was second nature. His masterful persona clashed with his training of doing the right thing as the leader for one of the world's major political entities.

Jerry Brown's struggle reflected virtually the same tension confronting tens of millions across California. On one hand, vast numbers of us pursued lifestyles at odds with the approaching crises. At the same time, repeated polling spanning many decades found large numbers indeed, frequent majorities confirmed numerous academic studies–moneyed interests had fundamentally corrupted everything from city hall to the halls of Congress while suppressing citizen activism to recast an inherently hazardous economy. The Pope may have jump started a novel undertaking: orchestrating a political campaign for elected leaders to take on the fossil fuel industry. The Vatican's conference in July 2015 was tactically thoughtful and purposeful. Rather than simply presenting a moral edict, the Vatican gathered political leaders from around the world to demonstrate the multiplicity of ways to begin dismantling the fossil fuel complex.

The Pontiff also signaled that large and powerful alliances already existed that could be brought together to move the economy. Previously, the California religious community occupied an isolated and largely irrelevant role in politics. Now, marshalling scientific information and a multiplicity of effective global initiatives (from Danish citizens purchasing wind energy at a long-term profit to the UK refusal to subsidize fracking) served as a forum to advance what seemingly everyone else had given up on: the power of the public to control and redefine the economic path of the state away from a doomsday machine.

The feasibility of advancing an economy no longer reliant on the burning of toxic substances was sufficiently demonstrated that various political entities around the world had embarked on aggressive programs to exit the fossil fueled era. The critical obstacles were largely, if not wholly deployed by those awaiting so-called market solutions while denying the rights and political responsibilities of citizens everywhere to control an out-of-control economy. At the global climate meetings, in Paris, Governor Brown and his entourage of agency directors, political leaders, regional and city staff from around the state united to present a common theme: the world could look to California for guidance about what to do about the climate crisis, at the close of 2015. It was a victory lap celebrating California laws and silently articulating what others around the globe already recognized: U.S. national climate policy was a disaster!

While many of those Californians attending the Paris meetings were well-versed in the decades-long and multifaceted laws and regulations laying the foundations for State success, the larger message drowned out the experience of flexibility. Among the Governor's entourage to Paris Tony Earley, the chief executive officer of the parent company of Pacific Gas and Electric had agreed to travel at the Governor's request because Jerry Brown's message resonated with him. "By and large, California has developed a very flexible model going forward, put in place programs like cap and trade, set aggressive goals for renewables and recognized that companies need to be able to thrive in this environment."[331] 'Flexibility' served as a code word understood as part of a 'demand driven' approach with emphasis on market mechanisms.

The conflict between the Pope and the Governor, while unresolved, would continue to resurface in Paris and beyond. Would decisions about a rapidly deteriorating global environment accommodate the economically powerful and the markets serving their interests, or prospective victims in the middle and lower classes? Largely absent from the discussion was an agenda aimed at achieving a simple imperative: a global plan of action for dismantling fossil fuels while building alternatives. Without a clear resolution of the problems cited by the Pope between markets and the Earth, the Paris agenda continued along the trajectory of an unchallenged premise recognized years before by Governor Brown, the myth of markets.

CHAPTER 17

Buying Our Way Out

When "you can simply buy your way out of any legal requirements to lessen emissions, this law has become nothing more than a joke." Throughout the fall of 2015, interests from across California lined up to take their share of prospective dollars accumulating from the trading of emission permits from the Solutions Act. For the chief Senate environmental adviser, Kip Lipper, it was déjà vu all over again.

Whenever new streams of revenue appeared at the capitol, lobbyists and legislators gathered in a ritual insiders referred to as "hogs at the feeding trough"; a comparison, no doubt, treated hogs unfairly. Distributing of emission revenues had been postponed before the close of 2015, due to both the rapidly expanding universe of claims and a lack of a comprehensive plan for prioritizing the best projects. While the law surrounding the Solutions Act and court cases regarding the legal use of fees provided a degree of clarity, political pressures made the exercise a tumult of competing interests. The legal architecture suggested that a hierarchy of expenditures should logically benefit those projects offering the greatest reduction of hazardous climate emissions.

While the "buying our way out" approach to toxic emissions fostered numerous isolated projects, it did little to displace larger and more damaging fossil fuel *sources.* To take but one example, several agricultural projects were designed around the theme of recycling of food and green wastes to improve soils. As a way to sequester carbon while building soils and reducing fertilizers, tillage, and irrigation, the projects emphasized the usefulness of co-benefits. Like earlier recycling projects, such expenditures did little to alter a basic premise of California's agriculture – the massive use of fossil fuels.

The widespread pumping of ground waters, the methane releases from animal feedlots, the intensive energy costs of transportation, processing of foods, harvesting of crops – all such activities indicated the need to fundamentally restructure the state's agriculture to properly address climate emissions. In this context, the expenditure of cap and trade money for vague and uncertain controls over dairy methane emissions neglected urgent action measures necessary across the entire structure of agriculture. Proposals to simply *examine* healthy soils or dairy cows posed the distinct possibility that the public, as well as their legislators, would check the box for agriculture without having addressed a more basic threat: an agribusiness complex in which the largest energy consumption and emission sources remained fugitive.

The bullet train project, pushed to the head of the line for claiming cap and trade auction proceeds paralleled a prior political calculus justifying early water projects. As staff constructed a tortured rationale for higher ranking, few serious analysts were convinced of its merits. Indeed, back-of-the-envelope calculations surrounding transportation priorities to address climate change threats – pointed to massive energy savings by investments promoting an electrified grid of buses and light rail to serve dense urban populations on a daily basis in the state's major urban hubs instead of catering to a much smaller and more affluent clientele traveling across the state by bullet train.

Many practiced negotiators recognized the futility of identifying a perfect hierarchy of projects since everyone involved could readily argue their case for a different metric moving their favoritet to the top ranking. Yet, picking projects according to a frenzied competition surely was not the answer. The chaos distracted everyone from the larger problem of dismantling the fossil-fueled economy. For Kip Lipper, any mention of California's 'Solution' released a flood of frustration. "It is no longer an environment program; it is nothing more than a funding program."

In Paris, the meetings have ended and the Governor's entourage, along with legislators, lobbyists, and others are returning to the Golden

State. In Sacramento, At day's end, Kip is walking away from the capitol shaking his head, still incredulous about the slow-motion train wreck following in the wake of the Global Warming Solutions Act. "People continue to ask me why I even concern myself with this legislation." As we walked along, Kip's preoccupation reflected what regularly occurs among professional staff. Often, even more than legislators whose names appear on the cover of proposed laws, staff such as Kip Lipper feel a personal responsibility for the laws appearing in the blue volumes of every legislative office in the capitol. When the result is bad law, despite great effort it is common for professionals to feel an even greater sense of outrage.

"I am," Kip explains, "concerned precisely because it [the Solutions Act] continues to have impacts not merely here in California, but beyond. And we now have 120 legislators [in the Senate and Assembly], who see it as a source of money for local projects." Kip next mentions where an infamous refinery in Wilmington, California purchased 500 million acres of forest land in Michigan to count against their emissions reduction under cap-and-trade. "Where is the environmental benefit in that?" As several of his former colleagues could attest, Kip possessed an intimate knowledge of how laws intended to preserve ancient forests had become undermined to the point where leading scientists no longer recognized their increasingly illusive environmental benefit.[332]

Among several mainstream environmental groups, a key source of support for cap-and-trade was rooted in the vast quantities of carbon stored in the trees and soils, along with the potential for forests to absorb CO_2. By maintaining sequestered carbon dioxide in forests, the stockpile of woodlands are converted into offset credits, then sold to those prepared to pay others to maintain healthy areas, as a trade for pollution elsewhere. Money generated as auction credits is invested, ostensibly into something that reduces carbon and improves the lives of local communities.

From a technical perspective, this use of forests posed problems including trades flooding the market with cheap offsets that lower the carbon price and further reduce incentives for industries to limit their use of fossil fuels. For Kip, the problems associated with the use of forests as a 'market mechanism' set in motion not merely technical issues; rather, this use served as a device effectively offering corporations a chance to meet obligations without actually reducing their own emissions. Certain of Kip's colleagues in the Legislature employed a more simple reference for the use of forests in cap-and-trade: fraud.

For professional staffers who interact with anyone living in the shadow of many California refineries, the answer is obvious. The benefit for neighborhoods holding California's largest sources of greenhouse gases and breathing contaminated air while the same refinery calculates credits for preserving a distant, pristine forest are an illusion: "And the cap? The truth is that the Solutions' caps are largely arbitrary and unenforceable. If you asked the members about how cap and trade works, they would not be able to tell you. They only want to know if they can fund a favorite project from the proceeds of this act,"

Within days of our walk, a group of local environmental activists illustrated the final, perhaps fatal flaw embedded in the Solutions Act. It was another version of the same question raised by Kip over the last decade: was the purpose of the Solutions Act to engage in trading or to eliminate the release of inherently hazardous emissions? While Schwarzenegger and many moderate legislators advanced 'trading' as the most efficient way to achieve an orderly reduction of greenhouse gases, a decade later cracks were appearing in the edifice of California's Solution.

The Market versus Citizens' Rights

The focal point of these activists concerned rules governing the air emissions from petroleum refineries in San Francisco. At its December 2015 meeting, the executive officer of the Bay Area Pollution Control Group explained that it was struggling about how to erect a limit or cap on refinery emissions. Noting district review of hundreds of comments representing sharply divided perspectives on *what to do* to limit emissions threats to public health of surrounding communities as well as the global climate, the executive officer concluded what should have been astonishing to everyone responsible for unleashing the California Solution. "It's doubtful the air district has the legal power to limit greenhouse gas emissions, because the state has the authority to do so with a cap-and-trade system, in which some industries buy pollution credits."[333]

Essentially unreported in mainstream media, the event outraged community activists who had cautioned against the use of market mechanisms as a device to address the ultimate hazard. If California represented successes for the rest of the world about how to lessen its reliance on fossil fuels, it also clung to notable failures. By 2015, petroleum companies expressed a reluctant willingness to negotiate cap-and-trade parameters. Ideally, there would be no fees. But, the promise of free credits and the offset system were far more inviting.

First, for nearly a decade the Global Warming Solutions Act delayed more effective and more decisive actions, including its failure to immediately restrict emissions of additional greenhouse gases such as methane. Second, 'Solutions' moved California into a regime of market mechanisms fraught with a lack of clarity about the allocation of free credits, the manipulation of prices, questions of legal jurisdiction, and as to when the program would finally impose sufficient disincentives to encourage a change to clean energy. Third, despite a series of laws mandating specific changes to swiftly address most egregious problems, Solutions now served as an obstacle to direct regulatory actions. Placing even greater reliance on pollution trading as a device for addressing emissions did not necessarily translate to stopping, slowing or even reducing dangerous emissions.

Fourth, the ambiguous language allowed agriculture to remain largely unregulated with respect to an overuse of fossil fuels in every facet of activities including planting and cultivation practices, irrigation, harvesting, processing, transportation, and marketing. Subsidizing a petroleum-intensive, massively polluting, and public health damaging, occupationally hazardous industry represented a massive and growing cost to taxpayers. In place of regulatory scrutiny and action, the Solutions Act offered a world of trading opportunities.

Fifth, pollution trading displaced other innovative policies and approaches. The most visible illustration occurred with Schwarzenegger's firing of the chief Air Board executive officer for pursuing direct regulatory actions against automobile companies. This single example, however, is but a part of the fact that among a suite of other laws from an earlier era, Solutions undermined the resources and budgets to advance a strict regulatory approach to alter the economy. An abundance of personnel dedicated to the state trading scheme fostered a locus in which fewer resources were available to facilitate clean energy projects.

Sixth, California, working in its capacity as a world leader on environmental policy, undermined the regulatory approach contained in a suite of laws set to address global climate disruptions by forwarding pollution trading as primary for use by other cities and states around the globe. California's 2007 pollution trading law obscures a fossil fueled economy built on inherent hazards involved in the extracting, processing, transporting and combusting of toxic substances. Yet, even these criticisms did not restore what was most lacking everywhere: a democratic infrastructure to ably challenge the influence and power of corporations.

Eyes on the Prize

Conversations with Air Board staff reflected a common perception among many inside the capitol: public workers performed outstanding service to the state. The many dozens of professionals laboring on California's Solutions Act provided the wherewithal for what was an open secret: few nations in the world possessed a comparable group of excellent public servants. This enviable record of protecting public health, the environment, and a thriving economy was anchored in a public infrastructure built by its citizens over many decades. In conversations I had been party to over years, involving dozens of professionals across a plethora of agencies, it was evident that in major instances excellent staff did their best to work within the context of deeply flawed programs. Paralleling experiments in which the participants were sometimes unaware of what they were recreating, where too often the basic premises went unquestioned.

A conversation with a senior staff member of the Air Board in 2016 confirmed the longstanding purposes of the state's principal climate laws as lost to the larger architecture of emissions trading. It was a situation in which the State's decisive direction of the economy had become subordinated. During our conversation, professional Air Board staff focused on a complex world of trading: encryption security, and transparent policies for non-leakage. In summarizing the purpose of the program, a refrain that characterized the Solutions Act was that it provides for a greater efficiency to address emissions than could be achieved via strict regulatory measures. Almost as an aside, was acknowledgement that the heart of the Solutions Act, pollution trading, unlike many other components of California's climate laws, did not enable the state directly and decisively to restructure the economy: But why not?

The scientific facts compelling the passage of California's landmark climate law in 2006 have only grown dramatically more compelling. Whatever efficiencies might be afforded to a small group of energy corporations, the public now faces a scenario ranging between grim and catastrophic. By the summer of 2016, elected leaders received more news that all was not well with California's Solution Act. Amidst a delayed distribution of cap-and-trade revenues from the previous budget year (2015/16), the final auction of the fiscal year witnessed a precipitous drop in revenues. With the first three auctions having yielded approximately $1.8 billion, the fourth auction expected to raise roughly $600 million totaled $10 million or slightly less than two percent of what had been anticipated.[334]

While the ensuing debate puzzled over whether this was a one-time aberration, the Legislature's fiscal analysts noted a more troubling legal question on the horizon: Were cap-and-trade revenues going to abruptly halt in 2020 due to drafting and legal errors contained in the original Solutions Act? As reported in the press, "...a policy analyst for the Legislative Analyst's Office said the volatility in this month's auction could be from skeptical buyers watching a lawsuit filed by the California Chamber of Commerce that contends the cap-and-trade program amounts to a tax that was never authorized through a required two-thirds vote in the Legislature. The cap-and-trade program extends only until 2020, leaving some statutory uncertainty in the program."[335]

Governor Brown's inclusion of high-speed rail, by the summer of 2016 having extracted some $850 million from cap-and-trade auction revenues was further compromised by its dubious use of monies gained for the purpose of reducing greenhouse gases. The Legislative Analysts' report was especially damning of the benefits to be derived from the uses of funds directed toward the high speed rail program, which would not be operational for another decade or more; "Once it does begin ferrying passengers up and down the state, according to state estimates, it will reduce state carbon emissions by 44 million tons over 50 years – less than 1 million tons a year."[336]

Nor were the use of cap-and-trade revenues for high speed rail the only problem. Air Board officials "struggled to rationalize forestry and agriculture initiatives and other transportation projects, for example, especially when costs are weighed against the emissions they cut."[337] While budget negotiators pondered the impact of volatile revenues on the construction of Jerry Brown's high-speed rail, a telling inquiry was whether its revenue source, the entire cap-and-trade architecture for pricing and trading carbon emissions, was not seriously flawed.

A decade later, the delays accompanying construction and launching of the emissions trading program initiated in 2006 confronting a renewed obstacle in the form of yet another corporate-sponsored campaign challenging the legal basis for conducting cap-and-trade beyond 2020. More than simply legal authority beyond 2020, the crucial challenge was whether the people of California could sustain the political means to dismantle fossil fuels and redirect their economy. The legal basis rooted in a trading scheme for emissions now characterized as "buying our way out" placed the state on the path to even greater harms, including the dismantling of citizen rights and democratic practices.

The Export Model Unleashed

As the California emission trading scheme confronted legal challenges at home, the export model achieved a notable victory at the close of 2016, offering one of the first global frameworks for limiting a specific category of greenhouse gas emissions: aircraft emissions. As reported by one of the world's most prominent financial news services, "Cheers rose from prominent voices around the world this month when almost all countries agreed to reduce the climate costs of international air travel... The United Nations and the White House applauded the deal, as did the airline industry and even some environmentalists."[338] Recognized as a high profile source of emissions, in 2016 airlines represented approximately 2 percent of emissions; a category everyone expected to expand, perhaps to as much as 6 percent by 2050.[339] Because the newly forged agreement progressed on a voluntary basis until 2027, airlines had a decade to decide how to respond to emission limits. The major weakness noted by the critique, however, did not simply end with delay and a low bar for success.

The harshest criticism mirrored those aimed at key concepts shared with California's trading scheme: "The signatories to the deal call the offsets a 'market-based mechanism'. But it has nothing to do with the market for jet fuel. A true market-based mechanism would be a price on the carbon content of that fuel, accounting for its toll on the atmosphere. Such a price would give jet-fuel buyers – the world[s airlines – an incentive to use lighter, more efficient aircraft, to change their routes or adopt other fuel-saving policies."[340] Over the last century, Californians have constructed an economy placing it among the world's largest and most innovative, and partially accounts for its importance as a center for production of law. Less well understood are incipient efforts to extinguish selected California laws and to largely obliterate persistent problems of a market state confronted by a legacy of democratic practices, gone south.

Many, no doubt, would point to detailed differences between the California law and the international agreement amongst airlines. Such quibbling, however, obscured the foreboding victory belonging to the architects and sponsors of a California pollution trading law that now constituted a new international regime. If passengers on this journey considered the purchase of offsets something to soothe their conscience, Kip Lipper would probably lean over and whisper in their ear, "You're simply trying to buy your way out."

CHAPTER 18

Dismantling Democracy

Look, "if anybody still wants to dispute the science around climate change, have at it. You'll be pretty lonely, because you'll be debating our military, most of America's business leaders, the majority of the American people, almost the entire scientific community, and 200 nations around the world who agree it's a problem and intend to solve it."[341]

Looking out across a chamber of steadfast opponents to his every effort, President Barack Obama delivered his final State of the Union address. Rather than demanding action by Congress, his talk outlined America's future. The speech captured a frequent focus on the world of promise that lay before us. Unsurprisingly, one of his central topics included climate change. Mirroring an approach adopted by a growing number of political leaders, he largely dismissed those wanting to deny its existence.

Hope Is Not a Strategy

The President noted that the country was already pursuing a more constructive project, based on the largest federal support in the nation's history: to combine wind and solar power with a transition away from 'dirty energy'. While he was able to pinpoint specific clean energy projects already deployed across the nation, the dismantling of dirty energy was more aspirational than real. "I'm going to push to change the way we manage our oil and coal resources, so that they better reflect the costs they impose on taxpayers and our planet."[342]

It may be that the President considered his partisan opponents the least of his problems. Obama hinted that the nub of difficulty was located among corporate lobbyists who held sway in both houses of Congress; "None of this will happen overnight, and yes, there are plenty of entrenched interests who want to protect the status quo. But the jobs we'll create, the money we'll save, and the planet we'll preserve — that's the kind of future our kids and grandkids deserve."[343] If the President expected Congress to embrace a program based on the needs of grandkids over immediate profits, we were indeed facing a world of trouble. For a public that had placed much trust in a campaign promising "hope," many citizens re-kindled a much older political adage: hope is not a strategy.

Only weeks prior to this speech before Congress, emphasizing the urgency of climate change measures, the House voted to block provisions of the Clean Power Plan set to curb greenhouse gas emissions, via two actions; "the first would bar the Environmental Protection Agency from enforcing rules aimed at cutting emissions from new power plants; the second would prevent the agency from enforcing rules targeted at existing power plants."[344] The Congressional action included a precaution blocking the President's Green Climate Fund, a $3 billion commitment to assist developing countries with adopting green energy systems.[345]

The actions of a Republican Congress to defeat even the most modest steps to address a deteriorating climate reflected more than a partisan difference of opinion. It was, rather, the product of yet another concerted effort led by a host of fossil fuel companies, to forge a business-friendly political climate. What citizens and their leader had expressed, time and time again as "hope," remained far from reality. Moreover, several of Obama's actions were fraught with contradictions in achieving these ends. As one observer noted, "The conservative revolution transformed our countries into authoritarian pro-business states, which are not just undemocratic but inherently anti-democratic. The last thing these people want is to give democratic power to a state that they cannot control, manipulate, make irrelevant or buy."[346] By the 21st century, the promotion of states dominated by corporations and their markets moved well beyond the realm of democratic institutions and toward an ascendant market state.

Contradictions

The President's promotion of market mechanisms over legal provisions was not limited to so-called free trade regimes. He fully supported what had become a centerpiece of his administration's work on climate change: pollution-trading auctions based on California's cap-and-trade program. Prior to his State of the Union speech, President Obama hosted a Chinese Premier who arrived in D.C. to announce his support for what was shaping up to be a major initiative at the December meeting in Paris on a new global climate treaty. The Chinese initiative embraced an approach already familiar to many in California: emissions trading.[347]

The announcement by a Chinese Premier and the White House included many common objectives to address climate change including "plans to start in 2017 its national emission trading system..."[348] While noting the value of many basic lessons about cap-and-trade, early analysis pointed to basic problems facing China, including the absence of essential information for tracking emissions, trades, leakage and related data.[349] Such obstacles, however, did not begin to capture the breadth of problems contained in the California experience. At a superficial level, the Chinese announcement underscored California's national and international leadership in advancing environmental policies. At the community level, many seasoned public interest advocates had detailed the host of problems already emerging from cap and trade. A more careful look revealed the perverse victory of industries bent on avoiding a fundamental mandate to immediately dismantle the use of fossil fuels.

A pollution trading scheme presented many attractive opportunities for fossil fuel corporations, including the avoidance of democratic controls over the direction of economic activities. As select legal heads put it, prior to enacting cap-and-trade, many foundational climate-related laws premised on state-directed economic activities to advance energy conservation and clean energy, impose greater restrictions on the use of fossil fuels coupled with legally-outlined citizen rights to sue, with provision of incentives and subsidies for energy conserving technologies, and their levy of increased fines and fees for damages. An enduring feature of the corporate lobby began with fundamental opposition to citizen-led controls over the pivotal economy. In its place, the corporate lobby offered consumer choice.

In 2015, fossil fuel interests narrowly dodged a law mandating a dramatically reduced dependence for one of the world's largest economies.[350] President Obama turned down the opportunity to advise the Chinese Premier to avoid a pollution trading program altogether; to mention that only a week before the Premier's visit, California's governor had signed what arguably was the most aggressive law in the United States: establishing a legal timetable to advance clean fuels while electrifying the state's transportation grid. Instead, the two largest nations responsible for ultra-hazardous emissions were united by a common trait: neither acting decisively to eliminate their national fossil dependence.

To be certain, President Obama's first term and his commitment to curtail climate catastrophe began with great promise: dedicating tens of billions in the 2009 stimulus package to energy efficiency and renewables (e.g., wind and solar investments, batteries for electric cars), proposing rules limiting new coal-fired plants, setting forth new requirements for states to adopt to limit carbon dioxide emissions from existing power plants, delivering numerous speeches to urge all Americans to act on climate challenges.[351] By the close of his second term in office, however, many were underwhelmed. One noted observer summarized the haunting parallel of President Obama's climate achievements to one of the Pope's encyclicals; "That's a good record, as far as it goes. The problem is, according to many concerned about climate change, it just does not rise to address the level of catastrophe we face. Not even close."[352] A more fundamental critique mirrored the contradictions evident across the globe. Obama's proposed regulations, plans and agreements on behalf of the environment were overwhelmed by contradictory actions further advancing the national dependence on fossil fuels.

During his presidency, Obama approved additional deep-water drilling for example, in the Arctic, Alaska's Beaufort Sea, the Atlantic Coast, the Gulf of Mexico. Indeed, in a speech delivered in 2012, presented a record of accomplishments that flew in the face of his alleged urgency to address climate change, "Over the last three years, I've directed my administration to open up millions of acres for gas and oil exploration across 23 different states. We're opening up more than 75 percent of our potential oil reserves offshore. We've quadrupled the number of operating rigs to a record high. We've added enough new oil and gas pipeline to encircle the Earth, and then some...In fact, the problem is that we're actually producing so much oil and gas...that we don't have enough pipeline capacity to transport all of it where it needs to go."[353]

As if international trade and environmental protections were each contained under entirely separate ledgers, while the President cast an image of standing with scientists against an onslaught of know-nothing partisans, such storylines missed the very public rebuke of his environmental policies "...best described as unadulterated 100 percent pure bullshit" by one of the world's most respected climate scientists, James Hansen and vowed during Obama's appearance at the climate treaty conference in Paris.[354] Hansen's anger was provoked by what the scientist regarded as a set of failed policies, ranging from carbon capture and storage to a vast maze of pipelines, to cap-and-trade.

At the same time that scientists and activists alike challenged the President's climate agenda, Naomi Klein spoke to hundreds at a more public venue in Paris, urging them not to linger on what promised to be another underwhelming meeting of world leaders. In place of non-binding resolutions that remain insufficient to address the worsening problems identified by climate scientists, Klein called for a mass mobilization of activists across the globe to re-double efforts for necessary changes that political leaders in Paris were failing to achieve.[355] In Klein's historic analysis, the aspirational national commitments to 'do better' faced a deepening of potential corporate blowback.

Trade Treaties

Among the paucity of voices indicating contradictions between climate change and trade treaties, a speaker joining Klein's confab outside the formal meetings noted; "If Canada were to take a real and serious position [on climate change], we would come back and be hit by investor state challenge from all of the American corporations under NAFTA, and all of the Chinese oil and energy corporations operating [in the] tar sands under a similar investor agreement [with China.]"[356] The speaker was not talking about North American Free Trade (NAFTA) as much as noting that the newly forged Trans Pacific Partnership might well undermine national efforts to curb fossil-fueled and related crises.

Comparing the Paris climate discussions to the recently negotiated trade treaty marked a striking world of differences. The Paris discussions were based on a transparent process involving a wide diversity of interests from around the globe. TPP conducted private meetings purposely designed to exclude popular participation. Going in Paris signers recognized that enforcement of climate treaties is essentially nonexistent, whereas the Trans Pacific Partnership was predicated on forging provisions including the ability of corporations to levy fines against nations (and therefore citizens) for violating the self-forged "rights" to achieve economic returns on investments, as a legally binding architecture.

For many, the President demonstrated a genuine commitment to the environment by denying a Canadian corporate plan to construct the Keystone Pipeline to carry 'dirty fuels' across America. One of the immediate consequences of this action was the filing of a $15 billion lawsuit against the U.S. government in damages for the loss of investment returns under prior provisions of North American Free Trade agreement. The contradiction of a U.S. president taking executive actions to address a specific project threatening the global climate while simultaneously forging international trade pacts where thousands of corporations from across the globe could now legally undermine a broad range of hard-fought victories by public interest groups across the fifty state designed to dismantle the extraction, processing, and sale of fossil fuels – predictably went largely unnoticed in major media reporting of the day.[357]

Indeed, trade deals marked the emergence of a qualitatively different politics. If the 20th century was characterized by the appearance of independent political entities possessing sovereignty demonstrated by the rule of law, the 21st century is better understood as a distinct movement from nation states to market states and a corresponding movement away from the creation of laws led by citizens. In California, hundreds, perhaps thousands, of laws had been shaped by countless community activists and their organizing efforts over decades. In many instances public interest advocates achieved significant success. Such victories convinced many corporations of the need to undermine democratic practices whereby citizens might effectively counter rules enfranchised by those same corporations. Public interest victories also revealed the subversive political agenda contained in an infamous soundbite: "government is the problem."

Nor was the public blind to the potential impacts of so-called trade deals. During the 2015 U.S. primary elections various political figures who otherwise appeared to support trade deals, delivered statements equivocating on the value of pending Congressional actions that advanced unrestrained trade. Multiple explanations responded to public sentiment running counter to the proclaimed benefits of unrestrained trade. The rise of outsiders challenging established interests in both parties reflected an enlarged body of opponents to free trade including many public interest groups.

Public Interest Challenges to the Market State

During the tumultuous 2016 election season the wonkish topic of international trade suddenly captured the attention of candidates for one simple reason: voters in many of the most important primary state elections expressed hostility toward innocuous sounding partnerships promoting so-called agreements to advance free trade among the United States and a number of other nations in the world. Forged behind the scenes, with provisions that actively excluded even legislative review, when mentioned by practitioners all, the agreements conveyed the image of sleepy technical/financial pacts, simply extending the fruits of global markets. The staging and timing of these agreements, originally scheduled to be approved by Congress before the election season, now precipitated an increasingly acrimonious debate resonate with a public informed that they would again be the beneficiaries of free trade.

On June 6, 2016 a letter transmitted to every representative in Washington D.C. conveyed a simple message: don't advance either of two so-called free trade deals awaiting action by Congress. Different than those received each day from individuals, this letter contained the signatures of more than 450 environmental, indigenous rights and other groups pointing to an issue paralleling the concerns of others representing public health, labor, and related organizations.[358] At first glance the Transatlantic Trade and Investment Partnership (TTIP) 450 letter contained yet another feature to distinguish it from so many campaigns that opposed proposed trade deals over the years; this letter alerted Congress that TPP and TTIP threatened to worsen national and subnational (e.g., a variety of California) efforts to address climate change. Specifically, the new trade regimes could undermine efforts to keep fossil fuels in the ground.

The most distinctive message of the letter, however, registered objection to a feature largely invisible in reporting by major media outlets – the creation of international tribunals not accountable to any domestic legal system. These tribunals, already present in other trade agreements (e.g., NAFTA), according to the 450 letter, would allow an unprecedented number of corporations, some of the world's largest polluters, to challenge U.S. policies and demand compensation for fossil fuel restrictions. Such demands would be decided not by any part of the U.S. judiciary, but by "investor-state dispute settlements." This new form of governance had been taking shape over years at meetings where hundreds of corporations participated as official advisors. The trade governors formally blocked the proceedings, in contrast to the dominant role offered to multinational corporations. Despite an effective cloak, drafts exposed via wikileaks and other sources provided a window.

A Sierra Club posting analyzed and summarized the potential consequences of the Transatlantic proposal in the following headings: 1) Open the floodgates for fossil fuel exports and fracking; 2) Allow more toxic chemicals; 3) Put corporate rights on steroids; and, 4) Revise law-making in favor of corporations.[359] As one of the world's most recognized environmental organizations, frequently portrayed as shrill by its corporate opponents, its message *understated* the essential threat posed by the pending trade agreements. A fair characterization of consequences included the broader impact of the destruction of democracy and citizen's rights, not simply damaging environmental impacts or a privileged corporate position.

This Is How Democracy Is Lost

Under provisions contained in earlier Congressional measures (e.g., NAFTA), Congress was being asked to approve 'fast-track' a new set of international trade regimes and to delegate detailed negotiations to the President. The blanket approval being requested by the President obscured public understanding that lengthy and detailed negotiations conducted in recent years were virtually secret: excluding the public while hundreds of representatives of multinational corporations were allowed to participate fully. The movement away from elected governments was further extended by the creation of investor-state dispute settlement (ISDS) with authorities that were neither elected by popular vote nor accountable to any body of the larger public. In their letter to Congress, the 450 public advocacy groups explained the worsened position of the United States in the proposed trade agreements:

"...TPP and TTIP would more than double the number of fossil fuel corporations that could ...challenge U.S. policies in private tribunals. Indeed, the pacts would be the first to allow the world's largest polluters– including all of the eight largest private greenhouse gas emitters outside the U.S.– to wield this tool against U.S. climate policies. The fossil fuel firms that would gain this right are currently fracking on our public lands, drilling for oil off our shores, building liquefied natural gas terminals on our coasts, running refineries in our cities, and operating fossil fuel pipelines and trains in nearly every region. No previous trade deal has given such broad rights to corporations with such broad interests in maintaining U.S. fossil fuel dependency." [360]

The 450 letter documented its arguments against the proposed trade pacts with specific cases in which fossil fuel corporations would undermine the authority of states 1) to restrict fracking, 2) to restrict offshore drilling, 3) to restrict oil and gas leases on public lands, and, 4) delay or deny the building of fossil fuel pipelines. The goal of dismantling a fossil fueled economy represented a public struggle against private political forces. Publicly defined rules of law were also dismantled by the promotion of international trade regimes by corporate interests that had been found complicit in a series of disasters, described here as a converging set of fossil-fuel crises of health now threatening the survival of civilization and the fate of the earth.

The Destruction of Law

The portrayal of law in so many parts of the United States assumes the character of secret agreements achieved behind closed doors and accompanied by bribes. There is an ample record to document that indeed many laws were forged in exactly this fashion during the 19th and 20th centuries. By the late 20th century, however, older stereotypes characterizing the usual process for making law misrepresented what, in certain places, was becoming a process more broadly participatory. The introduction of greater citizen input by no means translated to a fair competition in the production of law. Yet the portrayal of laws as a mere mechanism owned and operated by the oligarchy discounts the numerous times and places where public interest advocates have not only prevented much worse outcomes, but decisively defeated the corporate lobby and their clients.

In California, in the late 20th and early 21st century, the history of laws forged constitutes one of the greatest grass-root's manufacturing marvels in the world. Over the course of several decades, tens of thousands of laws were created in every imaginable arena of human activity. Without question, many older, powerful and private interests held sway. A full accounting of this period, however, includes public interest advocates, who became a vigilant and potent force challenging corporate dominance in varied domains.

As we have seen, public interest advocates have forged victories in a variety of arenas. Perhaps most striking, in the past four decades, several ballot initiatives have banned or swiftly phased out of existence thousands of products containing lead, mercury, and extremely hazardous pesticides, toxic art materials in schools and classrooms, hazardous occupational materials, dangerous furnishings, food contaminants, and on and on. The public gradually learned the lesson that the decision to remove these hazards would rarely occur if left to the marketplace Indeed, as the first chapter of this work illustrates, corporations frequently resorted to reversing many of these same laws having broad public support.

The construction of California law thus achieved by numerous communities and activists representing thousands upon thousands of volunteer citizens to define the rules regarding fair conditions of work, environmental protections, public health, energy policy, transportation, and more. As crazy as the political scene had become in 2016, no candidate advanced a proposal as audacious as that contained in the trade agreements – a breadth of political change largely inconceivable within the older framework of democratic institutions.. In addition to establishing rules with the potential to invalidate sweeping sections of law (many painstakingly crafted by public interest advocates), the latest trade agreements proposed establishing investor-state dispute settlements having the authority to impose substantial fines on taxpayers standing in the way of potential corporate profits. For the corporate lobby, it was the deal of the century!

CHAPTER 19

The War on California

Doesn't "the U.S. election simply illustrate the underlying inequality of classes and their access to power?" Following the election of Donald Trump, I decided it might be a good time to leave the United States. Although I had forecast Hillary Clinton's defeat nearly six months earlier during a dinner with two journalist friends, the stretch of political consequences was much less predictable. It was time to reflect on the altered political climate.

Since my early childhood, I found the wealth of perspectives gained by travel to other places often sharpened my thinking about politics in the United States. And so, by mid-January, I traded California's stormy weather for an early morning regimen that included walking through a centuries old city, Cartagena, on the coast of Colombia. Arriving before cruise ships discharged masses of tourists, I slowly made my way to a small plaza to gain a Colombian perspective on the day's events. I was speaking with a new acquaintance who spent all of his life in Cartagena. That elderly fellow introduced me to his sometimes-assistants, including a young street vendor who turned to me, adding: "Is this not part of a legacy of domination by the oligarchy? Does this not signal a worsening of relations between the United States and the rest of the world?" Following each question, he peppered me with a rhetorical device I encountered elsewhere in Colombia: "Yes or No?"

Seeking refuge from this nimble mind, I countered with my own question as we stood in front of the load of coconuts. "Who are you reading?" Without missing a beat, the street vendor responded "Well Noam Chomsky, of course!"

Only after returning to the U. S. and engaging in literary catch-up did I examine more closely the title, on prominent display in many bookstores across Colombia: Who Rules the World? With an echo of my own early training as a political scientist, I found Chomsky's introductory passages to summarize my earlier conversation with the street vendor:

> "Other studies have demonstrated that the large majority of the population at the lower end of the income scale, are effectively excluded from the political system...while a tiny sector at the top has overwhelming influence.
>
> One consequence is so-called apathy: not bothering to vote has a significant class correlation. Likely reasons were discussed thirty-five years ago…the total absence of a socialist or laborite mass party as an organized competitor in the electoral market, which accounts for much of the class-skewed abstention rates as well as downplaying of policy options that may be supported by the general population but are opposed to elite interests. The observations reach to the present."[361]

I found it richly entertaining: that a young Colombian street vendor could one-up me about U.S. politics. For all the bravado and theater, the 45th president of the United States very much followed his many predecessors, per Chomsky's text. Several days after my return, Bernie Sanders succinctly characterized Trump's tactics in winning working class voters. "This Guy is a Fraud," was his assessment of the adoption of populist rhetoric during election speeches but then extending the rule of private sector interests, upon becoming president.[362]

While Trump openly favors one corporation or one rich celebrity over another, there is no preference given to the poor or even middle classes over the elite. As Chomsky and his Colombian pupil told me, the trajectory of U.S. politics under Trump only further excludes most Americans from effectively participating. Particularly absent is anything approximating a popular control over the content and direction of the economy. With the new president's first days in office, a cascade of astoundingly erosive executive actions were issued from the Oval Office (ranging from suspending due process for immigrants to dismissing conflict of interest laws traditionally applicable to the presidency). Trump and the Republican Congress simultaneously pursued various measures to lift the burden of regulatory law in a sweeping executive order calling to eliminate two existing regulations for every one newly adopted.

The abundant historical documents from one decade earlier, all conveniently forgotten by Trump, detailed how an absence of strict regulations on banking and financial corporations brought about one of the worst financial disasters in the nation's history. As a bevy of scientists added warnings about humanity reaching crucial ecological tipping points in the fossil-fueled crises of the 21st century, the *petroleros* achieved a stunning victory to extend the burning of fossil fuels. In the first weeks of this new administration, Washington D.C.'s corporate lobby already had received commitments for astonishing shifts in law (e.g., a rewrite of Dodd-Frank banking regulations, and an executive order reversing fiduciary responsibility by financial advisors), and they hadn't even had to *ask* for favors. No less dramatic, indeed more worrisome than the unfolding environmental agenda was an executive threat to extinguish newly emerging alternatives to archaic, ultra-hazardous fossil fuel industries.

A Victory for Oil

The shock expressed by so many on the morning of the election of Donald Trump, November 9, 2016, was followed by a slow motion realization that a volatile billionaire/reality television host might just lack the requisite skills necessary to guide one of the world's most prominent nations. While the early days of his administration were filled with a series of missteps verging on Constitutional crises (e.g., judicial challenges to his 'ban on Muslims', refusals to fully disclose extensive financial holdings, or even to remove himself from family-related businesses) the nation found largely compliant Republican allies controlling both houses of Congress and a majority of governors and state legislatures actively applauding their new President.

President Trump's pursuit of the themes of earlier Republican administrations (e.g., downsizing government, reversing wide swaths of regulatory law, promoting the privatization of public services and education, increasing support for prisons, police, and the American military, expanding the ties between select religions and the state, and endorsing tax schemes benefitting corporations and the wealthy) contrasted with earlier proclamations of "draining the swamp" of corruption in D.C. His vows to represent "ordinary Americans" quickly morphed into an agenda designed by and for America's elite, featuring cabinet appointees recorded as the wealthiest in American history – holding personal assets reaching into the many billions of dollars.[363]

Naming the chief executive for Exxon Corporation, Rex Tillerson, as Secretary of State, Donald Trump drew an upsurge of questions about whether this signaled greater levels of corruption. "In nominating Tillerson, Trump is handing the State Department to a man who has worked his whole life running a parallel quasi-state, for the benefit of shareholders, fashioning relationships with foreign leaders that may or may not conform to the interests of the U.S. government."[364]

This appointment occurred at a moment in history marked by the filing of legal actions by New York's Attorney General, seeking further evidence as to whether Exxon had engaged in one of the largest acts of fraud in American history. This legal case rested on documented evidence of corporate deception regarding the extraordinary global threats posed by the burning of fossil fuels, even as Exxon's own scientists accumulated evidence underscoring explicit hazards.[365]

At the close of the 2016 election, Bernie Sanders, Hillary Clinton, and a group of Congressional members called for a federal probe into Exxon activities.[366] Exxon's initial cooperation with the New York Attorney General quickly shifted to a counter-suit blocking access to its files. Exxon's recalcitrance was backed by sympathetic Attorneys General from eleven other states.[367] Yet, "ExxonMobil and its precursors were responsible for directly or indirectly emitting 20.3 billion metric tons of CO_2 and 199 million metric tons of methane, or between 4.7 percent and 5.3 percent of all of humanity's industrial greenhouse gas emissions since 1882."[368] With the business of burning fossil fuels representing a doomsday machine, Trump could not have chosen anyone to better personify a negative image of America than Exxon's chief executive officer.

Others in President Trump's cabinet openly shared Tillerson's support for petroleum. Conventional news sources effectively missed the most important financial and environmental story of the day when they failed to highlight a President, his cabinet, and a Congress largely dismissive of the unfolding global disaster, incontrovertibly identified by scientists from around the world. In addition to a Congress held captive by fossil fuel interests and their corporate lobbyists, cabinet officials with serious personal conflicts of interest, and presidential support for a dangerously outdated industry, fossil fuels had otherwise been on the cusp of losing competitive price advantage over clean energy alternatives.

Just prior to the inauguration, a dry financial news service reported a remarkable transformation in energy prices: for much of the world, clean energy would soon be cheaper than either coal or petroleum. The team of energy analysts implicitly defeated central premises of Trump's support for fossil fuels. No one expected to find Republicans abandoning support for oil simply because it was opposed by nearly every climate scientist in the world. The daunting news for elected leaders holding firm to a dollars-and-cents reasoning that coal and oil afforded humanity with the cheapest sources of energy was that "renewables are robustly entering an era of undercutting" fossil fuel prices around the world.[369]

The problem facing U.S. renewables, according to Bloomberg as well as other energy analysts, commenced with the cost advantage already held by billion dollar coal and gas plants.[370] In unraveling the premise of cheap sources one could discern the house of cards built by fossil fueled interests. Arguments for deregulating fossil fuels, for easing their path with discretionary choices afforded by pollution trading schemes, for allowing subsidies in the form of tax relief, or funding and fighting foreign wars to maintain cheap oil -- all of these devices delaying the arrival of a new economy now took an image of a Potemkin village, built solely to make things look better than they are, and led by imbeciles.

Many in the public were awakening to the truth of an economy, political structure and public manipulated to achieve private purposes with one extraordinary twist on an old theme: this time the manipulation entails a level of destruction unparalleled in human history. The absence of discussion regarding either fossil-fueled crises or the viability of clean energy alternatives yielded a growing conflict reminiscent of an earlier war between the states. Parallel to the destructive economy based on slavery in the 1860s, the current insistence by *petroleros t*o continue with America's archaic fossil-fueled economy poses an existential threat to humanity on a global scale. In 2017 the emerging clash over the direction of the U.S. economy had no better poster child for opposition than the roughly forty million Californians.

The War on California

President Trump, just prior to the televised airing of the Super Bowl, declared to a national audience that "California is out of control."[371] Apparently provoked by the State Senate voting to expand protections for undocumented residents, Trump response contained a thinly veiled threat to withhold federal funding.[372] Residents openly worried as a new President and his Congress prepared to reverse broad swaths of California law ranging from support for undocumented immigrants to women's reproductive health services, to restrictive gun controls, to consumer warnings on hazardous products, to regulations on payday lending shops, to the expansion of bilingual education, to funding for mass transit, to prohibitions against the use and transport of coal, to the promotion of clean fuels, to protections for endangered species, to curtailing private prisons, to legalizing marijuana, to enforcing actions against banking fraud, to equal pay provisions... seemingly without end.

Within days following the election, many political discussions across the nation assumed the character of how best to work across partisan differences. Such even-handedness overlooked a political agenda anchored to the doomsday machine. President Trump and his cabinet readily embraced an agenda scripted "straight from the talking points of top energy industry officials and their lavishly financed allies in Congress"... " to lift environmental restrictions on oil and natural gas extraction, build the Keystone XL and Dakota Access pipelines, open more federal lands to drilling, withdraw from the Paris climate agreement, kill Obama's Clean Power Plan, revive the coal mining industry..."[373] Scott Pruitt, DJT's nominee to head the U.S. Environmental Protection Agency, succinctly characterized his role as a soldier in the emerging war on alternative energy, in 2015, by declaring: "The Clean Power Plan an unlawful attempt to expand federal bureaucrats' authority over states' energy economies in order to shut coal-fired power plants and eventually other sources of fossil-fuel generated electricity."[374]

Californian's successes in cleaning the air, water and the environment, along with creating safer workplaces, healthy communities, and green sprouts of an economy dismantling fossil fuels in favor of renewable energy meant that Trump's war centered on California: And with good reason. California held a leading majority of voters who had caused the latest president to lose the popular vote (achieving office only by archaic and tortured Electoral College calculations). For the new and notoriously thin-skinned President, California encapsulated his political failure; as "Trump drew a smaller percentage of the California vote - 31.6% - than any GOP presidential candidate in 160 years."[375] The divide between Trump and California ran much deeper.

The historic underpinnings of this undeclared war included the successes of organized labor and the blossoming of a vast network of public interest activists who shaped thousands of individual laws and, by so participating, fostered more expansive notions of democratic practice. The decades of activism by nurses, school teachers, farm/service workers, and millions of allied voters advanced a central principle: After decades of victories, citizens understood how the state's prominence as one of the largest and most dynamic economies in the world had resulted from the interplay of a public continuously engaged in directing the content and nature of private sector activities. By the beginning of the 21st century, the fruits of a decades-long struggle to control the increasingly negative consequences of fossil fuels resulted in an obvious political imperative: creating a thriving economy based on clean energy entails defeating the political power of *petroleros* and their corporate allies.

Californians found themselves on a collision course with a regime that, in place of this state's design for a post-fossil fuel economy, quickly advanced multifaceted preparations to purge clean fuel programs while *increasing* federal support for dirty fuels.[376] In his anticipation of useful targets, the state environmental policy arena loomed large for the new president. Dismissal of climate change as a hoax meant that chief targets immediately undercut the architecture for regulatory laws - most importantly Clean Air Act provisions for restrictive state emission controls and mileage standards: And the celebrated cap-and-trade solution to the global crisis? Few in Washington appeared concerned.

A Not So Different Presidency

For all of the shock and awe accompanying presidential edicts for 'alternative facts' and for the press to 'shut up and listen,' a central tenet of the new regime extolled a familiar theme: lifting the burdens of regulations on corporations. In the arena of fiscal policy, for example, President Trump vigorously supported lifting the burden of corporate taxes declared 'among the highest' despite empirical evidence to the contrary. "Republican pleas for tax reform relied-on the argument that America has one of the highest corporate tax rates in the world at 35%. Not so. Of the S&P 500's largest 50 corporations, the average tax rate (including state, local and foreign regulations) is 24%. U.S. Corporations rank among the world's most lightly, as opposed to heavily, taxed."[377]

After decades of stagnant wages, the resultant populist uprising against old guard politicians from both parties largely explained Trump's popularity. If Donald delivered a winning election slogan of promoting jobs, his transition into the Oval Office suggested a grim future for the working poor and unemployed. "[H]is policies of greater defense and infrastructure spending combined with lower corporate taxes to invigorate the private sector continue to favor capital versus labor, markets versus wages, and a continuation of the status quo."[378]

Nor were the criticisms limited to only one party. "Both the Clinton Democrats and almost all Republicans represent the corporate status quo that favors markets versus wages, Wall Street versus Main Street.... Neither party as they now stand has bold policies beyond the reach of K Street [D.C.'s corporate] lobbyists."[379] Even as most Republican leaders and many of their moderate colleagues voiced a shared insistence for deregulation, various critics castigated both parties' disregard for the working class.[380] Most notable, critics of the Dem's abandonment of blue collar workers dovetailed with stunning electoral losses in traditional strongholds (e.g., Wisconsin, Michigan, Pennsylvania)...

The shift of both parties toward *corporados* yielded a lack of enthusiasm in voting booths for either candidate. Even as the president-elect assembled panels of economic advisors dominated by corporate leaders notorious for their betrayal of America's working class, the question remained: Who are Americans left to turn to in a search for an economic transition benefitting workers, communities, the environment and the well-being of future generations? The answer could be found in the campaign of public interest advocates for a just transition to alternative fuels and an economy led by citizens.

A Capitalist Climate Solution

In the midst of the 2016 election various companies had already shifting away from fossil fuels. "On Nov. 4, Walmart had announced an aggressive plan to increase its investments in renewable energy, pledging to power half its operations from wind, solar, and other renewables by 2025 and to cut the carbon footprint of its operations by 18 percent over the same interval. Ten days later, Microsoft enacted its largest wind-power purchase ever, with a deal to buy 237 megawatts of electricity from turbines in Kansas and Wyoming to run data centers in Cheyenne. In between those announcements, Donald Trump was elected president, in part by calling climate change a hoax and vowing to gut most of Obama's clean-energy policies and revive coal mining."[381] A more careful parsing of corporate sector climate policies, however, displayed different levels of commitment. "Sixty percent of Fortune 100 companies have renewable-electricity or climate change policies, and 81 companies globally have committed to get 100 percent of their energy from renewable sources."[382]

Beneath their statement of broad long-term commitments, "companies parsed their investments in renewable energy in one of three ways: sourcing clean power from wind and solar projects through long-term agreements; purchasing a stake in green power projects; or using renewable-energy credits to offset the dirtier power they consume."[383]

The purchase of renewable energy credits, of course, fit perfectly with California's emission trading scheme; it also reflected the weakest commitment of any investment approach, by maintaining economies anchored in ultra-hazardous fuels. In this sense, California's trading scheme was proving to be the weakest instrument for aggressively dismantling the fossil fuel economy; and, because of this feature, it held a certain appeal for President Trump and the Republican Congress.

While simply suspending all fossil-fuel related regulations clearly held favor among many corporate lobbyists, the pollution trading scheme or a similar market-based approach offered great potential as a means to delay regulatory actions. On November 16, 2016, 300 U.S. businesses including General Mills, EBay and Intel called on Trump to support the Paris accord, reaffirming the symbolic commitment to alternative energy.[384] The state's celebrated pollution trading law provided broad latitude, coupled with minimal threats to fossil-fueled interests.

Vague corporate commitments to renewable energy, accompanying emissions trading in particular, hardly involved date-certain requirements for ending the burning of fossil fuels. Arguing against forcing automakers to build more electric cars than warranted by customer demand, the Ford chief executive announced a plan to lobby President-elect Trump to "soften U.S. and state fuel-economy rules."[385] Under President Barack Obama's rule, the auto industry agreed to double average fuel economy in order to achieve 50.8 miles per gallon by 2025 and to work with California to sell more zero-emission cars. Responding to an agreed-upon mid-term review, the U.S. EPA also determined in November, 2016, to maintain the 2025 targets.

For compliance alternatives to rigorous emission standards, the Ford CEO suggested "the auto industry may seek clean-air credits for self-driving cars, which could reduce fuel consumption and emissions by helping traffic move more smoothly."[386] This counterproposal not only undermined key legal provisions to lessen the burning of fossil fuels, it utilized California's emission trading as a platform for avoiding the certainty of regulatory law. The proposal captured perfectly the corrosive effect of market mechanism on the suite of regulatory laws that represented California's decades-long successes in dismantling a fossil fuel-based economy.

Before completing his first 100 days in office, the President acted in accordance with the proposal set forth by Ford and company. Governor Brown reacted with an angry letter to the administrator of the U.S. EPA: "President Trump's decision today to weaken emission standards in cars is an unconscionable gift to polluters. Once again, you've put the interests of big oil ahead of clean air and politics ahead of science." When Trump, his administrator, and the Republican Congress savaged the strict regulatory foundations for dismantling fossil fuels – cap-and-trade received the silent blessings of a new regime.

The erosive effects of cap-and-trade's 'buying our way out' found root in a *petrolero*-supported proposal known as the "capitalist solution to climate change." The former advisors to presidents Nixon, Reagan, George H.W., and George W. Bush authored op-eds in the New York Times, and the Wall Street Journal arguing for a carbon tax, stating: "The opposition of many Republicans to meaningfully address climate change reflects poor science and poor economics, and is at odds with the Party's own noble tradition of stewardship. A carbon dividends plan could realign the GOP with that longstanding tradition and with popular opinion."[387] It also dovetailed with the broad outlines of a plan offered in January 2009 by Exxon's Tillerson.[388]

The concept for a Republican-supported carbon tax contained a particularly attractive feature designed to gain the backing of *petroleros* and their corporate allies; it was predicated on phasing out most of the EPA's power to regulate carbon dioxide pollution - touting the virtues of a market-based tool to address the climate problem.[389] Indeed, the architect of the proposed Republican climate change solution - also referred to as "a capitalist climate solution" - was built on four basic 'pillars': a gradually rising carbon tax, carbon dividends for citizens, a border carbon adjustment, and a significant regulatory rollback.[390]

Various environmental groups expressed their opposition to eliminating regulatory rules, but, in a certain sense, the table for negotiating away regulatory controls had already been set in California a decade earlier when the *corporados* of both parties worked with the corporate lobby to perform a classic bait-and-switch: the fossil fuel industry could buy their way out by offering consumers token payments in exchange for the 'flexibility' to avoid more costly regulations. Meanwhile poor communities were poisoned, the well-being of everyone was further imperiled and the planet burned.

The final pillar of the capitalist climate solution–a border carbon adjustment–was simultaneously the most obscure and most interesting. Explained as a provision for 'leveling the playing field', an elaboration revealed that its purpose was to ensure that America's trading partners would follow with a similarly structured approach to shared climate problems.[391] The significance was not so different than what had appeared in the recently proposed trade agreements: to dismantle the harsh regulatory approaches designed in places like California.

Trade Regimes & the Authoritarian President

One dimension of the Trump presidency garnering popular support emerged with his expedient termination of the Trans Pacific Partnership (TPP) and a renewed commitment to renegotiate the North American Free Trade Agreement (NAFTA). What trade regimes would take their place? Trump's stated preference for bilateral treaties left the distinct possibility of agreements featuring many of the same elements of TPP and NAFTA, firmly embracing an industrial venue unrestrained by laws. While political leaders would come and go, the essential political agenda contained in recent trade treaties left little reason to expect President Trump to reverse the course. "U.S. first!" suggested the merging of corporations and the state: keeping democracy subordinate to market mechanisms. Indeed, the most troubling written assessments of President Trump compared his governance to authoritarian regimes of the 20th century.

More than mere hyperbole, authors writing in this vein noted the use of language and political symbolism, the structure of government, leadership and related features evinced by President Trump and shared with the rise of fascism in the 1930s, by a variety of post-World War II authoritarian regimes in Latin America, Africa, Asia and in the wake of the Soviet Union's collapse. As the 21st century unfolds the rights of states and corporations become merged, eclipsing rights of citizens to challenge either sphere. Voter suppression of immigrants is poised to expand into a broader agenda of restricting avenues for popular protest, as the tweets of President-elect Trump singled-out protesters on Main Street, critics in media, performers on stage, labor leaders and political opponents. In the meantime, a cabinet of "patriots" included those long antagonistic to people of color, campaign managers practiced in voter suppression, law and order zealots supporting expanded use of torture, and investors backing privatized prisons with a military presence in all spheres of life.

Would the bellicose and crude statements targeting immigrants, women and Muslims be replaced with more reasoned and careful statecraft? Among the many ironies within Donald Trump's agenda for the downplay of democratic rights and thinly veiled threats aimed at many of the nation's ethnic communities – it is especially to the staggering achievements of a state firmly anchored in diverse immigrant communities, and many escaping authoritarian regimes that fellow citizens across America owe their protection and enfranchisement.

At first glance, the stories of public interest advocates in California appear to reflect isolated struggles of unfamiliar communities. A larger historic view, however, reveals combat against polluted waters, hazardous workplaces, dangerous products, birth defects, financial fraud, and a world of additional harms in which public interest advocacy has defended tens of millions, perhaps hundreds of millions, of other Americans. Indeed, those laws generated by the work in California and borrowed across America for the protection of citizens, often originated in those diverse communities - by the same people so often categorically demonized by the architects of a new tyranny.

CHAPTER 20

The Climate of Change

Did "you notice that we just witnessed another magic act?" Sitting next to me in the empty chambers at the end of another committee hearing, my colleague Michael Endicott accompanied his comment with one of his signature cryptic smiles. Having long ago given up pretending not to play the straight man in our comedic routine, I asked "How so?"

"We were a part of the unrecorded history where our public interest friends drove another corporate-sponsored bill into the ditch. No one may ever know about this event, but the public will sleep soundly tonight, little realizing that they were saved by a group of advocates they have probably never heard about." His memorable observation, this was "a perfect disappearing act." Years later, it was a memory that would remind me about the importance of bringing greater public attention to the tireless and invaluable work conducted by public interest groups - and not just in California, but across the nation.

Despite all of the shock and awe that surrounded the election of Donald Trump, California's public interest groups were continuing their largely invisible acts up and down the state. Renewed efforts on behalf of immigrants, those facing the loss of health insurance, the religiously persecuted, as well as supporting the rights of women, voters, and workers continued across the state. One of the most important events overshadowed by the tumultuous election season and subsequent national chaos involved the little noticed actions by an expanding coalition of groups working steadfastly to dismantle fossil fuels: the California

Environmental Justice Alliance (CEJA). The long standing concerns by the Alliance and its partners over the state's emissions trading program was underscored once more with the release of a new report.

In the fall of 2016, a group of health researchers at the University of Southern California released a study examining the consequences of cap-and-trade for disadvantaged communities, a more nuanced way of referring to poor people and communities of color. While environmental justice advocates praised the researchers, they substituted their own title for the USC report, "It's the I-told-you-so report!"[392] Martha Argüello provided a succinct summary of its findings: "This report confirms all of our lived experiences with cap and trade. This program fails communities that need real changes the most. Emissions in environmental justice communities are not changing, and when they are, it's for the worse. The assessment also confirms that the areas most impacted by greenhouse gas emitters are low-income communities of color. The current system is not working. We need to do better. We need climate solutions that build on equity, and the unique needs of impacted communities from the start. This means regulations that prioritize public health, neighborhood resiliency, and a just transition to a clean economy."[393]

Not content to just be talking the talk, Strela Cervas, Martha and their partners with the California Environmental Justice Alliance had already been at work, searching for avenues to move beyond the failures of California's emissions trading scheme. Indeed, by the close of the 2016 legislative session, the Alliance had scored major victories with the enactment of six priority legislative measures as well as supporting the passage of many other bills.[394] Among its legislative projects, one measure merited particular attention as a law aimed at redirecting the purposes of the Global Warming Solutions Act. Assembly Bill 197 (Equity & Transparency in Climate Act, AB 197) recast the priorities away from trading and toward what had served as a centerpiece for shaping one of the world's largest economies: increasingly restrictive controls coupled with a fuller accounting of emissions for multiple greenhouse gas and related emissions.

As described by the final legislative analysis of the bill, AB 197 now required the Air Board "to prioritize regulations that result in direct emission reductions at large stationary, mobile and other sources."[395]

Linked to its companion measure (Greenhouse Gas Reduction Targets, Senate Bill 32) authorizing the State to pursue a further reduction of GHG emissions of least 40 percent below the 1990 baseline by 2030, the Alliance advanced the role of strict regulatory controls over emissions trading. Equally significant was the fact that the Alliance and its partner organizations were joined in a broader undertaking involving greater numbers of citizens exercising their control over the nature and direction of the Golden State's economy and future.

Victories in the California Legislature, especially by public interest advocates, were always a moving target. As the corporate lobbyists knew so well, the opportunities to reverse any advances by public-interest advocates were as close as the next election. If anyone needed any reminders, the corporate domination of the nation's legislative and executive branches opened new opportunities to preempt California laws or threaten the withdrawal of federal budget support for state programs. The great news is Californians have benefited for decades from an army of public interest organizations such as the California Alliance for Environmental Justice. From my earlier career, deep inside the capitol, some of the most notable actors in these scenes included people who show up to demonstrate their commitment as part of an organized coalition with many motivated by a vision of achieving broader social goals. These are the signs that we may be on the cusp of a new political movement; it is a political orientation emerging in stark contrast to what many observers see happening in the nation's capitol.

It is not surprising to find many citizens searching for an authoritative leader to deliver decisive solutions in chaotic times. Having someone make sense of an out-of-control world, and offer measures for restoring political order holds great appeal – especially for those people whose lives, work, and households have stalled and stagnated. These are the neighborhoods where elected representatives have typically avoided or even repressed voters and political activism for years, if not decades. The anger is palpable and the direction it might take uncertain. For select leaders, such as Donald Trump, channeling popular anger along a path to achieve personal power is foremost, even as elders from his own party likened him to a dictator.[396] Interwoven with this rise in popular support for a new kind of American authoritarianism is another trait of such regimes: to distort and misrepresent the major threats facing society.

One of the clearest threats to society is an out-of-control fossil fuel industry, literally endangering the survival of life on this planet. The most important agents of this destruction are an assemblage of large, private financial interests directing oil and coal companies and their many complicit associates including closely linked industries, allied corporate lobbyists, and, of course, compromised politicians, the so-called business-friendly moderates.

This last category, the *corporados*, play a crucial role in the political realm by often negotiating compromises to weaken, if not to destroy the ability of public interest lobbyists to achieve more sweeping changes. The prime example at the center of many stories in this book is California's cap-and-trade law and its pollution-trading scheme. Despite heroic and quite longstanding resistance by a coalition of community-based advocates, the legal instrument giving polluters major flexibility in the ultra-hazardous converging fossil-fueled crises has undercut the public's ability to expeditiously launch a new economy. With climate scientists issuing ever more alarming warnings against any further delay of an immediate dismantle of fossil fuels, *petroleros* and *corporados* have set in motion a law perfectly designed to relax more decisive actions.

From the perspective of arguably the most important story in the world - the fossil-fueled crises of the 21st century – California's celebrated solution to this global apocalypse, cap-and-trade can be framed as perhaps the great betrayal of a public trust. Intertwined with the destruction of our planet, is a parallel, no less astonishing story: the corporate war on democracy. After observing pitched battles between public interest groups and the corporate lobby inside one of the world's largest economies, the contours of this conflict as manifest.

Public interest advocates have often made their most important contributions in this lesser recognized war by bolstering citizens to fight for their democratic rights as well as an economic transition to decent jobs and protections for healthy communities. A statement issued by Martha Dina Argüello, one of the principal characters in this book, perfectly illustrates the contemporary struggle: "The current system is not working. We need to do better. We need climate solutions that build in equity, and the unique needs of impacted communities, from the start. This means regulations that prioritize public health, neighborhood resiliency, and a *just transition to a clean economy*...and to fully explore alternatives to cap-and-trade."[397]

The sensitivity to the issues surrounding how those currently engaged will fare under any dismantling of fossil fuels displays a maturity absent from so many older and D.C. bound groups, especially organizations with expensive addresses but little in the way of local activists. The dynamic of fostering coalitions between workers and environmentalists is a crucial political link. Quoting from the leader for one of my former unions, the Oil, Chemical and Atomic Workers, Steve Early reminds us of this dynamic in his skillfully written analysis in Refinery Town: "As Tony Mazzocchi, who died in 2002, often reminded us, trade unionists will not join "blue-green" alliances in large numbers unless they're assured of a "just transition" to non-polluting employment. To facilitate that shift for refinery operators and others he represented, Mazzocchi proposed that a federal "superfund" for workers be created to pay for their retraining and job transitioning."[398] The point made by Steve Early reflects a more vital lesson surrounding a conflict involving not solely California, but on the rest of the United States and the world: the campaign for a new democracy and new economy needs to be grounded in the economic reality facing people in their communities. At the same time, the now swiftly worsening crises make it essential for broadening coalitions to devise actions for a *rapid* transition away from fossil fuels.

It was late 2016, during a meeting at the headquarters for California's environmental agencies that Dr. Richard Jackson, the State Public Health Officer, called for a vastly more massive undertaking to address the threats of a fossil-fueled economy.[399] Dr. Jackson's diagnostic of the threat to global health and well-being has been joined by a growing chorus of voices in public health,[400] merging with climate scientists, to demand for the creation of a new Marshall Plan, the expeditious transformation of an archaic and ultra-hazardous fossil-fueled economy. Echoed in many similar discussions over the decades, these words outline the initial plans for for crafting a new economy that will transform neighborhoods, cities, states and beyond. The spark to reassert the rights of citizens and a flourishing democracy may be the only antidote to the authoritarian impulse that has gripped the nation's capital.

We no longer confront an absence of alternatives. The *petroleros* insistence that fossil fuels will remain essential for decades to come has yielded to their early replacement by wind, solar and other clean energy sources. Even more exciting than the spread of clean energy is the expanding global resistance to oil and ensuing support for alternatives. It is, after all, the collective political muscle flexed by millions, if not billions of individuals that will create a new future with the construction of an economy and bodies of governance that serve a broad public interest, not one privately-fashioned.

Organizing Political Turning Points

How to initiate change is a perennial question in politics. There is no single best answer; yet, mobilizing a broad cross-section of people to make their force overwhelming is necessary to overcome the power of money over our political institutions. A dynamic sometimes described inside the capitol as "the coalition of everyone", once achieved, often marks a crucial turning point away from an older political regime. Having observed multi-year struggles to create broader political change firsthand, one favorite example is farmworker campaigns to lessen exposure to especially hazardous pesticides, and to achieve justice in their workplaces, communities and the society at large.

A gathering in another capitol hearing room reflected this ongoing struggle. The legislation was titled 'occupational health', but most in the room recognized the matter more plainly: the poisoning of farmworkers from pesticides sprayed on the fields, sometimes even as they picked fruits and vegetables for distant markets. The opponents - major agribusinesses - were already smugly confident that they possessed the votes necessary to easily prevail. A quick calculus of those representatives seated in the committee hearing room decidedly reaffirmed the asymmetry of the political battle: What did a group of public interest attorneys have to offer elected officials that could not be matched many times over by corporate agribusinesses?

As the advocates came forward to testify on behalf of their seemingly powerless clients, they were joined by an uncommon coalition.[401] Corporate lobbyists watched with growing alarm as an expanding group of pediatricians, environmentalists, consumer allies, children's organizations and organized labor voiced support for the protection of field workers. Most of the business-friendly legislators on the committee had already calculated far too many opposition groups, reflecting a large cross section of citizens in their districts, to side with the corporate lobby. By the time the major agribusinesses presented opposition, their defeat had been sealed. The farmworker protection measure was signed by a governor who chastised the agribusinesses, noting that that their excuses no longer worked, they were outnumbered. While not an everyday occurrence, I would witness similar public interest victories in the years to come.

Following on the work of public interest advocates, I often spent hours fostering broad, permanent coalitions to achieve common social purposes. My political work nearly always turned on a necessary, but too often neglected, element: How do we use this particular issue to encourage a more expansive democracy? The common theme: the public must possess a practical basis for controlling private interests, typically those represented by multinational corporations and their lobbyists, from unleashing ever greater harms.

Even as a new president and his allies in Congress double down on support for a fossil-fueled economy in 2017, it is evident they are being eclipsed by real world events. The urgency is increasingly reflected in a broadening public realization of multiple hazards arising from fossil-fuel-dependent regimes around the world – from microscopic human reproductive damages and malformed fetuses, to the extinction of bees, fish and critters living on the planet, to contaminated aquifers and regional air basins, to disrupted climates and poisoned atmospheres, to social dislocations. The empty promises of tax cuts, saving hazardous industries and dangerous jobs, or pollution-trading dividends offer cold comfort for communities living amid hollowed-out industries and the continuing wreckage of fossil-fueled economies.

Are we prepared to exercise our democratic rights? The most important source of support for fossil fuel is not simply an obedient

Republican Congress, the Democrat *corporados*, or even the vast resources of *petroleros*. Pivotal support rests with the many clinging to the myth of markets, including a belief in the captains of capitalism as our saviors.

Organizing a New Economy

By employing symbols and images in his candidacy, telling many in the heartland that they were not only viewed as lesser beings by urban American coastal elites, but as racist, communities of narrow-minded people, Donald Trump gave voice to the pent-up frustrations of those painfully aware of living in another America, a place abused and disregarded by those in New York, Seattle, Washington, D.C., or Los Angeles. The Democrats, for their part, only deepened the divide with a smug nod at 'deplorables' in the fly-over states. In my world, such stereotyping reflected a rookie error in politics: instead of making assumptions about other neighborhoods, try walking and talking with these people to discover what it feels like to live in different parts of America.

Among the ironies of the 2016 election is that the answer to the plight of workers in so many parts of our heartland resides with those who do public interest work on behalf of immigrants, communities of color, nurses, organized labor, students, tenants, and many who labor for food, shelter, employment, and protections of their civil rights. While legions of the unemployed and the working poor were subjected to a barrage of negative campaign propaganda attacking Muslims, immigrants, African Americans, the media, people with disabilities and others, corporate lobbyists had already orchestrated the demise of middle America in the form of predatory corporate takeovers, free trade agreements, stagnant wages, closed health clinics, eroded social safety nets and an array of added assaults.

Unknown to heart-landers who stoically endured the destruction of their hopes, and livelihood, another America was taking shape. Distinguishing features of this other America included vibrant and enthusiastic voices challenging the myth of markets. Paralleling the suppression of voters and of civic participation in Middle America, public interest advocates, including importantly organized labor, assumed a growing power and influence elsewhere. California's pivotal political struggles hinged on public versus private control. In place of concerted corporate efforts to promulgate policies to undercut wages, benefits, and occupational protections; to demand the privatization of schools, medical care, transportation, and utilities; to suppress voters from direct initiation and enforcement of laws – California's public interest advocates crafted measures to expand the rights of citizens to achieve wide-ranging improvements.

By championing public well-being in just these ways, California has become a very different place than sister states in America's heartland. The difference didn't translate to a worker's paradise, or correct the shameful living and working conditions confronting immigrants, field labor, and people of color. None of this record of shame allowed for smug superiority over other states. What did distinguish the Golden State was the richness and diversity of advocates actively shaping politics and economy to work toward the widely shared principle that allowing capitalism to trump democracy is a bad idea. Traveling beyond California, I have frequently encountered a question posed by legislators, staff and advocates in other states: "How did you get away with unleashing all of these crazy programs?" In many instances, "crazy" served as subtle code for, "How did you defeat obvious corporate opponents?"

Recalling my early political mentor, I gave the same response: "The people of California demanded it." A more detailed answer would probably include a vital caveat: "... with the help and assistance of many public interest advocates coupled with mobilizing activists and ordinary people."[402] When California legislators posed a similar question to me, I sometimes answered by arranging public hearings. Whether massive reduction of pesticides in agriculture or banning toxic substances in consumer products or giving communities broader authority to enforce environmental laws was their focus, enthusiastic community members acted side-by-side with their public advocates and a wealth of voters to share a familiar template: we have a problem, things need to change and here is our plan about how to do it!

America and the Tradition of Public Activism

The achievements generated from many hundreds of laws are far from complete, but the history of recent decades reveals that public interest groups actively supported by voters represent a potent political force in shaping both economic and political decisions. The economic withering of communities left to slowly die had many explanations, but often included messengers extolling the virtues of a free market and calling on its casualties to be patient. Plutocratic assurances were issued to heartland Americans that deregulation, lower corporate taxation, repatriation of corporate profits, restrictions on immigrants, and expanded police powers would restore their economic well-being. Such promises, however, belied the snide laughter Casey had witnessed from inside the corporate suites. Their private assessment of the working classes: "Oh yeah, these people are the walking dead and don't know it; their jobs are never coming back!"

This dismissal had little to do with differences over religion, abortion, ethnicity, gays, guns or the Constitution. The dismantling of America's heartland proceeded with the cold corporate financial calculus that a people and their communities no longer offered a sufficient financial reward to maintain their jobs. The solution to the plight of workers abandoned over the decades, in so many parts of America's heartland, is never going to come from those who extinguished their economic lives. The striking difference between Americans centers both on those facing the travails of homelessness, unemployment, poverty, and abandonment, all on their own, and those engaged in a struggle to impose democratic controls over the conditions of pay, workplaces, and the economy. In heartland America, the idea of exercising worker rights and communities demanding a just economic transition has been distanced beyond the realm of citizen action. This distancing reflects the destruction of organized labor as a force for advancing the voices of other public interests in many parts of America.

Past experience with collective bargaining for decent wages revealed at least one dimension of why organized labor was so essential to my own political battles inside California's Legislature. Decades of experience in negotiating directly with corporate America gave labor a singular advantage: a willingness to engage in political hardball. At day's end, organized labor adopted a tactic borrowed from the corporate lobby itself: if negotiations go against us, you will see us in your next bid for re-election. Many legislators sided with labor not out of love, but because they feared the consequences of hundreds, perhaps thousands of workers mobilized in their districts. While I often drew on a coalition of community-based groups to support statewide policies, many coalitions actively sought the power of organized labor as a means of having an equal political footing with their corporate lobby adversaries.

Through the serendipity of geography, political borders, natural resources, and history, California's residents, at least until recently, have been most fortunate in their representation. When conversations with counterparts in other states end with a resigned sigh, "We couldn't possibly do that here!" my thought is, "Have you looked closely at the successes of public interest advocates and activists and considered how to broaden their political reach?"

Asserting Citizens' Rights

'Pretending the use of fossil fuels is somehow the natural workings of the market is not a serious proposition. It might be politically convenient for conservatives who want to assist fossil fuel interests. Pretending the fossil-fueled crises of the 21st century are unintended consequences of an otherwise virtuous market is convenient for the beneficiaries of inequality. But we should not structure our future according to what benefits fossil fuel interests. There is no way of escaping the fact that the continued burning of fossil fuels and the existential threat to life on this planet is guided by laws affecting such matters as transportation, agriculture, energy, a multitude of products, and so on.'[403]

I would like to claim the above words as my own, but they are the very slightly altered writing of noted economist, Dean Baker. While Dr. Baker in this instance addressed the beneficiaries of inequality, I find his thinking aptly applies to the dismissal of public control of markets: "The people who would treat these and other policy decisions determining the distribution of income as somehow given are not being honest. We debate the merits of a policy, but there is no policy-free option out there. This may be discomforting to people who want to believe that we can fall back upon a set of market outcomes, but this is the real world. If we want to be serious, we have to get used to it."[404] For my part: getting serious about fossil-fueled crises means mobilizing citizens to reclaim their state legislatures, and to reorient an out-of-control economy.

Even as Donald Trump and his cabinet of billionaires consolidated their hostile takeover of the Republican Party in November 2016, voters in California handed Democrats a supermajority, comprised of two-thirds of the legislators in both houses. Where 60 percent of California voters embraced the view that government should do more, nationally the view was the opposite.[405] The difference could also be measured by the Democrats' national loss of roughly 1,000 elected representatives from state houses to Congress since the beginnings of the new century. Such metrics supported a narrative of the growing partisan divide between 'red' and 'blue' states.

Americans are notorious for marking of differences between regions and states based on cultural traits: inflections in speech, favorite foods, or even partisan allegiances, as artificial divisions separating a common heritage. There are, to be certain, distinctions to be drawn from the experiences of survivors in Appalachia, Louisiana's cancer alley, Ohio's rust belt, a degraded West Virginia coal country, Montana's contaminated mining towns, New Mexico's irradiated sacrifice zones, or the polluted drinking water of Michigan. For a huge swath of Americans, a vicious, self-inflicted notion of personal responsibility is the explanation for their plight – even though everyone knows this game is rigged. A mechanism is set in motion to divide Americans, especially those living most precariously on the margins. We both blame and separate ourselves from one another - unless we operate from the vantage of community-based public interest advocacy.

Many in the world of politics voiced dismay in the weeks following Barack Obama's victory in his first term as President: It wasn't the failure to fully indict banking executives, although this was clearly a momentous mistake. It wasn't his inability to enact a cap-and-trade bill (this, of course, was a great stroke of good luck). A failure that would haunt his presidency resulted from turning off the massive public support acquired in his electoral campaign. The political disaster arrived in the form of silence, in which hopeful citizens awaited the president's call to march forward and craft a new America. It may be that neither President Obama nor his advisors knew what they were up against: a fight requiring citizens everywhere to actively participate. Instead, tens of millions poised to help craft a new American economy were effectively told to go back home and go to sleep.

In my work over years with political struggles, the groups of citizens willing to show up... in hearings, in town hall meetings, in neighborhood gatherings, protest marches, legislators' district offices, and especially via community-based organizations joined with larger coalitions have almost always defined the parameters of the political change. A snapshot of my most difficult times captures a common image – me, sitting alone, across the table from a group of corporate lobbyists who recognized the absence of political support in that room as a clear sign of there being little to keep them from achieving their private purposes. There are many signs that mass-based coalitions of public interest advocates may be re-emerging at a crucial moment. The growing awareness of the war being waged on many of the nation's poor and working poor, immigrants, women, and others underscores the value of mobilizing citizens in a common political project. What people are mobilized to, of course matters (e.g., expanding democratic rights versus the police state).

Nearly a decade ago, an independent research group examined a question long on the minds of many political junkies: "What If California's Non-voters Voted?" The results confirmed what many of us suspected. "If California's adult population made their voices heard at the ballot box, much of the political status quo could change – dramatically .. [and]...There could be some radically different outcomes."[406] The study concluded that non-voter participants would shift the direction of politics in an even greater progressive direction, suggesting even greater support for progressive taxation, expanded health care, and environmental protections. The report caused many to wonder if this finding extended to other states, especially those with a legacy of voter suppression among poor and disadvantaged communities.

The net effect over many years of "encouraging" legislators with monetary gifts, trips, contributions, honoraria and a promise of lucrative careers after public life and threats to support political opponents' run of negative advertising, and fund local campaigns to move constituents against them if they stray, has been to produce a generation of elected officials who accurately sense the dangers of going against specific corporate interests or of offering a critique of free markets, free trade, or their corporate lobbyists. If they voice doubts about the trajectory of capitalism, they do so behind closed doors. A permanently activated citizenry, directly intervening through democratic institutions, to immediate dismantle fossil-fueled threats to the survival of the planet is what so many public interest advocates view as the only viable solution to the problem of money in politics.

These factors make the difference for the tens of thousands of advocates working in the public interest. In place of vague platitudes, their stories point us toward tens of millions of supporters poised to advance democratic rights and a just economic transition. There are many ways to join one of the most important struggles of our era. As for time and interest it takes, you may be surprised to find the truth behind what motivates so many public interest activists: it can be one of the most stimulating, rewarding and meaningful activities in life.

The People's House

Another late morning in the capitol and, as my partner was fond of saying about my daily routine, 'I had miles to go before I sleep'. Swiftly descending the staircase from my office, I paused to greet one of my favorite acquaintances, José Carmona. José operated under the impression that I served as a political mentor of sorts, when it was I who regularly sought his counsel on any number of legislative issues. Indeed, among the highest honors I received over the years was when José introduced me to other public interest-oriented associates in the capitol with the simple line, "He's one of ours."

On this morning, José stopped me mid-way in my mad dash, and introduced three women, noting that they had traveled from homes in the southern reaches of the state (Imperial County) to visit the capitol. These visitors clearly came from a position of disadvantage; there were none of the displays of wealth or privilege portrayed by the powerful lobbyists who passed us on the upper floors. As such, I was prompted to welcome them to the capitol with an even greater flourish than usual. Motioning their attention to the impressive open-aired rotunda rising above us, I voiced a refrain known from my earliest years, "Welcome to your home!" I don't know if they thought me corny, too high on coffee, or simply one of José's more oddball friends, but the looks on their faces caught me by surprise.

The three women looked awestruck, proud, and pleased by the notion that all of this was something *they* possessed. That moment crystallized a potential to foster democracy that I had spent years trying to share with many young legislators. We stood in a place where the people can set rules governing...really everything. Even in the context of corrupt officials or the tweeted posts of a self-indulgent president, the potential for the exercise of democratic power remains strong. The more serious obstacles, including the corporate lobby, the moderate/business friendly legislators, Supreme Court rulings that treat multinational corporations like persons, *petroleros* and their support for a doomsday machine - all of these obstacles can be overcome by an activated and engaged citizenry.

Serving the Public Interest: Profiles of Advocates

In addition to the cast of many characters celebrated in this book there are innumerable public interest advocates who are unnamed. Many of you will justifiably wonder, "Where am I?" I must offer observation by one of my earliest readers, an esteemed UC professor, whose pithy response pointedly objected to an even larger cast of original characters, "What in the hell is this: a new Russian novel? I cannot keep up with this multitude of people!" So, my apologies to the many others, who while deserving greater recognition, will hopefully gain some modicum of recognition in my blog, if not the hereafter. One important caveat for the reader is to understand that I am not speaking for others. I am neither a spokesperson for any individual named nor any of various organizations identified – who will very ably speak for themselves.

Abascal, Ralph Santiago a disciplined legal mind, guiding spirit of California Rural Legal Assistance organization crafted central provisions of Proposition 128 "Big Green", featured in Ch. 3. While pursuing a doctorate, Abascal assisted César Chavez and Dolores Huerta to ban the short-handled hoe and DDT. He received the Thurgood Marshall Award, the Kutak-Dodds Prize of the National Legal Aid Association and was honored as a "Legal Hero" with a Fellowship at Hastings to fund transactional policy work.

Altieri, Miguel A., Chilean-American Agro-ecology professor, UC, Berkeley [Ch. 2] provides productive, natural resource conserving, culturally-sensitive, socially-just and economically viable" basics with focus on biodiversity. UN Development Program Sustainable Agriculture coordinator and founder of the Latin American Scientific Society of Agroecology, Miguel authored more than 250 publications.

Argüello, Martha Dina, feted for expanding the Los Angeles' Physicians for Social Responsibility's Health Care Without Harm Coalition [featured in Ch. 6, 9, 15, 20] serves with Californians for Pesticide Reform, Californians for a Health and Green Economy, and the CARB Global Warming Environmental Justice Advisory Panel. Committed to protecting vulnerable communities, Martha co-created the Toxies Awards to retire 'bad actor' chemicals, as co-chair for Standing Together against Neighborhood Drilling.

California's Public Employees: Among the less celebrated individuals serving the public each day hundreds of thousands of fire fighters, teachers, engineers, scientists, laborers, secretaries, and scores of additional occupations - are a bedrock supporting one of the world's most dynamic economies' achievements in health, environmental protection, clean energy, innovative technologies, sustainable business practices, clean production, and occupational safety – all built by the state's organized public workers.

Carmona, José M. (featured in Ch. 20), Energy Foundation Program Director served as former Chief of Staff, Assembly Majority Floor Leader V. Manuel Perez 2008-2014 and earlier as Advocacy Director for V. John White and Assoc. Center for Energy Efficiency and Renewable Technologies, 2003-2008.

Cervas, Strela co-Director of the California Environmental Justice Alliance, manages Energy Equity, coordinates new Civic Engagement, and Organizational Development. Work featured in Ch. 18 led to historic legislative policies bringing local renewable energy to hard-hit communities. An Environmental injustice activist with the Pilipino Workers'

Center in LA, Strela helped launch the California Household Worker Bill of Rights campaign: given that asthma and allergies are connected to living next to toxic sites

Chernow, Derek former Chief Deputy Director of the California Department of Conservation has a long history of leading environmental programs in the public, private, and nonprofit sectors. Deputy Executive Director at California Pollution Control Financing Authority Cheronow and Elena Miller were fired from the Division of Oil, Gas and Geothermal Resources by Governor Brown for "holding up drilling permits" to oil industry dismay, by requiring oil companies to follow long-standing state and federal laws [featured in Ch. 12].

del Aguila, Elma a youth member of the Central Coast Alliance United for a Sustainable Economy (CAUSE) attended California Public Utilities Commission hearing in Oxnard to demand 'Not One More Power Plant'. Elma was featured in Ch. 15, as a speaker at the 2015 CEJA Congreso

Del Chiaro, Bernadette Director CA Solar Energy Industries Assoc. lead the Million Solar Roofs campaign/ directed Environment California's Clean Energy L.A campaign. Featured in Ch.5, Del Chiaro works with the Energy Foundation to secure funding for low-income/ high unemployment areas.

Early, Steve labor activist, lawyer, cited the Richmond Progressive Alliance to show how progressive politics at the municipal level can make real change: [in Ch. 15, 16, and 20]. Author of Refinery Town: Big Oil, Big Money, and the Remaking of an American City, and articles on "The Gay Cop Who Turned Around One of America's Most Dangerous Cities" and "Breakfast with [Panther] Chairman Bobby."

Endicott, Michael B. former consultant for State Senator Tom Hayden; for the California Assembly Committee on Environmental Safety & Toxic Materials, Sierra Club California Resource Sustainability Advocate, featured in Ch. 20. Bill Magavern honored Attorney Endicott "as a point person for the environmental community inside the Capitol, doing a great job in pointing out flaws in proposals."

Filter, Gale M. started his 'official' environmental work in 1991 in the Imperial County District Attorney office where, with murders and felonies, he took on the prosecution of people responsible for harming the environment. Former first Deputy Director-Enforcement and Emergency Response, State Dept. of Toxic Substances Control, the Ash Center at Harvard honored his on-going Environmental Justice Enforcement community-based task force as a "Bright Idea in American Government:" featured in Chapter 14.

Intergovernmental Panel on Climate Change includes experts from more than 130 countries, with 450 lead, 800 contributing authors, 2,500 experts review drafts based on published, peer reviewed scientific technical literature. After the 1997 Kyoto Protocol, IPCC in 2001 concluded that temperature increases could be significantly larger than prior thought. James Hansen spoke against cap-and-trade, and was arrested 2011 and 2014 at the White House to urge rejection of the Keystone pipeline extension.

Jackson, Dr. Richard J. served as California State Public Health Officer and as longtime Director of the Center for Disease Control & Prevention, featured in Ch. 2, 5, 9 and throughout. As chair of American Academy of Pediatrics Committee on Environmental Health, he instituted federal efforts to "bio-monitor" chemical levels in the US population, received a Breast Cancer *Hero,* and *Lifetime Achievement Award* from the Public Health Law Association and the New Partners for Smart Growth, a John Heinz Award for national environmental leadership, and the Henry Hope Reed Award for his contributions to Architecture.

Jennings, Robert Case completed a degree in economics at the U.C. Berkeley and began his finance career performing Internal Revenue Service field collection in Watts, Compton, and Newport Beach. After work with at the Pacific Stock Exchange in San Francisco, the largest slice of his varied financial service career was spent at GE Capital, with focus on new product development and execution. Casey, featured in Ch. 5, 6, 10 and 16, is the COO of 13th Avenue Funding – a California 501(c)(3) that uses Income Share agreements instead of debt as a way for low-income households to fund their college costs.

Johnson Meszaros, Angela as General Counsel, Earth Justice employs litigation; community legal education and mediations, was co-chair of the Environmental Justice Advisory Committee on(AB 32 2007-2013 with focus on air pollution, energy issues, lead poisoning, land use, Superfund clean-up freeway siting, and particular research into the health impacts of oil and gas extraction [Ch. 9, 12, 15]. Among many honors, Angela was an Echoing Green Environmental Justice Resource Network Fellow.

Kanouse, Randele Sacramento lobbyist for East Bay Municipal Utility District [Ch. 1] was instrumental in advancing California legislation with the toughest lead-content standard for drinking water plumbing in the world. Randy worked for 11 years to enact a requirement that water supply availability be proven before large-scale projects may be approved, via SB 221(Kuehl) and SB 610 (Costa) enacted in 2001.

Lipper, Kip helped craft many of California's groundbreaking laws - and amendments over the decades, as the environmental expert for the state Senate's ruling Democrats, as air and water and ecological ethos are his specialty: [Featured in Ch. 8, 17]. California Clean Air Act, the state Safe Drinking Water Act and curbs on greenhouse gas emissions, bills to boost recycling, reduced landfill dumping, clean power plants ... all bear his fingerprints, as advisor to California State Senate President Pro Tempore and guest lecturer.

Magavern, Bill Policy Director for the Coalition for Clean Air since 2012, author of numerous reports on energy, environmental issues, and frequently testimony before the State Legislature and public agencies, is featured in Chapters 6, 7, 8, 12 and throughout. Bill represented Sierra Club California, 2000-2011, earning the Mary Ferguson and John Zierold Awards for outstanding legislative advocacy, a Clean Air Champion and Consumer Advocate of the Year Award. Bill's prior work was in D.C. as a staff attorney for the U.S. Public Interest Research Group, director of Public Citizen's Critical Mass Energy Project.

Marquez, Jesse N., member of California Communities Against Toxics, the L.A. Environmental Justice Network, the Coalition for Clean & Safe Ports, Harbor Vision Task Force and *many* related organizations founded the Coalition For a Safe Environment [CFASE, featured in Ch. 14], to mitigate, reduce, eliminate public health impacts caused by pollution generated by the goods transportation industry. He established the L.A. Community Environmental Enforcement Network in 2014. Author of varied publications, Jesse is a professional photographer and a student of Aztec history.

Moses, Dr. Marion Health Program for the United Farm Workers, Pesticide Education Center Director, and Medical Director for the National Farm Health Group in Keene California, director of the Pesticide Education Center in San Francisco, author of Designer Poisons, was honored by the Wonder Woman Foundation, Women of Courage Award. Professional writings center on pesticides, herbicides, toxic substances, worker rights. M.M. M.D. is a frequent public speaker: [organophosphates Ch. 9, 11, 20].

Newell, Brent Oakland Legal Director, the Center on Race, Poverty and the Environment since 2008 serves on the Animal Agriculture Reform Collaborative "steering" committee, and the Ralph Santiago Abascal Fellowship Committee. Featured in Ch. 14, Brent's environmental justice litigation and policy experience on climate change, civil rights, and the San Joaquin Valley Air Quality Project earned him a Breathe California Clean Air Award for Leadership in 2008.

Opal Plant, Pennie Yaqui, Mexican, English, Choctaw, Cherokee & European activist on environmental indigenous rights, a founding member of Idle No More, is part of the team leading SF Bay Area Refinery Corridor Healing Walks and a member of the UN Women's WECAN [featured in Ch. 16 at COP21].

Sawyer, Robert F. Chaired the California Air Resources Board, 2005-7. A UC Berkeley Professor of Energy, senior US EPA policy advisor, National Academy of Sciences Committee member, International Combustion Institute president, chair of the Bay Area Air Quality Management: featured in Ch. 11.

Takvorian, Diane Executive Director of the Environmental Health Coalition [Ch. 15's Comngreso], in 2009 President Obama-appointed to the Joint Public Advisory Committee, the NAFTA Commission for Environmental Cooperation and, in 2008 received the James Irvine Foundation Leadership Award.

Tickner, Joel - Dept. of Community Sustainability & Health, U. Mass Lowell, co-author: Massachusetts Toxic Use Reduction Act, of 1980 [in Ch. 9] demonstrates continuing focus on pollution prevention, epidemiology, green chemistry: an innovative gold standard of legislative models for toxic- prevention.

Valdez, Martha Senate Office of Research, head of the California Waste Control Board an ,Ensenada native featured in Ch. 4 joined the Environmental Health Coalition in San Diego. Martha Valdez offered early, cogent critique of EPA recalcitrance to fulfill its duty.

Van Dyck, Thomas (CIMA®) a leader in As You Sow investment advocacy -to engage corporations in environmental, human / labor rights and corporate social responsibility initiatives- offered legislative testimony [featured in Ch. 10] to discuss the Divest/Invest movement that he helped to initiate.

Wei, Angie Commission on Health, Safety & Workers' Compensation member appointed as legislative director of the state AFL-CIO Labor Federation, acting chief of staff since 2000, also of the Northern CA Coalition for Immigrant Rights PolicyLink Oakland, responding to federal welfare reform law cuts, 1996 Organized Labor [Ch. 15, 17, 20] represents 1,200 union affiliates/2 million collective bargaining workers

Witherspoon, Catherine advises the ClimateWorks Foundation on mitigating short lived climate pollutants, served as Executive Officer of the California Air Resources Board where In 2007, she was forced out by the Schwarzenegger Administration: [featured in Ch. 11] mistakenly intent on delaying substantive work on climate mitigation until the U.S. Congress acted (before the effective date of AB 32).

Yoshitani, Miya Executive Director, Asian Pacific Environmental Network, co-drafter of Principles of Environmental Justice, honored (with Mari Rose Taruc, Bernadette Del Chiaro, Strela Cervas, Darryl Molina Sarmiento, Shana Lazerow-CBE, Carolina Martinez, Ingrid Brostrom-CRPE, Laura Melgarejo, Nicole Capretz, Assemblymember Susan Eggman) as "Solar Sisters: Fighting for Equitable Clean Energy".

Zayas, Rossmery Youth Organizer, Communities for a Better Environment L.A., was active to shutdown Exide battery plant, polluting the soil of 10,000 homes for 30 years. Member of the LA Equity Alliance opposing South Gate's chronic disinvestment, Zayas [Intro, Ch. 14, and 16] joined a 2016 Grassroots Global Justice Alliance People's Caravan during the D National Convention, and protest at Paris' COP21.

Acknowledgements

This book has many origins, but one of its points of inception occurred during a bus ride several years ago with Tom Hayden. We had not met for some years, but he recognized me from our episodic exchanges at the capitol. When I asked why he had not already written something about his experiences in the Legislature, his wry response resonated with me: "I haven't gained enough distance from that experience to put things in perspective. It has taken me years to gain sufficient distance not to be overwhelmed by political commitments or works that often envelop our lives.

Central sources for my inspiration with this writing project are the numerous people I have encountered over the years. While some have worked very directly with this book, others are no less responsible for their mentoring, guidance and advice. In some other world, I would have found a way to include many, but my skills are not sufficiently honed to accomplish such a feat. So for now, I must limit my gratitude to this acknowledgement.

My political work has often hinged on confidentiality. When contacting individuals with state and federal agencies, lobbying firms, university programs or even certain legislative offices, I would often leave a message from "Carlos", a neutral alter ego better received than a call from "that trouble-maker" with the California Legislature. Many of my off-the-record meetings began with a common greeting, "*todos somos* Carlos!" I owe those of you who assisted Carlos over the years a substantial debt of gratitude.

For early guidance and brief conversations to extensive comments and suggested revisions. those who have been especially important in advancing this writing project include John Syer, Barbara Perkins, David Weir, Randy Kanouse, Joel Tickner, Bill Friedland, Ann Dubay, Ginger Rutland and Don Fields, Rebecca Newhouse, and V. John White. Special appreciation goes to A.T. Birmingham Young for her patience and good humor in (with?) addressing the challenging quirks of my version of writing: (Or should that be "my version of English."?)

In a similar vein, I want to call attention to a cast of political leaders who should receive credit for their outstanding public service. For each of these individuals, a separate publication could easily be composed around their many notable contributions extending over years, often challenging some political orthodoxy as well as constantly urging public interest advocates to press for expanded democratic practices. These individuals include Congress members George Miller, Alan Lowenthal, Barbara Lee, and Judy Chu; current and former members of California's Legislature: the Honorable Byron Sher, Lloyd Connelly, Fred Keeley, Bill Monning, Sheila Kuehl, Hannah Beth Jackson; and seat mates subjected to my many visits to the Senate Chambers, who have moved on to other venues.

I count many of the most prominent public interest advocates in this work as close colleagues, but offer only a glimpse of their complicated lives. I have frequently endeavored to rely on their published words. Many, if not all, of these individuals are better positioned to write on important topics including environmental justice, citizen activism, and civil rights; I am hopeful that many of them will share their valuable experiences and lessons in their own future writing projects. The words and errors in this text are mine- alone.

While at times critical, my written words are never intended to disparage even those indicted by the Federal Bureau of Investigation. While my partner and many close friends believe that I simply thrive on conflict, I have also learned from many older hands not to take things personally. It is difficult not to recall adversarial encounters with even my closest allies, but I trust that these and others have never mistaken the respect I have for even my political adversaries. (Well, maybe except for...) Like much of my political work, these writings are in large part collaborations involving many others. It is true that those named cannot be blamed for what appears herein; nevertheless, they do share a responsibility for having encouraged my own works or have demonstrated by example the courage that all of us should pursue in the short we have on this planet:.

The cast of notable public interest lobbyists who have assisted many endeavors over the years is impossible to list, but here goes: Bonnie Holms-Gen, Gary Patton, Dan Jacobson, Jane Williams, Andy Igregas, Mark Schacht, Tom Rankin, Jody Sparks, Michael Green, Caroline Cox, Joe Lyou, Angie Wei, Steve Smith, Barry Broad, Elizabeth Martin, Kelly Moran, Still others who have inspired my work over the decades include an extraordinary team of legal activists: Al Meyerhoff, Ralph Abascal, Luke Cole, Jim Wheaton, Vic Sher, Tim Malloy, David Roe, Mike Axline, Jon Bonine, Scott Valor and Martha McCabe: one of Jim Hightower's earliest, most sage counselors. One of the most gifted and talented of this esteemed group, Claudia Polsky, is a faculty member with UC Berkeley's School of Law.

Additionally, there are numerous professionals from the arena of public and environmental health who have often served as my science guides in last minute tutorials preceding committee hearings, floor debates, and other political encounters that have often proven invaluable. Those in my continuing education practicum include: Carl Cranor, Amy Kyle, Joel Tickner, George Alexeeff, Tracy Woodruff, Louis Guillette, Stefan Lorenzato and, my most constant collaborator, Richard J. Jackson.

Finally, there is my partner in life and most important force in this work, Cheri Lucas Jennings. In a collaboration extending over more than four decades, Cheri has been steadfast; passionately supportive of my tilting at windmills of every imaginable sort. With an activism originating in civil rights marches, Professor Emeritus Lucas Jennings has carried on the good fight, always challenging those who might prefer to ignore everyday injustices. She insists that authorship of this book belongs solely to me: But, those familiar with Cheri's advocacy will see her influence on the style, direction and content of this work: For all of that, and so much more...

About the Author

Bruce H. Jennings was born in Oakland, California and in his early years lived in Spain, Argentina and Mexico. He graduated with honors from the University of California, Berkeley and received his doctorate in Political Science at the University of Hawai'i. Bruce balanced his academic studies with extra-curricular activities including membership with the International Brotherhood of Teamsters and the Oil, Chemical and Atomic Workers.

Bruce has taught at several institutions, including the University of California at Berkeley, the University of Montana, and the Evergreen State College. He has delivered lectures at the *Universidad Autonoma de Chapingo* and the London School of Economics and Political Science. Bruce's research includes several appointments as a visiting scholar at UC Berkeley and as a Fulbright Scholar conducting research on the North American Free Trade Agreement in Mexico.

Bruce retired as one of the co-directors for the Senate Committee on Environmental Quality after having served as a senior advisor to the California Legislature for environmental policy over a period spanning approximately twenty-five years. He began his career as a Senate Fellow and served as a senior consultant to the Senate Office of Research as well as the chief of staff to the Assembly Committee on Environmental Safety and Toxic Materials.

Bruce's partner, Cheri Lucas Jennings, is a professor emeritus at the Evergreen State College in Olympia, Washington. In addition to collaborating on various writing projects, they host a blog post on California politics at Calpolitico [http://calpolitico.blogspot.com/]. Bruce launched a collaborative venture in 2017, Collective Political Strategies in Santa Rosa, California.

END NOTES

Introduction

1. Studs Terkel, Hope Dies Last: Keeping the Faith in Difficult Times (NY: The New Press, 2003) p. 222.
2. Allison Dunne, " Zephyr Teachout Is Among Activists Delivering Petitions To Trump Tower," On the Media (WAMC: December 15, 2016).
3. Don Lee, "Trump... the Richest Cabinet in U.S. History," Los Angeles Times (December 7, 2016).
4. Bill O'Reilly Show, Interview with Donald Trump (Fox News Network: February 5, 2017).
5. George Skelton, "California Democrats relish opposing Trump on immigration - but they could go too far," Los Angeles Times (February 2, 2017).
6. Michael Klare, "Donald Trump's Energy Nostalgia and the Path to Hell," (TomDispatch.com) December 1, 2016.
7. Bloomberg News, "Scott Pruitt, critic of Clean Power Plan, picked to lead U.S. environmental agency": (Bloomberg News) December 8, 2016.
8. George Skelton, op cit.
9. Simon Thomsen, "'I don't give a damn if we agree': Arnold Schwarzenegger just gave a climate-change speech that will give you chills," Business Insider Australia (December 8, 2015).
10. Ibid.
11. Sammy Lyon, "System Change Not Climate Change," (posted at Lyonideas.com, March 8, 2016).
12. California's cap and trade program as defined in legislation enacted in 2006 would become known by its bill number, Assembly Bill 32 or AB 32 as well as the bill's title, The Global Warming Solutions Act and more formally cited as Chapter 488, Statutes of 2006.
13. Dan Morain, "How Oil Won the Battle for SB 350," The Sacramento Bee, September 12, 2015.
14. James Hansen, et al., "Ice melt, sea level rise and superstorms: evidence from paleoclimate data, climate modeling, and modern

observations that 2 ◦C global warming is highly dangerous," The Journal of Atmospheric Chemistry and Physics, Discussion Paper, 15, pp 20059 -20179.

15. Naomi Klein, This Changes Everything: Capitalism vs. the Climate (NY: Simon & Shuster, 2014).
16. Neela Banerjee, Lisa Song, David Hasemyer, "Exxon's Own Research Confirmed Fossil Fuels' Role in Global Warming Decades Ago:" InsideClimate News (September 16, 2015).
17. Forecast the Facts appears to have been the originator of this term in twitter messages designed to emphasize that Hurricane Sandy far from being a "natural disaster" was a largely industrial event based on pumping huge amounts of carbon into the atmosphere, most intensively during the twentieth century.
18. Jess Shankleman, "Eight Fuel Majors Seen Polluting as Much as the U.S." (Bloomberg, March 8, 2017): For a more extensive discussion of the importance of fossil fuels in framing the discussion of worsening climate crises, see Thomas Princen, Jack P. Manno, Pamela Martin, editors, Ending the Fossil Fuel Era (MIT Press, 2015) pp 3 - 4.
19. Chris Megerian, "World is on a collision course with fossil fuels, Governor Jerry Brown Says," Los Angeles Times, July 8, 2015.
20. David Baker, "Pope Blasts California's Cap and Trade system," San Francisco Chronicle (SFGATE: June 18, 2015). More generally, see Pope Francis, Encyclical on Climate Change & Inequality: On Care for Our Common Home (Brooklyn: Melville House, 2015).
21. The 'corporate lobby' refers generally to those representing larger, typically multinational firms as distinct from the very large number of small businesses with effectively no representation.
22. As an explanatory example, see Michael Hoexter, "Living in the Web of Soft Climate Denial," posted on Naked Capitalism (September 10, 2016) and first published on New Economic Perspectives: "The common but lazy use of the term "market" for the private sector as a whole, adopted by neoliberalism, is an ubiquitous ideological mislabeling, that enables the diverse assemblage of economic actors in the private sector to claim that they represent the virtues of the

supposedly optimal economic organization of "free" markets. The conception of society embedded in neoliberal ideas is based on the ahistorical abstractions of neoclassical and Austrian economics in which society is either already or should soon be a "free" or minimally-regulated market. The simultaneous, paradoxical assertion of the not-yet-achieved model ideal and the already-existent reality of an all-encompassing market, in real political practice, tends to hide from public view, the dealings within the private and public sectors of the wealthy, the financial sector and non-market and quasi-market corporate monopolies and oligopolies."

23. The comment made by Warren Buffett during an interview on September 30, 2011 with reference to the differential tax treatment for upper income earners and others has been widely quoted. A large body of empirical studies have documented this broader trend (e.g., analysis of gini index regarding the increasing disparity between economic classes) and led to a discussion regarding rich and poor.

Chapter 1 Climate of Conflict

24. The legislative measure, Senate Bill 651, was presented on August 28, 2007 in room 112 of the State Capitol at a regularly scheduled hearing o≈f the Senate Environmental Quality Committee.
25. Assembly Bill 1953, by Assemblymember Wilma Chan (Chapter 853, Statutes of 2006).
26. For appreciation of the politics of occupational health standards see David Noble's America by Design: Science, Technology, and the Rise of Corporate Capitalism (Oxford University Press, 1979).
27. Technically, the motion on Senate Bill 651 was recorded as "held in committee without recommendation" which the author recognized as essentially a defeat with the courtesy of not requiring members of the committee to actually cast votes in opposition.
28. While water quality is primarily under purview of the State Water Resources Control Board, it is a jurisdiction also shared with other agencies responsible for public health and toxic substances.

29. aka former State Senator Ron Calderon.
30. Federal Bureau of Investigation, "State Senator Ron Calderon Charged....," (U.S. Attorney's Office, Central District of California, February 21, 2014) Press Release
31. Ibid.
32. Who also sponsored a series of bills authored by Assembly member Lloyd Connelly and Senator Nicholas C. Petris, among others, during the 1980s. See also the Birth Defects Prevention Act of 1984 and the Pesticide Contamination Prevention Act of 1985.
33. David Rosner and Gerald Markowitz, "Two, Three... Many Flints: America's Coast-to-Coast Toxic Crisis," posted February 9, 2016 at TomDispatch.com
34. David Rosner and Gerald Markowitz, Lead Wars: The Politics of Science and the Fate of America's Children (University of California Press, 2014).
35. Ibid.
36. Tony Barboza, "Higher levels of lead found in the blood of children near Exide plant in Vernon," Los Angeles Times, April 8, 2016.
37. Leslie Carothers, Upholding EPA Regulation of Greenhouse Gases: The Precautionary Principle Redux, 41 Ecology Law Quarterly (University of California, Berkeley: 2015).
38. Most specifically the Health and Safety Code relating to the cleanup of underground tank leaks, remediation of hazardous waste, permitting refinery emission, penalties for violations of law as evidence that much regulation is constructed around recognized hazards in processing, use, and disposal of petroleum.
39. An amendment attempted during the committee hearing on Senate Bill 651 was defeated when the staff questioned the premise that such a group was independent from industry influence.
40. It is important to note that the California standard does not precisely equate to lead-free, although from a practical view no water passing through such faucets allows for any lead content and the faucets themselves allow for only de minimus amounts anywhere else in the faucet.

Chapter 2 Inside the Law Machine

41. The Senate Fellows program selects applicants from a statewide competition. Past recipients of the fellowship have included individuals, like I, who had little or no connection to elected officials or their wealthy donors. Over time, the fellowships became coveted as a vehicle for the heirs of the powerful to enter a career in politics.
42. Linkage to the politics of agricultural research had taken shape long before I arrived in Sacramento, principally in the form of my doctoral research (see Foundations of International Agricultural Research (Westview Press in 1988).
43. Senate Bill 872 (Chapter 1188, Statutes of 1986), was brought to Senator Petris in 1984 by organic farmers (Kay Thornley, Drew Rivers, "Amigo" Bob Cantisano), recognized activists such as Sibella Kraus, and eventual backing from organizations across the state, including the luminary owner of Chez Panisse Alice Waters, one of the state's larger raisin growers Steve Pavich, and Lundberg Farms, the first members of California Certified Organic Farmers.
44. Narda Zacchino, California Comeback: How a 'Failed State' Became a Model for the Nation (New York: St. Martin's Press, 2016) p 175.
45. "Smoke & Fumes," The Center for International Environmental Law (as posted on May 19, 2016).
46. Zacchino, op cit., p 175.
47. Ibid. In addition to the documents collected by the Center for International Environmental Law are the analyses collected by InsideClimate News as well as the Los Angeles Times.
48. Birth Defects Prevention Act regulatory apparatus (see section 13121 et seq. of the Food and Agriculture Code) is celebrated for eliminating many thousands of pesticide products posing long-term health hazards. In later years, original supporters became dismayed with the calculus of risks instead of a legal device to expeditiously eliminate known hazards from commerce.
49. The many individuals leading the assault included Marion Moses, Laurie Mott, Al Meyerhoff, Ralph Santiago Abascal and many public health and alternative agricultural research officials.

50. Dr. Jackson's service as a branch chief was in a predecessor agency to what would later become known as the Office of Environmental Health Hazard Assessment. This was before he became the State Public Health Officer.
51. See the Pesticide Contamination Prevention Act, a series of field posting of hazards statutes, school pesticide prevention, and the toxic air contaminants programs, among others.
52. Sacramento Bee, October 1, 2012 Jerry Brown surpasses Reagan, Deukmejian for most bills signed," Gov. J. Brown had signed more regular session bills - 12,744 - than any other governor since 1967, according to a Senate Committee on Governance & Finance analysis. The third-term Democratic governor signed 876 regular session bills in one year. Deukmejian and Reagan signed 12,530 bills and 12,486 bills, respectively. Brown, a governor before from 1975 to 1983, had now vetoed a total of 773 regular session bills, the fewest of any governor since the "pocket veto" era ended in 1967. His veto rate of 12% is slightly lower than the 14% rate he posted in 2011, and the average veto rate of 13% since 1967. He vetoed fewer than 5% priorly. http://blogs.sacbee.com/capitolalertlatest/2012/10/ brown-surpasses-reagan-deukmejian-for-most-bills-signed.html#storylink=cpy
53. The comparison with laws enacted in D.C. owes especially to the combining of many topics in a single Congressional measure or conflating budget with policy elements. Many in Congress typically have very few measures for which they are the principal architects. More often, a California a sole-author legislator will have fewer measures signed into law by the governor during their first two years but more subsequently than federal legislators.
54. "Measures enacted by the U.S. Congress from 1981 to 2010," posted on Statista (June, 2015).
55. The number and complexity of negotiations for taxes, constitutional measures, and such become more challenging in terms of vote requirements (27 in the Senate, 54 in the Assembly).
56. Statista, op cit.

57. The legislator mentioned herein, although not 'Jack', is based on conversations with staff over the years echoing the experiences of California legislators, after being elected to Congress.
58. The allocation of the fund being negotiated at the time, the Petroleum Violation Escrow Account, was a matter over which Petris exercised potentially considerable authority, as a member of the Senate Rules' Committee. The purposes for utilizing such funds in agriculture, in the eyes of many, fit perfectly with a mechanism that was designed to reimburse Californian's generally for having been overcharged by petroleum companies; an agriculture that was excessively reliant on petroleum inputs for every facet of cultivating, processing and transporting food.
59. In later years the same energy-reliant agricultural system would be subject to critical review for utilizing excessive amounts of fossil fuels and damaging the earth's climate on a global scale.
60. Dahlsten and Altieri's challenges to dominant agricultural methods, especially to the use of synthetic pesticides, each provoked controversy. In response to a challenge that select UC program directors were not conflicted by subsidy from pesticide manufacturers, U.C.'s administrators argued that virtually all faculty were tainted. After Altieri or Dahlsten were chosen to head the unit, the University switched arguments, saying that Berkeley was an inappropriate location, statewide.
61. Senate Bill 872: Chapter 1188, 1986 Statutes. The beginning passages in this bill include the following language: "Section 552 The purpose of this article is to promote more research and education on sustainable agricultural practices... [including methods designed to accomplish all of the following:] (a) The control of pests and diseases of agricultural importance through alternatives that reduce or eliminate the use of pesticides and petrochemicals. (b) Produce, process, and distribute food and fiber in ways that consider the interactions among soil, plant, water, air, animals, tillage, machinery, labor, energy, and transportation to enhance agricultural efficiency, public health, and resource conservation."

Chapter 3 Taking the Initiative

62. Big Brown or the California corporate farming initiative included supporters from the Western Growers Association, the Agricultural Council of California, California's Citrus Mutual; Farm Bureau, and the Western Agricultural Chemicals Association (WACA). Using the acronym CAREFUL (the "Consumer Pesticide Enforcement Act For Food, Water and Worker Safety), Big Brown's provisions emphasized the protection of consumers based on expanded programs including scientific advisory panels, scientific data reviews, pesticide monitoring and risk assessment programs, none of which were actually meant to initiate changes.
63. The Senate Office of Research (SOR) frequently devised decisive innovations in California law. Often compared to the Congressional Research Service and its detailed analyses of federal laws, a more apt comparison was with the Congressional Office of Technology Assessment (OTA). Like OTA, various staff aggressively pursued effort to combat "regulatory capture," by which agencies became zombies, controlled by the very industries they were mandated to regulate. Formally non-partisan, the SOR displayed an independence from the control of Democrats' dominance as political leaders. Consultants both criticized existing policies and formulated more progressive solutions to deal with intransigent bureaucracies. SOR briefings by a brain-trust had the additional responsibility of providing both reviews and questions for the governor's appointees that required Senate confirmation.

    The Office frequently linked the California Legislature to a range of other policy-making groups from regional to Congressional to non-governmental/private sector associations to Think Tanks. Especially extensive links to a vast network of faculty and researchers within public and private state universities aided the monitor of policy across the U.S. and beyond, while synthesizing and delivering proposals for innovative policies. The Research Office also served over the years in both the Senate and the Assembly, as a training ground for consultants, back-stopping the work of standing committees.

Many SOR consultants later assumed senior Assembly and Senate positions.

Ronald T. Libby, Eco-Wars: Political Campaigns and Social Movements (Columbia Press, 1998).

64. Ibid.
65. See California Secretary of State website, "History of Initiatives Voted into Law" et al.
66. Proposition 65 is the Safe Drinking Water and Toxic Enforcement Act of 1986. Enacted by the people of California as a voter initiative, it may be found in Sections 25180, 25180.7, 25192 and 25249.5. through 25249.13 of the Health and Safety Code.
67. While a comprehensive listing would prove impossible, recognized legal talent included such individuals as Vic Sher, David Roe, Al Meyerhoff, Ralph Abascal, Harry Schneider, Judith Bell, Ralph Lightstone, Mike Axline, John Bonine, Luke Cole, David Beckman, Martha McCabe as well as a very large number of attorneys working for local, state and federal agencies (many of whom are probably advantaged by not being named publicly).
68. Bruce Jennings, California's Experience with Proposition 65: Implementing the Safe Drinking Water and Toxic Enforcement Act (Sacramento: the Senate Office of Research, March 1990) p. 27.
69. Ibid. pp 3-4.
70. Ibid. pp 3-4.
71. Ibid.
72. Incisive discussion of this phenomena found in David Noble's seminal work, America By Design.
73. Samuel S. Epstein, "Are We Losing the War Against Cancer?", Congressional Record, Vol 133, No. 135 (Washington, D.C.: September 9, 1987) p E 3449.
74. AFL- CIO v. Deukmejian, Third Appellate District (Sacramento, California) July 20, 1989, Superior Court No. 348195, p 21
75. For an analysis of provisions, among other reviews, see: Bruce Jennings, et al: Proposition 128: Environmental Protection Act of 1990 (Sacramento: The Senate Office of Research, Undated).
76. Ibid. pp 21 - 22.

77. From 27 to 54 miles per gallon equals forty percent of mandated reductions
78. Phone interview with John Van de Kamp. August 11, 2014.
79. Ibid.
80. Barry M. Casper, Lost in Washington: Finding the Way Back to Democracy in America (Boston: University of Massachusetts Press, 2000) p. 308.
81. Ibid.
82. Neela Banerjee, Lisa Song, David Hasemyer, Exxon: The Road Not Taken, Inside Climate News (Sept 16, 2015).
83. Neela Banerjee, "Exxon's Oil Industry Peers Knew About Climate Dangers in the 1970s, Too," InsideClimate News (December 22, 2015) vis a briefing by Stanford Professor John Laurmann.
84. Ibid.
85. Ibid.
86. Ibid.
87. David Hasemyer and John H. Cushman Jr., "Exxon Sowed Doubt About Climate Science for Decades by Stressing Uncertainty," InsideClimate News (October 22, 2015).
88. Ibid.
89. Banerjee, Song and Hasemyer, , op. cit.
90. The estimates are taken from Peter Schrag, California: America's High-Stakes Experiment (UC Press, 2006) p 152. As someone who worked within SOR our shared perspective was that research offices largely ceased to operate as they once had functioned, from the resulting loss of staff.
91. David Hasemyer and John H. Cushman Jr., "Exxon Sowed Doubt About Climate Science for Decades by Stressing Uncertainty," InsideClimate News (October 22, 2015).
92. Speaking at an event occurring before the Kyoto Protocol, Exxon's chief executive articulated a position that had already been dismissed by his own internal scientific team, "It is highly unlikely that the temperatures in the middle of the next century will be significantly affected, whether policies are enacted now or twenty years from now."

Chapter 4 So Far from California

93. For unrelenting detail on these points, see my related book, Foundations of International Agricultural Research: Science and Politics in Mexican Agriculture (Boulder Colorado: Westview Press, 1988).
94. Literature on forcing Mexican peasantry from the countryside resulting from "modernization" of agriculture is voluminous, especially those works authored by Mexican scholars including David Barkin, Blanca Suarez, Victor Toledo, Cynthia Hewitt de Alcantara, Javier Trujillo de Arriaga and certain others outside of Mexico with special mention of Angus Wright's notable work: The Death of Ramon Gonzalez (University of Texas Press, 2005).
95. Joel Hirschhorn, Serious Reduction of Hazardous Waste (Washington, D.C.: Congressional Office of Technology Assessment: US Government Printing Office, Sept. 1986).
96. The study was a Fulbright Research Award allowing me approximately six months to travel freely throughout Mexico gathering materials and interviewing people.
97. Tom Athanasiou, Divided Planet: The Ecology of Rich and Poor (Boston: Little, Brown & Co. 1996) p 265.
98. Mark Dowie op cit., p 186.
99. The original phrase uttered by Mexican President Porfirio Diaz at the turn of the 20th century, translated is more popularly known as "Poor Mexico, so far from God and so close to the United States!"

Chapter 5 A Path Not Taken

100. For a useful fuller description of these events and the period, see Kevin Starr's Coast of Dreams: California on the Edge, 1990-2003 (New York: Knopf, 2004), especially the most relevant chapter, "The Boys from Texas."
101. Christopher Weare. California Electricity Crisis (San Francisco: Public Policy Institute of California) 2003.

102. Peter Schrag, California: America's High-Stakes Experiment (Berkeley: UC Press, 2006) page 161.
103. Narda Zacchino, California Comeback (NY: St Martin's Press, 2016) pp 86 - 87.
104. Kevin Starr, Coast of Dreams: California on the Edge, 1990-2003 (N.Y.: Knopf, 2004). p. 591
105. Bethany McLean and Peter Elkin, The Smartest Guys in the Room: The Amazing Rise and Scandalous Fall of Enron (NY: Penguin Group, 2003) p. 264.
106. V. John White, registered lobbyist and executive director, Center for Energy Efficiency and Renewable Technologies (CEERT), Interview Sacramento, January 2016.
107. Ibid: p 593.
108. Weare, op. cit.
109. Ken Alex, testimony for the Senate Select Committee on Climate Change, State Capitol, Jan 7, 2010.
110. The quote from the former Senator Bowen is contained in Peter Schrag's work, California: America's High-Stakes Experiment (Berkeley: UC Press, 2006) p. 154
111. McLean and Elkin, op cit., page 267.
112. Assembly member Fred Keeley (representing Santa Cruz), played a pivotal role exploring the radical notion that a public entity might purchase a private entity. Without his leadership, it is unlikely that any legislative workgroup would ever have been formed or alternative approaches even considered in the Legislature.
113. Kevin Daehnke, one of the partners in the law firm Daehnke Cruz, played a leadership role in gathering together a cross section of private sector associations in Los Angeles.
114. Weare, op. cit.
115. Weare, op. cit. It is important that even though various casual observers thought California was simply a victim of a "perfect storm" of natural events (e.g., see Starr's Coast of Dreams, p. 593) subsequent investigations mirror assessments by the UC economist, Casey Jennings and others who briefed legislative

staff and legislators that the State was being gamed by energy traders.

116. V. John White, CEERT, Interview Sacramento, 2016.
117. Claudia Assis. "J.P. Morgan, energy regulator near settlement." Wall Street Journal (July 17, 2013).
118. David R. Baker, "Enron Redux: Shell Bilked California in Energy Crisis, Judge Finds," San Francisco Chronicle (April 15, 2016).
119. Ibid.

Chapter 6 A Tale of Two Lobbies

120. At the time of this scene, the legislative directors for the Sierra Club and Physicians for Social Responsibility - Los Angeles, respectively.
121. Martin Gilens and Benjamin I. Page, "Testing Theories of American Politics: Elites, Interest Groups, and Average Citizens," American Political Science Review (September, 2014). A summary of their findings penned by one of the largest bond managers in the world, Jeremy Grantham, provided this summary in an opinion piece for Barron's (July 28, 2015): "Their extensive review of federal legislation documents that the average bill in the U.S. Congress has a 31% chance of passing; this chance falls to 30% when the proposed legislation is hated by average citizens and rises to 32% when they love it! In contrast, love from the economic elite, although not absolutely guaranteeing success raises the chances of its passing to 60%. But when the elite truly detest an issue, it is like passing a death sentence: About 1% of these bills pass."
122. As difficult as it is to draw on two individuals to characterize California's environmental lobby, my purpose is to juxtapose their work with their counterparts in the corporate lobby. Shown in the profiles at the end of this book is a much wider and deeper group of public interest organizations actively engaged in the state capitol on a regular basis.
123. For a fuller history surrounding the 'new wave' of environmentalism, see the excellent discussion in Mark Dowie's analysis of contemporary

environmentalism: Losing Ground: American Environmentalism at the Close of the Twentieth Century (Cambridge: MIT Press, 1995).

124. Personal interview with Bill Magavern, Sacramento (2014). For a more extensive background of Bill's work see Lost in Washington: Finding the Way Back to Democracy in America by Barry M. Casper (University of Massachusetts Press, 2000).
125. Capitol Weekly listing of "the most powerful movers and shakers in California politics", 2009.
126. Laurie, with Randlett Nelson Madden since 1985, represents business clients on cutting edge issues including green chemistry, bio-monitoring labeling, hazardous waste disposal and air quality legislation regulations as they relate to consumer products.
127. Marisa Lagos, "The Cost of a Seat: California Legislators Raise More than $1,000 a Day," KQED, June 24, 2015 with data provided by MapLight.
128. Patrick McGreevy, "Lobbyists Set Spending Record in Sacramento," The LA Times: Feb 2, 2012.
129. The examples are not hypotheticals, but reflect my personal involvement in conflicts over specific bills, bond and initiative measures.
130. Dowie, op. cit. pp 40 - 42.
131. Reports focusing on specific corporate-based efforts (e.g., the American Legislative Exchange Committee or ALEC) misapprehend that state legislative agendas are increasingly dominated by a much broader corporate presence - framing a larger public narrative and political agenda (e.g., the vital role of private sector jobs versus urgency to create jobs decoupled from industries that are destructive to public health and the environment).
132. The primary lobbyist served for several years as an advisor to Speaker Willie Brown. Indeed, many of Speaker Brown's staff eventually became prominent members of California's corporate lobby.
133. The reference is to one of California's most respected legislators, the Honorable Byron Sher.
134. Staffing resources - such as Research Offices for the Senate (SOR) provide some opportunity for an in-depth analysis of legislation not available to many other states or even Congress.

135. See Kahl Pownall Website heading Public Relations" see Appendix A
136. Ibid

Chapter 7 Market Solutions for Market Failures

137. Denny Carpenter in comments before a closed meeting of the Senate Fellows during the Fall 1984, among many others holding a similar perspective.
138. Kevin Hechtkopf, "Arnold Says Now Is Time for Action," Associated Press, June 2, 2005.
139. Executive Order S-3-05 issued by Governor Schwarzenegger on June 1, 2005.
140. Tom Athanasiou, Divided Planet: The Ecology of Rich and Poor (Boston: Little Brown, 1996) p 66.
141. Assembly Bill 32 is formally cited as Chapter 488, Statutes of 2006 commencing with Section 38500 of the Health and Safety Code. Also related are agency regulations, memoranda of agreements, budgetary actions, executive orders, and the work of specialized groups (e.g., Section 12812.6 of the Government Code relating to the Climate Action Team Report).
142. California's climate related laws include statutes on renewable energy portfolio standards, appliance standards, interstate transmission of energy, building efficiency programs, vehicle emission standards, tire replacement inflation standards, recycling mandates, restrictions on truck and rail idling, and a state Clean Air Act restricting emissions for a broadening range of particulates, gases and combustion materials, including carbon dioxide. Since the beginning of the 21st century, many argued that by adopting California's suite of regulatory standards the nation as a whole could rapidly and aggressively reduce greenhouse gases.
143. Known as the "Legislative Counsel", a group of several dozen attorneys perform the too little appreciated task of ensuring that legislation achieves a much higher degree of excellence than the ideas

copied on the back of napkins or the marginal notes of harried committee consultants.

144. "shorting" a term used by investors, is used here to imply California's declining financial position by engaging in emissions trading, hence 'shorting' California signifies that wise investors would bet against the state as benefitting from emission trading.
145. Brevity is the standard in legislative communications: so too with committee analyses. Documents summarizing existing law, proposed law, and an analysis of the proposal are typically 3-5 pages.
146. Naomi Klein, This Changes Everything (NY: Simon & Schuster: 2014) p 218.
147. To establish GHG emissions' reductions as a baseline threshold used to set a limit on aggregate emissions. The aggregate emissions would then be limited by declining caps on total emissions over time as a means of decreasing the release of GHGs. In combination with this decreasing cap, the law would create allowances or trade-credits equal to the numeric value of the cap.
148. This paragraph paraphrases a passage written by the Legislative Analyst 2014-15 Budget, "How Cap-and -Trade Works to Reduce Emissions," (Sacramento, February 24, 2014) p 2.
149. "Business as usual" in this sense meaning to what extent might one expect various industries to reduce their emissions based on existing law and prevailing economic conditions? (such as conformity with Clean Air Act and clean energy requirements for the sale of electrical energy from sources outside the state, Toxic Air Contaminant Act requirements affecting co-pollutants).
150. Later: approached by a group of scientists supporting the bill, including professionals with Ames/ NASA, Lawrence Livermore, and other research labs, I proposed a conference call for discussion of a basic premise: was AB 32 asking enough reduction in GHG emissions? Neither the scientists nor the national environmental group sponsoring their visit returned my call.

151. One example is found in the extensive regulatory provisions of hazardous waste law contained in California's Health and Safety Codes.
152. Robert D. Bullard, Dumping in Dixie: Race, Class, and Environmental Quality (Boulder, CO: Westview Press, 1990): Back cover of paperback edition.
153. Ann Katten, California Rural Legal Assistance Foundation.
154. Set by the US EPA and known as the National Ambient Air Quality Standards (NAAQS).
155. Gordon Morris Bakken, "Reclaim and Pollution Credit Training: Aiming the Spotlight on the 'Energy Crisis Profiteers Leaving the Public in the Dark," University of West Los Angeles Law Review 33 (2001) p 175.
156. RGGI refers to the Regional Greenhouse Gas Initiative established by a memorandum of agreement in 2005 among nine East coast states to reduce carbon dioxide emissions. It has achieved notable successes in reducing emissions it also differs significantly from California's program with respect to a smaller universe of facilities, the number and kinds of pollutants, auction prices, and the complexity of emission sources.
157. Kim Hoofs, "Property Rights in Legal History." Property Law and Economics: edited by Boudewijn Bouckaert (Cheltan, 2010). p 248.
158. See for example, the Floor Analysis of Senate Bill 2170 of 1996. "..with RECLAIM on the books and other market-based measures on the horizon, variance limitations have become crucial…an interconnected system of mass emission caps, declining balances, and tradable currency, RECLAIM depends on each company making choices – between applying controls or buying credits on the open market... If companies can effectively 'leave the system' by getting variances, the market will be undermined, credit values will drop, emissions will not be fully offset and the overall program could collapse."
159. The quote represents a common response among community-based environmental organizations arriving to the capitol and speaking to me about their concerns about AB 32.
160. Section 38565 of the Health and Safety Code.

Chapter 8 The Climate of Subversion

161. While personally familiar with this particular episode, I revisited it with Kip Lipper on December 10, 2015 at his capitol office.
162. Among the unresolved controversies in the Senate Environmental Quality Committee hearing on AB 32 was the issue of defining greenhouse gases. In prevailing with rejecting the inclusion of what I had understood to be an accepted amendment to broaden the definition. This back-room deal stopped decisive action on a pivotal group of contaminants, by as much as a decade.
163. Arnold Schwarzenegger with Peter Petre, Total Recall: My Unbelievably True Life Story (Simon & Schuster, 2012) p 549. BP is the acronym for British Petroleum.
164. Ibid., p 549-550.
165. Catherine Witherspoon, personal communication (March 15, 2017).
166. Appointed to chair the Air Resources Board on December 22, 2005, Governor Schwarzenegger praised Dr. Sawyer as "an exceptionally accomplished scientist, environmental policy expert and teacher who devoted his career to use science and technology to improve air quality, not only in California, but across our country and the world..."
167. President pro Tempore Don Perata and Speaker Fabian Núñez correspondence to Robert Sawyer, Chair, California Air Resources Board (The California Legislature: September 7, 2006).
168. Executive Order S-17-06 - Implementation of Global Warming Solutions Act: As with other official actions, it remains unclear to what extent the Governor was even aware of potential controversies surrounding the soon-to-be rescinded executive order. Speaker Nunez's quote is in:
169. President pro Tempore Don Perata to Governor Arnold Schwarzenegger, October 23, 2006.
170. Terry Tamminen, Lives Per Gallon: The True Cost of Our Oil Addiction (Washington, D.C. Island Press, 2006).
171. Ibid. book jacket
172. AB 32 authorized discrete early action greenhouse gas emission reduction measures to be initiated on June 30, 2007 and adopted on

or before January 2010 pursuant to Section 38560.5 of the Health and Safety Code.

173. Dr. Sawyer voted against a package of three global warming early action measures regarded as inadequate, based on an understanding of the law by knowledgeable capitol staff. He was, he demurred, simply a matter of his carrying out his duties as Chair, for "the state board to adopt rules and regulations in an open public process."

174. Paul Rosenberg, "Governor Schwarzenegger's Global Warming Act Called Hot Air," Consumer Watchdog (http//www.consumerwatchdog) July 7, 2007. "The week Sawyer's firing became public, his communications director, Adam Mendelsohn, stated that the Gov. wanted the California Air Resources Board to adopt more items, a message consistent with the Governor's carefully-crafted image, but also another lie.

The next Monday, Sawyer released a transcript of Executive Aid Dunmoyer's voice message saying the governor's office was "very comfortable' with the three items," adding, "We really prefer you to stick to the three that we believe are vetted well, that are likely to succeed. That's the direction." Dunmoyer, acted as a key aide in Sawyer's firing and was known in Sacramento as a former insurance industry lobbyist who authored a 2002 Karl Rove-styled memo calling for "all-out war on the industry's enemies."

175. Catherine Witherspoon, op. cit.

176. Angela Johnson Mezaros, Clean Air Matters [http://cleanairmatters.net/blog] March 31, 2011.

177. Paul Rosenberg, "Governor Schwarzenegger's Global Warming Act Called Hot Air", Consumer Watchdog, July 7, 2007

178. Ibid.

179. Peter Huynh, Muhammad T. Salam, Tricia Morphew, Kenny Y. C. Kwong, and Lynne Scott, "Residential Proximity to Freeways is Associated with Uncontrolled Asthma in Inner-City Hispanic Children and Adolescents," SCIENCEOPEN 13 (June 2010): noted the importance of environmental justice impacts of climate change in transportation, "even more sobering when you consider that 45 million Americans live within 300 feet of a highway and the far greatest percentage are poor children of families of color."

180. Ibid. quoting Judy Dugan.
181. See, for example Mark Dowie's Losing Ground: American Environmentalism at the Close of the Twentieth Century (Cambridge: MIT Press, 1995) p. 182.
182. Sir Nicholas Stern, The Stern Review on the Economic Effects of Climate Change (London: Her Majesty's Treasury: 2006).
183. Juliette Jowit and Patrick Wintour, "Cost of Tackling Global Climate Change has Doubled, Warns Stern," The Guardian (London: June 25, 2008).
184. Michael P. Wilson, Daniel A. Chia and Bryan C. Ehlers, "Green Chemistry in California: A Framework for Leadership in Chemicals Policy and Innovation," (Berkeley: The California Policy Research Center: 2006) Executive Summary.
185. Background information on Martha Argüello's discussion about the toxies and related work in archives of the Collaborative on Health and the Environment, Science and Action to Protect Public Health: How Health Care Professionals Are Changing Chemical Policy (January 11, 2012)
186. *Promotoras* is a female noun referring to those who promote health protective practices, but are not necessarily formally trained in all avenues of public health.
187. From the original oath, swearing by Apollo physician: The modern version (by Louis Lasagna, Tufts, 1964) does "not treat a fever, chart a cancerous growth, but a sick human being, whose illness may affect the person's family and economic stability. My responsibility includes these related problems, if I am to care adequately for the sick."
188. Bruce Jennings, Summary of SB 2767 for Senator Nicholas C. Petris (Sacramento: Unpublished, Mar 7, 1988). Specific elements of the California legislation were: 1) A toxic substance inventory; 2) A toxics use reduction plan for each facility to ensure regular industry reviews for less toxic materials; 3) A Toxics Use Reduction Institute to assist industry in transition; 4) An enforcement program authorizing citizens suit; 5) A provision to expeditiously remove problematic toxics from the marketplace; 6) Establishing the Department of Toxics Use Reduction to ensure

an appropriate priority; 7) A financing, tiered taxation mechanism for raw materials, to forsake toxics.

189. Hazardous Waste Source Reduction and Management Review Act of 1989, § 25244.12 et seq.
190. Gerald Markowitz and David Rosner, Deceit and Denial: The Deadly Politics of Industrial Pollution (Berkeley: UC Press, 2002) p 297.
191. A classic technique described by Ivan Illich in Tools for Conviviality (Harper & Row, 1973) when heroin was first devised as a solution for the addictive properties of morphine, during WWII.
192. Michael E. Belliveau, "The Drive for a Safer Chemicals Policy in the United States." New Solutions. Vol 21(3) 359-386 (Baywood Publishing, 2011).
193. "Confronting Toxic Contamination in Our Communities: Women's Health and California's Future," (The Women's Foundation of California: September, 2003).

Chapter 9 Hazardous Traits

194. Mike Wilson, with Daniel A. Chia, Bryan C. Ehlers, Green Chemistry in California: A Framework for Leadership in Chemicals Policy and Innovation (UC Policy Research Center: 2006). pp 59-60
195. Ken Geiser, Materials Matter: Toward a Sustainable Materials Policy (Boston: MIT Press, 2001)
196. Ibid: to consider chemicals as components of the broad system of production in which they are used, not as isolated individual entities, which is never how they actually show up... to disseminate more complete information on whole classes of chemicals, develop less toxic alternatives, and convert industry sector by sector to chemicals that represent a low hazard.
197. Joel Tickner, editor. Precaution: Environmental Science and Preventive Public Policy (Island Press, 2003).
198. Seeking rapid phase-out of groups of chemicals not predicated on exhaustive data reviews. The memo advanced that putting force behind initiatives at the state level made much more sense.

199. For an excellent, thorough analysis of toxics law in the judicial setting, and specific issues, see Carl F. Cranor's Toxic Torts: Science, Law, and the Possibility of Justice (NY: Cambridge University Press, 2006), particularly the end discussion in the chapter "Science and Law in Conflict."

Chapter 10 Cassandra Does Sacramento

200. The Joint Committee Hearing by the Senate Environmental Quality Committee, et al., "The State of California's Environment: Obstacles and Opportunities," The State Capitol (Sacramento: March 2, 2005).
201. Robert F. Kennedy, Jr., Crimes Against Nature: How George W. Bush and His Corporate Pals Are Plundering the Country and Hijacking Our Democracy (NY: Harper-Collins, 2004) p. 3.
202. . cit., Joint Legislative Hearing.
203. Ibid., The full title of his talk appeared as "The Importance of California's Environment to the Economic Engine: A Private Sector Perspective."
204. The comments are based on my best recollection of the hearing, but do not represent a verbatim account in the absence of a recorded version or transcript.
205. Real Estate Prices Roller Coaster (Flixxy.com spectacularbubble.com) U.S. housing prices plotted as a roller coaster ride simulation, based on a graph by Yale University economist Robert Schiller.
206. Subsequent reviews following the great recession would document that the collapse of real estate prices had little to do with the magic hand of the market and much more to do with financial firms constructing what would be known as instruments of financial destruction. Among the many corporate culprits, Countrywide Financial would emerge as a notorious actor.
207. Michael Lewis' *The Big Short: Inside the Doomsday Machine* W. W. Norton & Company (March 15, 2010). The NY Times bestseller and award winning movie is the story of several financial traders

who, recognizing the reckless and manipulative actions by a group of financial firms, seek to demonstrate that the only smart investment parallels what Schiller and others conclude elsewhere: an impending financial disaster.

208. A high-yield insurance-linked instrument meant to raise money in case of a catastrophe has a special condition that states if the issuer suffers a loss, then its obligation to pay interest and/or repay the principal is either deferred or completely forgiven. CAT bonds are used to transfer risk to investors.
209. Collateralized Debt Obligations backed by receivables, loans or bonds that banks sell to investors in order to reduce the risk of default. Banks offer higher interest rates to investors willing to buy CDOs backed by higher-risk loans. CDOs also reduce capital requirements,, when banks can raise funds through their issue.
210. Matt Taibbi, "The Great American Bubble Machine," The Rolling Stone (June 23, 2009).

Chapter 11 The Climate of Austerity

211. Among my many extracurricular activities around the capitol were unofficial seminars, including one on this topic, where an invited speaker introduced a committee to financial engineering built on offshore accounts, the harvesting of state and federal codes, the deferral of state and federal tax bills, and other forms of tax avoidance often reaping decades-long benefits for major businesses, including the most notorious measure sanctioned by California voters: the freezing of commercial property taxes arising from a so-called tax revolt of Proposition 13.
212. The alleged absence of law relating to financial crimes against the state explains, in part, why individuals in the regulatory realm were stymied during the financial meltdown when challenged to produce those provisions of law that were violated. The regulatory folks were secondarily challenged that with the rapid unfolding of the crisis, there was not a consensus to act in a timely and decisive way, even if applicable law *could* be found.

213. Joseph E. Stiglitz, "The Globalization of Protest," Common Dreams (November 4, 2011 by Project Syndicate*). See Project Syndicate link*
214. Ibid.
215. Simon Constable, "Barton Biggs: U.S. Needs a Massive Public Works Program" The Wall Street Journal (July 1, 2011). I first came across the WSJ article by way of an even better article authored by Susan Feiner, "What Deficit Hawks Don't Know Will Hurt Us All. Monday, July 18, 2011. See Ms. Magazine Blog posted July 18, 2011.
216. Ibid.
217. Brown's budget would be based on raising income taxes for individuals making at least $250,000 a year to 10.3 percent from 9.3 percent. Among those earning $300,000 to $500,000, the rate would climb to 10.8 percent. For single filers with income above $500,000, the tax would rise to 11.3 percent. Californians with income of more than $1 million are now taxed at 10.3 percent.
218. Robert A.G. Monks, "The corporate Capture of the U. S.," (Cambridge: The Harvard Law School Forum on Corporate Governance and Financial Regulation (Harvard University, Thursday January 5, 2012 at 10:21 am)
219. Gretchen Morgenson, writer for the New York Times appearing on Bill Moyer and Co, January 20, 2012.

Chapter 12 Private Profits and a Punished Public

220. Studs Terkel, Hope Dies Last: Keeping the Faith in Difficult Times (NY: New Press, 2003) p. 222.
221. Angela Johnson Meszaros, Clean Air Matters, [htp://cleanair matters.net/blog] "Energy, Air Quality, and Climate Change from an Environmental Justice Perspective" (April 25, 2011).
222. Bill Gallegos, Angela Johnson Meszaros, et al. "Climate Law Implementation to Halt Deal to Limit Court Ruling Fails to Materialize," (Sacramento, CA March 31, 2011): Press Release by the Center on Race, Poverty and the Environment and Communities for a Better Environment.

223. Judge Ernest H. Goldsmith, Superior Court of State of California, County of San Francisco (Case # CPF - 09- 509562) December 8, 2011.
224. Cap-and-Trade Market Issues, The Legislative Analyst's Office (Sacramento: June 29, 2011). http://www.lao.ca.gov/handouts/resources/2011/Cap_and_Trade_Market_Issues_062911.pdf
225. LAO, op cit.
226. Ibid.
227. This portion of the discussion is based on a concise summary of issues authored by Dan Morain, "Can Market for Clean-Air Credits Resist Profiteers," Sacramento Bee (May 27, 2012).
228. Ibid.
229. Ibid. "Cap-and-trade does have a familiar feel. Back in 1996, the Legislature approved a bill to deregulate energy. The promise was that there'd be competition among electricity providers, and rates would fall by up to 20%. Then Senator Steve Peace helped write legislation, and remembers the fallout. Enron and other buccaneers manipulated a deregulated market. The state had rolling blackouts. Traders made millions. A few went to jail. Others remain in the business...involved in cap and trade. Peace predicts cap and trade markets will 'work for a while', and then the traders get the opportunity to cash in...These guys will make a lifetime's income in that moment." Nichols demurs: "This is not restructuring the electricity system. We're not effecting changes in the way business operate. We're just getting them to think about carbon emissions." "I hope she's right."
230. Bärbel Hönisch, Andy Ridgwell, Daniela N. Schmidt, Ellen Thomas, Samantha J. Gibbs, Appy Sluijs, Richard Zeebe, Lee Kump, Rowan C. Martindale, Sarah E. Greene, Wolfgang Kiessling, Justin Ries, James C. Zachos, Dana L. Royer, Stephen Barker, Thomas M. Marchitto Jr., Ryan Moyer, Carles Pelejero, Patrizia Ziveri, Gavin L. Foster, and Branwen Williams, The Geological Record of Ocean Acidification. *Science*, March 2, 2012 DOI:10.1126/science.1208277

231. Fiona Harvey, "Global Carbon Trading System Has 'Essentially Collapsed," The Guardian Newspaper (September 10, 2012).
232. Steve Suppan, "Climate Finance Debated While Climate Change Rages," Institute for Agriculture and Trade Policy (December 4, 2012). See especially Dr. Suppan's comments on the dysfunction of the emissions trading markets; "A British consultancy, boasting the health of London exchanges, reported that the global value of carbon emissions credit transactions had increased to $176 billion in 2011. However, the vast majority of these transactions are re-circulating the value of carbon credits given for free by the European Commission to power plants and heavy energy users in the EU. According to a June Carbon Trade Watch report, these free credits have amounted to an average annual seven billion euro windfall profit for European polluters since 2005. At a November auction of European Union ETS credits, which begins the 2013-2020 phase of the ETS, the price had fallen to 6.7 euros a metric ton of GHGs from about 20 euros in 2009."

    However, just one percent of the transactions on the soon to be defunct Blue Next carbon exchange in Paris are "spot" transactions used by non-financial firms to meet their emissions limits. The remaining transactions are financial derivative contracts based on the value of carbon credits. Returns and fees on derivatives may enrich carbon traders and exchanges, but they do not "leverage" revenue for adaptation or mitigation projects. Because of the falling price of ETS credits, the European Commission debated how to increase carbon prices sufficiently to prompt emitters to reduce their output.
233. Naomi Klein, op cit., p. 225.
234. Chris Hedges, "Stand Still for the Apocalypse," as posted on Truthdig (November 26, 2012).
235. Peter Barnes Who Owns the Sky? Common Assets and the Future of Capitalism (Washington D.C.: Island Press, 2001).
236. Legislative Analyst, 2014-15 Budget, "Cap-and-Trade Auction Revenue Expenditure Plan," (Sacramento, February 24, 2014) page 1.

237. Joint Hearing of the Senate Environmental Quality Committee and the Select Committee on Climate Change, AB 32 Implementation, (State Capitol, Room 4203, March 12, 2014).
238. The most striking part of the hearing was the announcement that the Air Board proposed to address short-lived pollutants as part of a package of regulations. The short-lived pollutants would now include black soot and methane: And given the change in legislators, staff, and others in hearing room 4203, probably only a handful remembered that approximately eight years had passed since Senator Pavley was requested, but refused to address this simple, but significant element of AB 32.
239. Legislative Analyst 2014-15, op cit.,"Potential Litigation Over Use of Auction Revenues." page 4.
240. Michael Hiltzik, "How refineries' greed sank an environmental program that was saving them millions," Los Angeles Times (March 26, 2017). Even as the Air District sought to remedy the situation, the *petroleros* resisted.

Chapter 13 Adding Fuels to the Fire

241. Denis Cuff, "Stricter pollution controls approved for Bay Area oil refineries," Inside Bay Area News (Group) Dec 17, 2015.
242. Legislative Analyst 2014-15 Budget, op cit., "Cap-and-Trade Auction Revenue," page 3.
243. Tony Wikrent, "Neo-liberalism, Decapitalization, and the Res Publica," in the blog, Naked Capitalism (June 5, 2012): Mr. Wikrent cogently summarizes the issues; "That oil and gas are such an outlier on the graph [of] the outsize political economy effect of the rentier influence exerted... If we were seriously trying to address resource constraints and climate change, we would not be seeing such an outsize impact by oil and gas...This lack of investment in what the country really needs shows why government regulations are crucial...to regulations and taxes that discourage economic activity that harms society. Now, everything wrong is incentivised, while support for education and clean energies is being cut in a

mad dash to austerity. We need regulations and policies that make it more profitable to invest in wind farms and solar arrays, than in credit default swaps and currency futures."

244. Tamminen, op cit.
245. Shawn Donnan, "Global Energy Subsidies Fuel Climate Change, IMF Study," Financial Times, May 18, 2015.
246. Ibid.
247. Ibid.
248. Passage taken from an interview with an anonymous source conducted on November 19, 2015.
249. Naomi Oreskes, "Wishful Thinking about Natural Gas: Why Fossil Fuels Can't Solve the Problems Created by Fossil Fuels," posted July 28, 2014 on Naked Capitalism.com.
250. Ibid.
251. BusinessWeek, "Governor Brown Fires Anti-Oil Regulators (Bloomberg News, November 5, 2011).
252. Derek Chernow served as the acting director for the Department of Conservation, Elena Miller as the oil and gas supervisor at the Division of Oil, Gas and Geothermal Resources.
253. Ellen Knickmeyer, "Governor Brown pushed to waive oil safeguards, ex-officials testify," The Associated Press, September 6, 2015
254. Ibid.
255. Ibid.
256. BusinessWeek, op cit.
257. Ellen Knickmeyer, op cit.
258. Michael J. Mishak, "Fracking bill moves forward in California Legislature." (The Los Angeles Times, April 10, 2012).
259. Ellen Cantarow, "The Frontline of Fracking" posted on TomDispatch (January 31, 2014).
260. Ibid.
261. National Drought Mitigation Center (Washington, D.C.: USDA, May 15, 2014).
262. See Marc Reisner's spell-binding portrayal in Cadillac Desert: The American West and Its Disappearing Water, Revised Edition, Penguin Books, 1993) pages 351-2 "One such project, to redirect water down to LA., was named to commemorate Governor Edmund G. 'Pat' Brown."

263. Jennifer Medina, "Governor Brings Climate Issues to the Fore," New York Times, May 19, 2014
264. The town of Mendocino, for example, issued calls for its citizens to cut their water use by 40% in April, having experienced an absence of water that had lasted for many weeks in 2013.
265. The question was posed by Dan Jacobson representing Environment California at the Environmental Summit, Sacramento, 2014.
266. Naomi Oreskes, "Wishful Thinking About Natural Gas: Why Fossil Fuels Can't Solve the Problems Created by Fossil Fuels," posted July 28, 2014 on Naked Capitalism.com
267. Gayathri Vaidyanathan, "How Bad a Greenhouse Gas Is Methane?" Scientific American (December 22, 2015) posted under the heading: ClimateWire.
268. Naomi Oreskes and Erik Conway, The Collapse of Western Civilization: A View from the Future (Columbia University Press, 2014).
269. See, for example, James Hansen, Storms of My Grandchildren: The Truth About the Coming Climate Catastrophe and Our Last Chance to Save Humanity (Bloomsbury: 2009).
270. California State Senate Committee on Natural Resources and Water, "Oversight/Informational Hearing: Senate Bill 4 (2013) Well Stimulation in California," (State Capitol, February 11, 2015).
271. Ibid., testimony by Dr. Jane Long on behalf of the California Council on Science and Technology.
272. Ibid.
273. Ibid., testimony by Andrew Grinberg, representative for Clean Water Action.
274. S. Conley, et al., "Methane emissions from the 2015 Aliso Canyon blowout in Los Angeles, CA," Science (February 25, 2016).

Chapter 14 Race, Poverty and Trading

275. Gene Maddaus, "Jesse Marquez: Thorn of Industry," LA Weekly (May, 19, 2011).
276. One of the better known works is the film based on the book by Jonathan Harr, A Civil Action (NY: Vintage Books, 1995).

277. See Jonathan Harr, A Civil Action for a more detailed discussion of Foley, Hoag & Eliot and the essence of law practices protecting powerful corporate clients at the expense of an endangered public. The primary regulatory authority, the US EPA is portrayed as having ineffective rules for dangerous chemicals - lacking even the most rudimentary of enforcement powers.
278. The largest settlement was another of Gale Filter's works, involving the illegal disposal of geothermal wastes, $1.7 million.
279. Gale Filter, "Community Action and Strategies for Empowerment," a series of electronic correspondences, including this one dated December 9, 2012.
280. California District Attorneys Association's "Advanced Topics in Environmental Enforcement" Annual Meeting (Asilomar, 2004).
281. Gale Filter recounted that one of the heroes working behind the scenes, an atmospheric scientist at UC Davis, Dr. Tim Cahill, helped provide a forensic fingerprint of particles from Exide and elsewhere as an essential step where a typical defense might begin with, "how do you know its coming from our plant and not somewhere else?"
282. Carbon Pollution Emission Guidelines for Existing Stationary Sources: Electric Utility Generating Units, Docket ID #EPA-HQ-OAR-2013-0602.
283. Center on Race, Poverty and the Environment petition to Gina McCarthy, Administrator, US EPA: Climate Justice Comments on Carbon Pollution Emission Guidelines, December 1, 2014.
284. Ibid., p 2
285. Ibid.
286. Ibid., p 7
287. Ibid.
288. Denis Cuff, "Stricter pollution controls approved for Bay Area oil refineries," Inside Bay Area News (Bay Area News Group) Dec 17, 2015.
289. California Environmental Justice Alliance Website (visited October 15, 2016).
290. Ibid.

Chapter 15 Climate of Compromise

291. Bill Magavern. "How to Read What the Legislature Did on Climate and Energy:" Coalition for Clean Air End-of-Session Blog, September 14, 2015.
292. Dan Morain, "How Oil Won the Battle for SB 350," The Sacramento Bee, September 12, 2015.
293. Steve Early, Refinery Town: Big Oil, Big Money, and the Remaking of an American City (Boston: Beacon Press, 2017) pp. 11-12.
294. Ibid., p. 17.
295. Ibid.
296. California Proposition 14, Top Two Primaries Act (June 2010).
297. Ibid., quoting Allan Hoffenblum, editor of the California Target Book.
298. Jessica Calefati, "Moderate Assembly Democrats emerge as powerful pro-business force," Contra Costa Times (September 26, 2015) quoting Professor Jessica Levinson, a campaign finance expert with Loyola School of Law.
299. Ibid: quoting Assembly member Adam Gray, former staff to the indicted Senator Ron Calderon who received nearly $400,000 from business and industry committees in 2012 and 2014.
300. "Study shows how to power California with wind, water and sun," Stanford News Service, July 24, 2014.
301. Kolya Abramsky, ed. Sparking a Worldwide Energy Revolution (AK Press, 2010).
302. Steve Early, Refinery Town, op. cit., p 185-186.
303. Mark Baldassare, President Public Policy Institute of California, "Californians and Climate Change," Fox & Hounds: Keeping Tabs on California Business and Politics (August 11, 2015).
304. California Proposition 14, Top Two Primaries Act (June 2010).
305. *Citizens United v. Federal Election Commission*, No. 08-205, 558 U.S. 310 (Argued: March 24, 2009, Decided: January 21, 2010), a corporate law.
306. California Environmental Justice Alliance CEJA Congreso 2015 People Power Policy (August 24 & 25, Sacramento, California).

307. Assembly Bill 1288 (commencing with Section 38562 of the Health and Safety Code).
308. CEJA Congreso Highlights (August 24 & 25, 2015).
309. California Environmental Justice Alliance website 2015.
310. Ibid.

Chapter 16 The Pontiff, Politicians, and Paris

311. Simon Thomsen, "'I don't give a d___if we agree': Arnold Schwarzenegger just gave a climate-change speech that will give you chills," Business Insider Australia (December 8, 2015
312. Sammy Lyon, "System Change Not Climate Change," (posted at Lyonideas.com, March 8, 2016).
313. California's cap and trade program as defined in legislation enacted in 2006 would become known by its bill number, Assembly Bill 32 or AB 32 as well as the bill's title, The Global Warming Solutions Act and more formally cited as Chapter 488, Statutes of 2006.
314. Will Parrish, "Cap and Clear Cut," East Bay Express (January 12, 2016).
315. For a fuller discussion of the roots of citizen and labor activism in Richmond, California, see Steve Early's excellent work - Refinery Townforeword by Bernie Sanders (Boston: Beacon Press, January 2017).
316. Ibid.
317. Pope Francis, Encyclical on Climate Change and Inequality: On Care for Our Common Home (Libreria Editrice Vaticana/Melville House Publishing, July 2015).
318. Ibid., quote contained in Introduction by Naomi Oreskes, p xix.
319. George Skelton, "Pope / Brown Part Ways on Cap-and-Trade," Los Angeles Times, July 20, 2015
320. Tom Kington, "Brown Blasts Climate Change Deniers During Vatican Conference," Los Angeles Times, July 21, 2015
321. Ibid.
322. Ibid.
323. Ibid.

324. Chris Megerian, "Governor Jerry Brown takes aim at oil companies over highly destructive product," Los Angeles Times, August 24, 2015.
325. Studs Terkel, Hope Dies Last: Keeping the Faith in Difficult Times (The New Press, 2003) p 222.
326. David R. Baker, "As California Pumps Out Oil, Governor Brown says World Must Cut Back," San Francisco Chronicle, July 21, 2015
327. Ibid.
328. George Skelton, op cit.
329. Pope Francis: with Naomi Oreskes' introductory remarks, op cit., p xiii.
330. David Coady, Ian Parry, Louis Sears, Baoping Shang, "How Large Are Global Energy Subsidies?"
(Washington, D.C.: International Monetary Fund, May 2015).
331. Kurtis Alexander, "Gov. Jerry Brown marches California climate agenda to Paris," San Francisco Chronicle November 27, 2015.

Chapter 17 Buying Our Way Out

332. Will Parrish, "Cap and Clear Cut," East Bay Express (January 20, 2016) includes concise review of how Senate Bill 812 of 2002 and forest protocols became "corrupted" as explained by Jeff Shellito, the lead staff on the Senate Environmental Quality Committee, Senator Byron Sher with Kip Lipper serving as the staff director.
333. Denis Cuff, "Stricter pollution controls approved for Bay Area oil refineries," Inside Bay Area News (Bay Area News Group) Dec 17, 2015.
334. Melody Gutierrez, "High-Speed Rail Takes Hit as Cap-and-Trade Cash Falls Short," San Francisco Chronicle, May 27, 2016.
335. Ibid.
336. Julie Cart, "With Cap-and-Trade in Doubt, Key Questions Go Unanswered," CalMatters (July 5, 2016).
337. Ibid.
338. The Editorial Board, "A Weak Deal on Airplane Emissions." (bloomberg.com, October 14, 2016).

339. Ibid.
340. Ibid.

Chapter 18 Dismantling Democracy

341. President Barack Obama, State of the Union, January 12, 2016.
342. Ibid.
343. Ibid.
344. Elizabeth Kolbert, "Congress Moves to Sabotage the US Climate Summit," The New Yorker December 4, 2015.
345. Ibid.
346. Will Denayer, "How Climate Change is rapidly Taking the Planet Apart" Ecology & Growth (July 20, 2016) p 8.
347. The White House, "U.S.-China Joint Presidential Statement on Climate Change," (Washington, D.C., Office of the Press Secretary, September 25, 2015). See also Mark Landler, "U.S. and China Reach Climate Deal After Months of Talks," New York Times, November 12, 2014.
348. Ibid. China described the trading system as eventually covering key industry sectors (iron and steel, power generation, chemicals, building materials, paper-making, and nonferrous metals).
349. John Flalka, "China Will Start the World's Largest Carbon Trading Market: Even though China has a non-market economy, it has learned from mistakes in Europe and California," Scientific American (May 16, 2016).
350. See earlier versions of Senate Bill 350 (2015) prior to enactment and chaptering.
351. Bill Press, Buyer's Remorse: How Obama Let Progressives Down," (NY: Simon & Schuster, 2016) pp 203-205.
352. Ibid., p 205.
353. Ibid., p 206-207. And he was arrested three times for Obama White House pipeline protests.
354. Eric Berger, "Prominent climate scientist offers scathing critique of Obama's Paris plans," ARS Technica (November 27, 2015) with a summation of actions pursued by James Hansen trying to

influence the President and others in his post, "Isolation of 1600 Pennsylvania Avenue: Part I.'

355. Mychaylo Prystupa, "Naomi Klein says politicians leading world to "very dangerous future,"
    National Observer, December 3, 2015
356. Klein, op cit., the statement was delivered by Maude Barlow with the Council of Canadians.
357. A notable exception appeared in "Keystone Lawsuit Shows TTIP's Threat to Climate Action," Transport & Environment (posted on February 26, 2016).
358. Sierra Club, "450+ Environmental, Landowner, Indigenous Rights, and Allied Organizations Letter to Congress: Pending Trade Deals Threaten Efforts to Keep Fossil Fuels in the Ground," (June 2016) sites Sierra Club report on trade. http://www.sierraclub.org/trade/truth-behind-ttip

    The market state, as response to original nation states discussed by philosophical leaders such as Aquinas is used by Philip Bobbitt to characterize the first wave of reaction to the end of the Cold War. To overstate only slightly, primary drivers of international politics are economic, yet our habits of thought and our institutions remain powerfully conditioned.
359. "The Truth Behind Transatlantic Trade and Investment Partnership," (The Sierra Club) (http://www.sierraclub.org/trade/truth-behind-ttip).
360. Ibid. op. cit. Sierra Club http://www.sierraclub.org/trade/truth-behind-ttip.

Chapter 19 The War on California

361. Noam Chomsky, Who Rules the World (NY: Metropolitan Books, 2016). p. 2.
362. Taylor Link, This Guy's a Fraud: Bernie Sanders sees right past President Trump's rhetoric about helping the middle class," Salon (February 6, 2017).

363. Don Lee, “Trump... the Richest Cabinet in U.S. History,” Los Angeles Times (December 7, 2016).
364. Steven Coll, “Rex Tillerson, From a Corporate Oil Sovereign to the State Department,” The New Yorker News Desk (Dec 11, 2016). Mr. Coll also authored Private Empire: ExxonMobil and American Power (Penguin, 2012).
365. David Hasemyer, “Exxon Now Seeks to Block New York Attorney General’s Climate Probe,” Inside Climate News (October 16, 2016).
366. Katherine Bagley, “Hillary Clinton Joins Call for Justice Department to Investigate Exxon,” InsideClimate News (October 29, 2016).
367. David Hasemyer, op.cit.
368. Dan Drollette, “Just 90 companies are accountable for more than 60 percent of greenhouse gases,” The Bulletin of Atomic Scientists,” (October 27, 2016).
369. Tom Randall, “World Energy Hits a Turning Point: Solar That‘s Cheaper than Wind Energy Markets Are Leapfrogging the Developed World Thanks to Cheap Panels,” Bloomberg New (Bloomberg technology: December 14, 2016).
370. Ibid.
371. Bill O‘Reilly Show, Interview with Donald Trump (Fox News Network: February 5, 2017).
372. George Skelton, “California Democrats relish opposing Trump on immigration - but they could go too far,” Los Angeles Times (February 2, 2017).
373. Michael Klare, “Donald Trump’s Energy Nostalgia and the Path to Hell,” (TomDispatch.com) Dec 1, 2016.
374. Bloomberg News, “Scott Pruitt, critic of Clean Power Plan, picked to lead U.S. environmental agency.” (Bloomberg News) December 8, 2016.
375. George Skelton, op cit.
376. Catherine Traywick and Jennifer A. Dlouhy, “Trump Team Memo Hints at Big Shake-Up of U.S. Energy Policy,” Bloomberg, December 8, 2016.
377. Bill Gross, “Low Wage Americans Will Suffer Most Under Trump” Financial Times (Nov 16, 2016).

378. Ibid.
379. Ibid.
380. See for example various essays by Thomas Franks, including one of his most recent publications, Listen Liberal (NY: Metropolitan Books, 2016).
381. Matthew Phillips, "Clean Power Is Too Hot for Even Trump to Cool," Bloomberg Businessweek (Nov 16 2016).
382. Ibid: according to Bloomberg New Energy Finance.
383. Ibid.
384. Ibid.
385. John Lippert and Jamie Butters, "Ford CEO Sees 'Pressure' on Business Without Softer Fuel Rules," Barron's December 2, 2016.
386. Ibid.
387. John Upton, "Conservatives Push Carbon Tax to Address Climate Crisis," Climate Central (February 8, 2017) Ibid., Edmund G. Brown, Jr. Governor's correspondence with U.S. EPA Administrator Scott Pruitt (March 15, 2009).
388. Robinson Meyer, "Rex Tillerson Says Climate Change Is Real, but..." The Atlantic (Jan 11, 2017).
389. Ibid.
390. Eric Roston, "Republicans Break Ranks with Pledge to Fight Climate Change," Bloomberg (March 15, 2017), including excerpts from a taped video with Ted Halstead, CEO and Founder of Climate Leadership Council.
391. Ibid.

Chapter 20 The Climate of Change

392. Lara J. Cushing et. al., "A Preliminary Environmental Equity Assessment of California's Cap-and-Trade Program," (University of Southern California: Program for Environmental and Regional Equity, Sept 14, 2016).
393. Martha Argüello commentary, California Environmental Justice Website (visited October 15, 2016).

394. The six measures included SB 1000 (Planning for Healthy Communities Act), AB 2722 (Transformative Climate Communities), SB 32 (GHG Reduction Targets), AB 197 (Equity & Transparency in Climate Act), AB 1550 (Increased Climate Investments), and AB 1937 (Environmental Justice in Power Plant Siting).
395. Lawrence Lingbloom, Assembly Floor Analysis of AB 197 (Concurrence in Senate Amendments) (Sacramento: The California Assembly, August 24, 2016).
396. Amy B. Wang, "That's how dictators get started: McCain criticizes Trump for calling media 'the enemy.'" The Washington Post, February 18, 2017.
397. California Environmental Justice Alliance website, by Martha Argüello (visited October 1, 2016).
398. Steve Early, Refinery Town: op. cit.
399. Richard Jackson address - CalEPA 2016.
400. To navigate the rising tide of public health research and discussions, see the excellent aggregation of information collected by the Collaborative on Health and Environment.
401. Central coalition figures often included Ralph Lightstone (California Rural Legal Assistance Foundation), Tom Rankin (AFL-CIO), Mike Paparian (Sierra Club California), Harry Schneider (Consumers Union), a primary lobbyist with the March of Dimes and Dr. Richard Jackson working behind the scenes.
402. Differences between advocacy and activism, organizing and mobilizing are thoughtfully parsed by Jane McAlevey in her recent work, No Shortcuts: Organizing for Power in the New Gilded Age (London: Oxford University Press, 2016).
403. Dean Baker, Rigged: How Globalization and the Rules of Modern Economy Were Structured to Make the Rich Richer, (Washington, D.C.: Center for Economic & Policy Research, 2016). This paragraph interprets a passage at the conclusion of Dr. Baker's book about income inequality (page 218) to place it in the context of climate change.
404. Ibid., p 218.

405. Ben Adler, "Pollsters: Election Results Show California Unlike the Rest of America," Cal Counts (Capital Public Radio, November 16, 2016) posted on capradio.org.
406. "What If California's Non-voters Voted?" (San Francisco: Public Policy Institute of California, September, 2006). press release

www.ingramcontent.com/pod-product-compliance
Lightning Source LLC
Chambersburg PA
CBHW021918190326
41519CB00009B/826